ARCHITECTURAL
DRAWING

ARCHITECTURAL DRAWING

REVISED EDITION

by

LAWTON M. PATTEN, B.F.A. and B. Arch.

Professor, Department of Architecture
Iowa State University

and

MILTON L. ROGNESS, B. Int. Arch., and M.S. Arch. Engr.

Associate Professor, Department of Engineering Graphics
Iowa State University

KENDALL/HUNT PUBLISHING COMPANY

2460 Kerper Boulevard,
Dubuque, Iowa 52001

FOREWORD

This textbook shows the student how to draw, not how to design.

It includes architectural graphics, building construction fundamentals, and methods of drawing considered prerequisite to architectural design.

Illustrations and explanations are arranged on a self-instructional system to save time for both student and instructor.

With this purpose the authors present the following pages.

L. M. Patten
M. L. Rogness

ACKNOWLEDGMENTS

Acknowledgment is made to Professor Leonard Wolf, late Head of the Department of Architecture, Iowa State University, and Professor James S. Rising, Head of the Department of Engineering Graphics, Iowa State University, for their valuable advice and assistance; to Professor Maurice W. Almfeldt of the Department of Engineering Graphics, Iowa State University for his help in securing many of the photographs used; and to Bruno Schiller for his assistance in preparing the proofs and the solution of problems.

Acknowledgment is also made to the architects, publishers, and photographers who granted permission to reproduce various photographs used as illustrations.

Lawton M. Patten
Milton L. Rogness

ARCHITECTURE

Architecture is the art and science of building, uniting in harmony its three fundamental requirements -- utility, structure, and beauty.

ROLE OF THE ARCHITECT

The architect exercises professional leadership in the art and science of planning and designing buildings. These buildings must be functional, efficient, safe, structurally sound, and beautiful.

The architect must not only be interested in imaginative work, but he must develop creative ideas into architecture, structurally and aesthetically adequate.

By means of presentation drawings he must be able to convey his idea to his client, and by means of working drawings and specifications, to the builder.

TRAINING OF THE ARCHITECT

This book is devoted to that phase of the architect's training that will enable him to communicate his creative ideas to others. It presents the fundamentals and techniques of architectural graphics, the drafting and geometrical interpretations of three-dimensional forms. It includes the general criteria for choosing materials and types of construction.

Lawton M. Patten
Milton L. Rogness

TABLE OF CONTENTS

TABLE OF CONTENTS (Cont.)

TABLE OF CONTENTS (Cont.)

THE SEGREGATION OF ALPHABETS IS BASED UPON THESE THREE GROUPS

All letters made with even width strokes are classified as Gothic (Text letters were originally called Gothic)

GOTHIC=ABCDEFGHIJKLMNOPQRSTUVWXYZJ

GOTHIC=ABCDEFGHIJKLMNOPQRSTUVWXYYZ abcdefghijklmnop

gothic= abcdefghijklmnopqrstuvwxyz = qrstuvwxyz=gothic

All letters made with "accented" strokes (thick and thin lines) are classified as Roman

ROMAN=ABCDEFGHIJKLMNOPQRSTUVWXYZ=abci

ROMAN=ABCDEFGHIJKLMNOPQRSTUVWXYZ=defghijkl

roman=abcdefghijklmnopqrstuvwxyz=mnopqrs,

Text= includes all the styles of Old English, Cloister, Church, German, Black texts=

ABCDEFGHIJKLMNOPQRSTUVWXYZ

ABCDEFGHIJKLMNOPQRSTUVWXYZ

abcdefghijklmnopqrstuvwxyz abcdefghijklmnopr

ALPHABET GROUPS
(Courtesy C. Howard Hunt Pen Co.)

TECHNIQUE OF GOOD LETTERING

"All normal persons can learn to letter if they are persistent and intelligent in their efforts." --
Giesecke, Mitchell, and Spencer.

PROPORTION: 1. Proportion is the relationship of height to width, not mathematical but a matter of good judgment.

              2. When necessary, proportions are changed to fit definite spaces.

FORM: 1. Draw round letters uniformly round, vertical letters exactly vertical, and sloped letters uniformly sloped.

              2. The simple basic shape is the most legible.

SPACING: 1. Space letters and words uniformly by eye rather than by measuring.

              2. Each letter is a unit of design in itself. When letters are combined they form a more complex design. This design will be legible and pleasing to the eye if the PROPORTION, FORM, and SPACING of the letters have been properly executed.

CONSISTENCY: 1. Don't mix alphabets.

              2. Watch proper use of serifs. If serifs are used on the "I" and "J," they should be used on all letters.

              3. Be consistent in use of capital and lower case letters.

"Like a well-drilled army, good letters wear a uniform, and act in a uniform way -- as an orderly group, not as a rabble of individuals. They work in common and must accept the discipline of a certain community of appearance."

-- Benson and Carey

GUIDE LINES: Experts use them, and on pencil lettering they are generally allowed to remain, enhancing the appearance.

PENCILS

9H
8H   The harder pencils in this group are used for graphical computations, charts, diagrams, and
7H   other drawings requiring a high degree of accuracy. The softer pencils in this group are used
6H   for line work in machine drawings.
5H
4H

3H
2H   This group is used for general-purpose work, for technical sketching, for architectural line
 H   drawings, for pencil tracings of architectural or machine drawings, for lettering, arrowheads,
 F   and for other freehand work.
HB
 B

2B
3B
4B   This group is used for freehand work of various kinds, for architectural rendering, and for full-
5B   size details in architectural drawings.
6B

The above gradations vary with different brands. The same pencil will also vary with the type of paper used and even be affected by the weather.

A good general rule to follow is: USE THE GRADE PENCIL THAT WILL GIVE YOU THE TYPE OF LINE SUITED TO THE JOB AT HAND. "Suited to the job at hand" means one which will give the intensity of line desired without requiring undue pressure or injury to the surface of the paper.

The lettering shown below and through page 5 was done by students in the beginning drawing course in architecture.

Aa Bb Cc Dd Ee Ff Gg Hh Ii
Jj Kk Ll Mm Nn Oo Pp Qq Rr
Ss Tt Uu Vv Ww Xx Yy Zz
1234567890 &

Method is fast and free Once control is acheived
full sets of guide lines are unnecessary Such
lettering works well for architectural notes
                                    Dave Schleiger

The above lettering is not done by a student, but is an example of good lettering in a style developed by an individual.

ABCDEFGHIJKLMNOPQRSTUVWXYZ
& 1234567890
VITRUVIUS: "WELL-BUILDING HATH THREE
CONDITIONS: COMMODITY, FIRMNESS,
AND BEAUTY."
                                    K. T. SCHNEPP

ABCDEFGHIJKLMNOPQRSTUV
WXYZ & 1234567890
VITRUVIUS :
"WELL-BUILDING HATH THREE
CONDITIONS: COMMODITY, FIRM-
NESS, AND BEAUTY."

TOM BALDWIN

ABCDEFGHIJKLMNOPQRSTUVWXYZ
& 1234567890

LE CORBUSIER : "THE SCHOOLS ARE THE
PRODUCT OF 19TH CENTURY THEORIES.
THEY HAVE KILLED ARCHITECTURE."

THOMAS F. WERDERITSCH

ABCDEFGHIJKLMNOPQRSTUVWXYZ
1234567890
LOUIS SULLIVAN: "FORM
FOLLOWS FUNCTION"

DON PRIMUS

ABCDEFGHIJKLMNOPQRST
UVWXYZ
& 1234567890
LUDWIG MIES VAN DER ROHE:
"LIKE MUSIC, ARCHIECTURE MUST
WAIT FOR REALIZATION ON SOME-
OTHER THAN ITS AUTHOR!"

J. C. GOETTSCH

ABCDEFGHIJKLMNOPQRSTUVWXYZ
1234567890
VITRUVIUS: "WELL-BUILDING HATH
THREE CONDITIONS: COMMODITY,
FIRMNESS AND BEAUTY."

JERRY QUEBE

ABCDEFGHIJKLMNOPQRSTUVWXYZ
& 1234567890

ARCHITECTURE IS THE ART AND
THE TECHNIQUE OF BUILDING EMPLOYED
TO FULLFILL THE PRACTICAL AND THE
EXPRESSIVE REQUIREMENTS OF CIVIL-
IZED PEOPLE.

MICHAEL McPHERSON

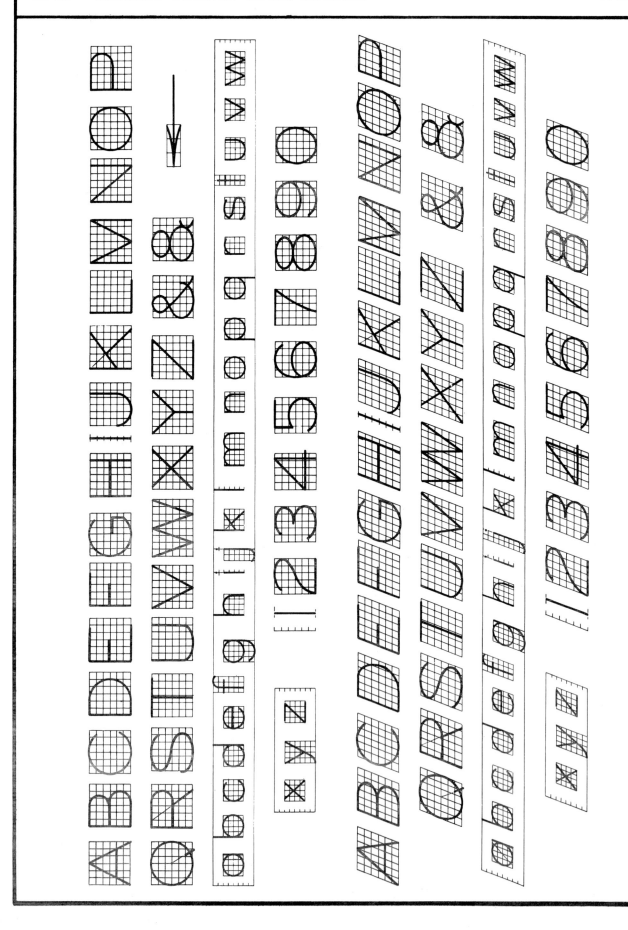

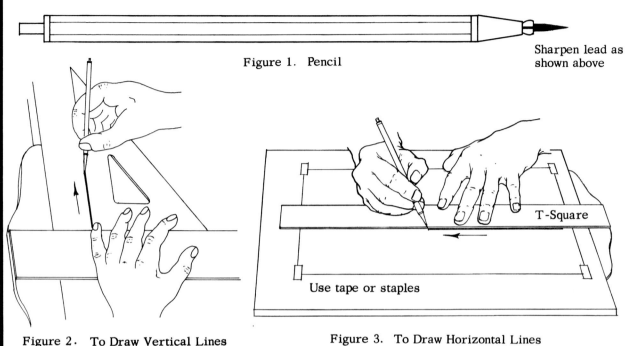

Figure 1. Pencil

Sharpen lead as shown above

Figure 2. To Draw Vertical Lines

Use tape or staples

T-Square

Figure 3. To Draw Horizontal Lines

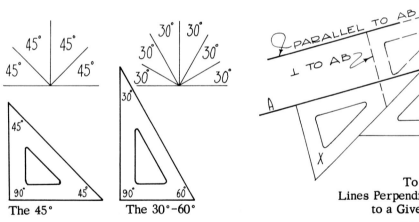

The 45°

The 30°-60°

Figure 4. Triangles

PARALLEL TO AB

⊥ TO AB

Slide triangle X to the desired position while holding triangle Y stationary.

To Draw
Lines Perpendicular or Parallel
to a Given Line (AB)

Figure 5.

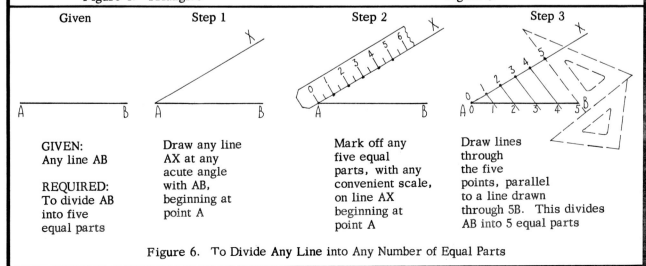

Given	Step 1	Step 2	Step 3
GIVEN: Any line AB

REQUIRED: To divide AB into five equal parts | Draw any line AX at any acute angle with AB, beginning at point A | Mark off any five equal parts, with any convenient scale, on line AX beginning at point A | Draw lines through the five points, parallel to a line drawn through 5B. This divides AB into 5 equal parts |

Figure 6. To Divide Any Line into Any Number of Equal Parts

Figure 1.

How to Fill a Ruling Pen

SUGGESTIONS FOR INKING LINES WITH A RULING PEN:

1. Have the pen properly sharpened. See Figure 2 and 3.

2. Figure 1 shows how to fill the pen.

3. Avoid excess ink in the pen.
   Approximate proper amount is shown in Figure 3.

4. For desired width of lines turn the adjusting screw.
   See Figures 2 and 3.

5. Maintain a uniform speed in drawing a line.

6. Prevent ink from drying in the pen. Refill often and wipe
   the pen clean between each filling and immediately after
   each use.

7. Maintain the 90° as shown in Figure 3 and approximately
   the 60° shown in Figure 2.

A person must discover for himself the importance of the
above suggestions to appreciate their value in executing a
good drawing in ink with a ruling pen.

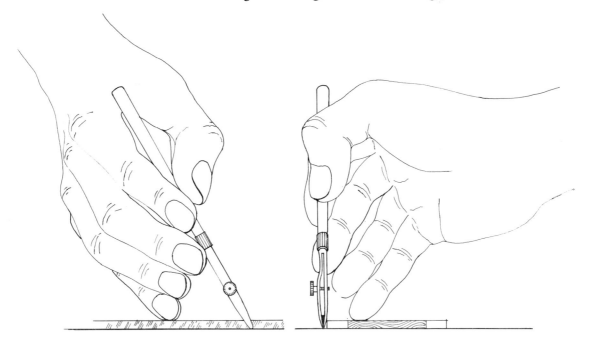

Figure 2.   Figure 3.

Hold the Pen at Approximately 60° Slope in a Vertical Plane

Other instruments for drawing and sketching lines, and for lettering are available in drawing
supply stores:

1. Fountain pens designed to hold India Ink are available with interchangeable points for
   different widths of lines.

2. Pen points that can be used in the conventional pen holder are available in a variety of
   sizes and shapes, varying from fine quill pens to wide speedball pens.

3. Felt-point fountain pens are available in various colors and are suitable for wide-line
   sketching and lettering.

4. LeRoy and Wrico lettering sets provide templates for lettering to be done mechanically.

TYPE OF LINE	WEIGHT	APPLICATION
	VERY HEAVY	
1. Border Lines		Border lines of this page
2. Cutting Plane Lines	$\frac{1}{8}$" $\frac{1}{32}$" A A	page 3 and 5, Chapter 6
3. Cutting Plane Lines	A A	page 4, Chapter 6
	HEAVY	
4. Outline of Parts		page 4 and 5, Chapter 2
	MEDIUM	
5. Hidden Lines		page 5, Chapter 6
6. Ditto Lines	$\frac{1}{8}$" $\frac{1}{32}$"	
7. Break Lines		page 3, Chapter 6
	LIGHT	
8. Dimension and Extention Lines	2'–3"	page 2, Chapter 8
9. Property Lines		page 20, Chapter 8
10. Phantom Lines		page 3, Chapter 6
	VERY LIGHT	
11. Break Lines		page 3, Chapter 7
12. Center Lines		page 5, Chapter 6
13. Section Lines		page 4, Chapter 6 and page 6, Chapter 7
14. Projection and Construction Lines		page 3, Chapter 4 and pages 2, 6, 7, 9, Chapter 10

In the interest of making drawings easier to read and interpret, it is important to use the proper type of lines as well as the proper relative line weight. The actual widths of the lines are not as critical as their relative contrast.

The successful draftsman makes all pencil lines as sharp and black as possible, different only in their widths and types. He emphasizes the ends of each line slightly, avoiding feathered ends and foggy lines. Blacker lines make clearer blueprints.

Inked lines, of course, will always be as black as the ink used, and depend entirely on their relative widths for contrast.

An architect uses tracing paper (1) when he makes drawings that will be blueprinted, and (2) when he makes preliminary studies of layouts and designs by tracing from one to another. Tracing paper is available in sheets and rolls of various sizes. (Other types of paper are usually used for presentation drawings.)

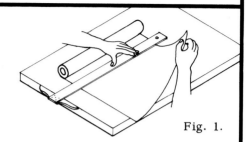

Fig. 1.

Figure 1: Tear off a sheet larger than needed.

Figure 2: Place on the drawing board as shown. This allows the draftsman a maximum reaching advantage.

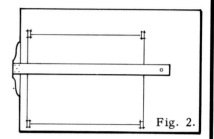

Fig. 2.

Figure 3: See pages 1 and 2 of Chapter 2 for drawing lines. If all lines are drawn lightly until the layout is completed, it will be easier to keep the drawing clean and allows corrections or changes to be made with less effort than after the final heavy lines have been drawn.

Three border lines are usually drawn. The tracing is trimmed on the dash line "A"; Blueprints are trimmed on line "B"; All drawing is done within "C"; and "D," the Title Block, represents space allowed for title information. The wide border on the left is space for binding.

Fig. 3a.   Fig. 3b.   Fig. 3c.

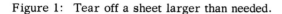

Fig. 3.

Figures 3a, 3b, and 3c show other variations of spaces allowed for title information: TITLE STRIPS or a combination of TITLE STRIPS and TITLE BLOCKS.

TITLE information includes names of CLIENT, PROJECT, ARCHITECT, DATE, PAGE NUMBER and other identification information, as well as a record of changes that may be made after the job has been awarded to the builder.

Fig. 4.

Figure 4: In the interest of time and convenience, draw the layout lines longer than needed. The excess lines can easily be erased. For symmetry make F less than E and G less than H.

Figure 5: Erase the surplus layout lines before drawing the final heavy lines. Lettering is done either before or after drawing the heavy lines.

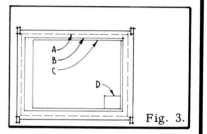

Fig. 5.

Figure 6: Draw the final heavy lines. The drawing is now ready to be blueprinted.

As mentioned above, the tracing is not trimmed back as far as the blueprint of it is. This extra portion protects the tracing when handled, filed, or returned to the drawing board for changes etc.

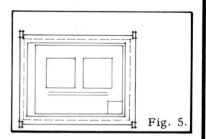

Fig. 6.

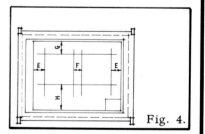
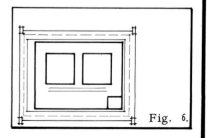

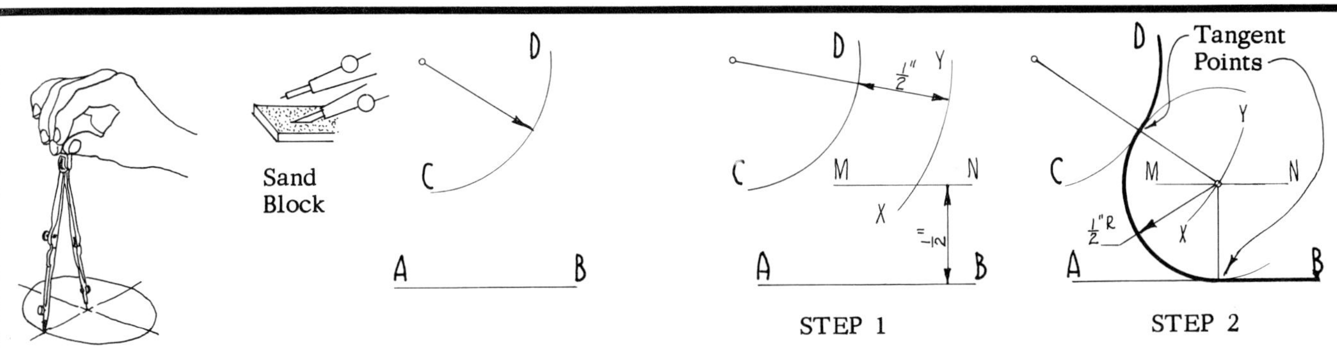

To sharpen compass lead, use a sand block or a file.

Sand Block

GIVEN: Lines AB & CD.
REQUIRED: to draw an arc 1/2" radius, tangent to the given lines.

STEP 1

Draw arc XY with a radius 1/2" larger than the radius of CD. Draw a line MN 1/2" away from and // to line AB.

STEP 2

The intersection of the two lines XY and MN locates the center of the required arc.

Tangent Points

Figure 1. Use of the Compass

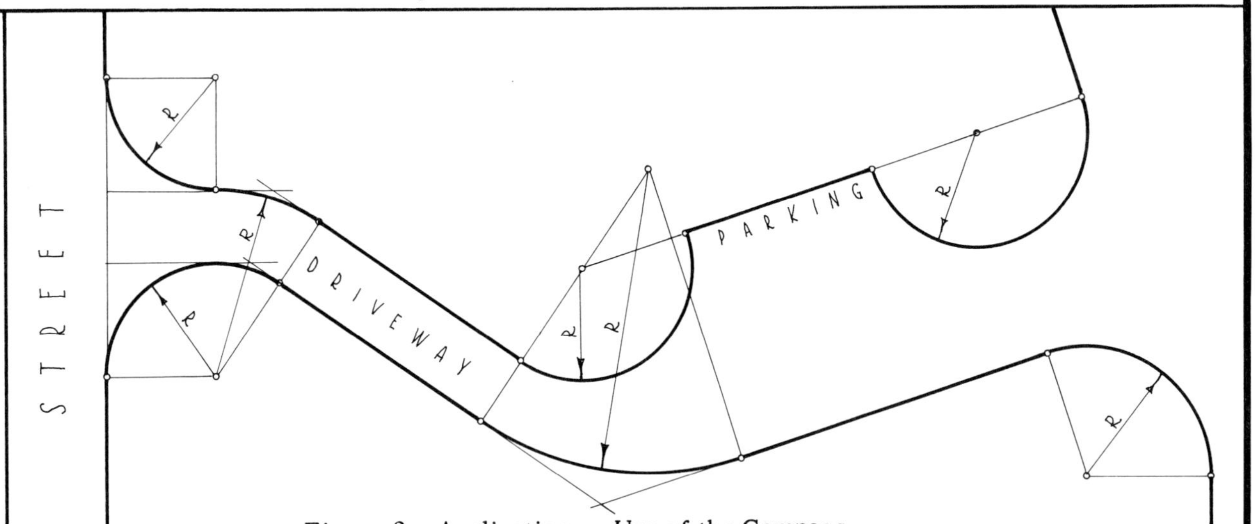

Figure 2. Application -- Use of the Compass

A FRENCH CURVE is used to draw an IR-REGULAR CURVE. It is important to make each setting of the French Curve tangent to its previous setting. This will insure a smooth continuous curved line. Note, the French Curve is set to include the small dots at each setting, but only the portion between the two larger dots is drawn at one setting.

Irregular Curve

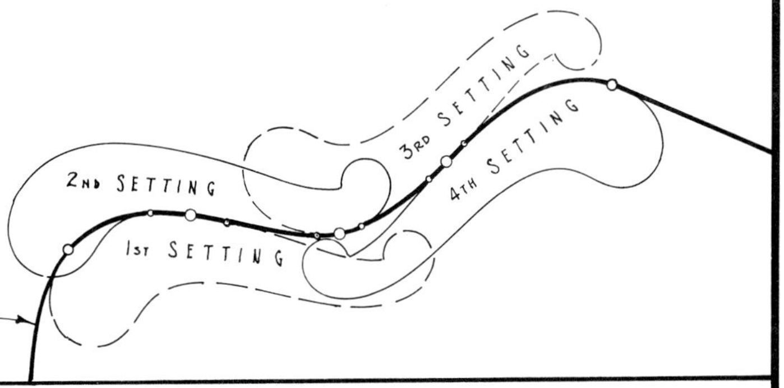

Figure 3. Use of French Curve

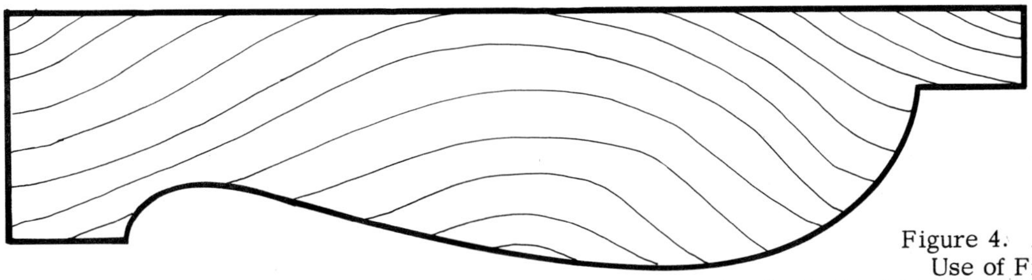

(The wood-grain section lines are always drawn freehand.)

Figure 4. Application -- Use of French Curve

SCALES

By use of scales, drawings can be made smaller than actual size, and even larger than actual size, without any computations. Buildings, of course, cannot be practicably drawn full size, and must be drawn to some smaller scale suitable to the size of the paper being used. The dimensions can be read accurately and directly on the chosen scale.

ARCHITECT'S SCALE

This scale is used in making most of the drawings for the building industry. It measures feet, inches, and fractions of inches. Standard units of scale represent 1 ft. as 1/16", 3/32", 1/8", 3/16", 1/4", 3/8", 1/2", 3/4", 1", 1 1/2", and 3", and are noted on the drawing as: 1/16" = 1'-0", 3/32" = 1'-0", 1/4" = 1'-0", etc.

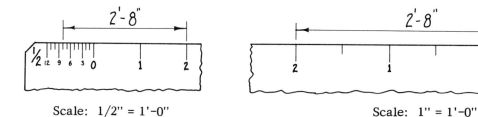

Scale: 1/2" = 1'-0"   Scale: 1" = 1'-0"

Figure 1.

The instrument called the ARCHITECT'S SCALE has many scales on it. Above is an example of one dimension (2'-8") as read on two of its different scales.

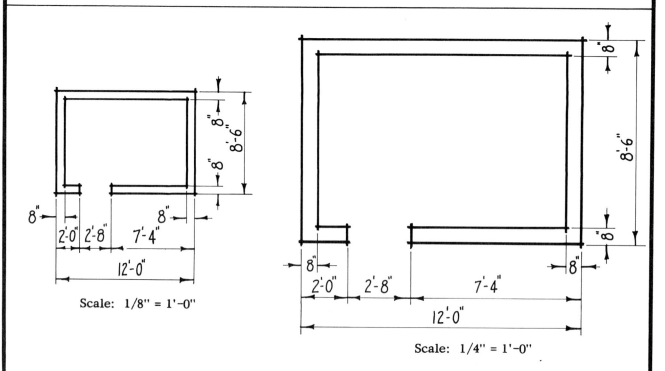

Scale: 1/8" = 1'-0"

Scale: 1/4" = 1'-0"

Figure 2.

A comparison of two drawings of the same floor
plan drawn at two different units of scale.

ENGINEER'S SCALE

This scale is used in most branches of Engineering. Its measurements are based on the decimal system. Standard units of scale are: 1" = 10, 1" = 20, 1" = 30, 1" = 40, 1" = 50, and 1" = 60. Each of these units of scale can be used to represent a number of different lengths, as shown below in Figure 1.

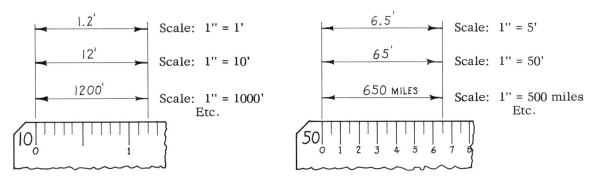

Figure 1.

Adaptability of the Engineer's Scale

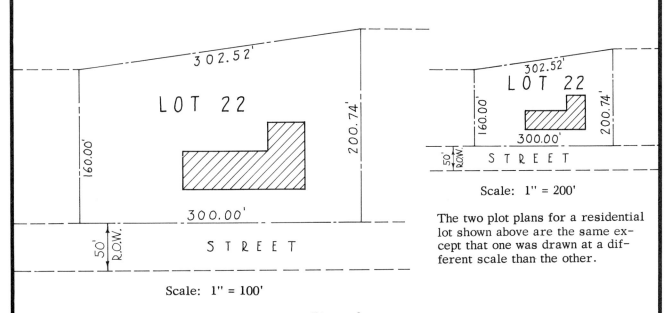

Scale: 1" = 100'

Scale: 1" = 200'

The two plot plans for a residential lot shown above are the same except that one was drawn at a different scale than the other.

Figure 2.

Note the above plot plans are not complete land descriptions (See Chapter 8 for land measurements.); they are showing some linear measurements to illustrate the use of scales. The 50 ft. R.O.W. (Right of Way) street includes sidewalks, parking, and pavement, all of which is city property.

IMPORTANCE OF ACCURACY IN DRAWING

1. Legally speaking, dimensions are important but accuracy of the drawing is not.

2. From a design standpoint, layouts and details need to be as accurate as possible. The larger the scale, the greater the possibility of accuracy.

3. Working drawings are more easily interpreted if they are reasonably accurate.

A person often finds it convenient to sketch freehand, orthographically or pictorially, for the purpose of preliminary studies or to illustrate his explanation during a discussion with others.

Therefore, in the interest of convenience and time, a freehand sketch is usually made with a pencil, without the aid of instruments. No attempt should be made to make a freehand sketch look like an instrument drawing.

However, it is often advantageous to block out the drawing to scale when sketching, especially when the object has parts that have definite standard dimensions. The success of the sketch may depend on the parts being shown quite near their true dimensions, particularly when it is preliminary to an instrument drawing.

SUGGESTIONS:

1. Use a soft pencil. (Grades of pencils best suited for freehand sketching are shown on page 2 of Chapter 1.)

2. As in instrument drawing, light layout lines are usually made before heavy finished lines. See page 4 of Chapter 2.

3. Sketch each line with a sweeping single stroke, not with short choppy lines.

4. Sketch short freehand lines (up to 3" or 4") with the ball of the hand resting on the paper and acting as a pivot, for better control of the direction of the lines and the pressure of the pencil on the paper. See Figures 1 and 2, page 9. Chapter 2.

5. Sketch long freehand lines using the movement of the entire arm but with the tip of the little finger sliding on the paper to control the pressure of the pencil. See Figure 3, page 9. Some prefer a longer grip on the pencil when sketching long lines.

Lines sketched from left to right and
downward are easier to control than
lines sketched in opposite directions.

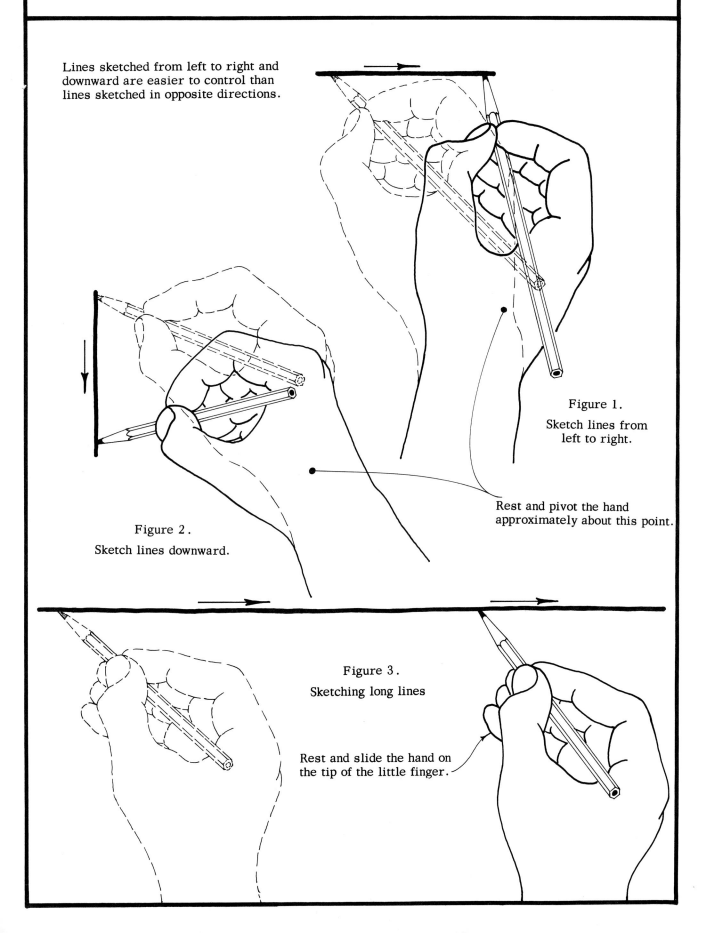

Figure 1.
Sketch lines from
left to right.

Rest and pivot the hand
approximately about this point.

Figure 2.
Sketch lines downward.

Figure 3.
Sketching long lines

Rest and slide the hand on
the tip of the little finger.

Below are shown some exercises that a beginner may follow in practicing freehand sketching.

It is easier to control short lines than long lines. Practice short lines and small sketches first. "Doodling" is good practice.

For circles, sketch a square lightly, then the four centerlines on which 8 points on the circumference of the circle can be located before the circle is sketched. See Step 1 and Step 2 in the exercises below.

Short vertical or horizontal lines sketched close together without lifting the pencil from the paper are often used to quickly indicate cross-sectioned areas or for shading pictorial sketches.

Refinements or improvements of a design are often accomplished by numerous freehand sketches on tracing paper laid over the original design.

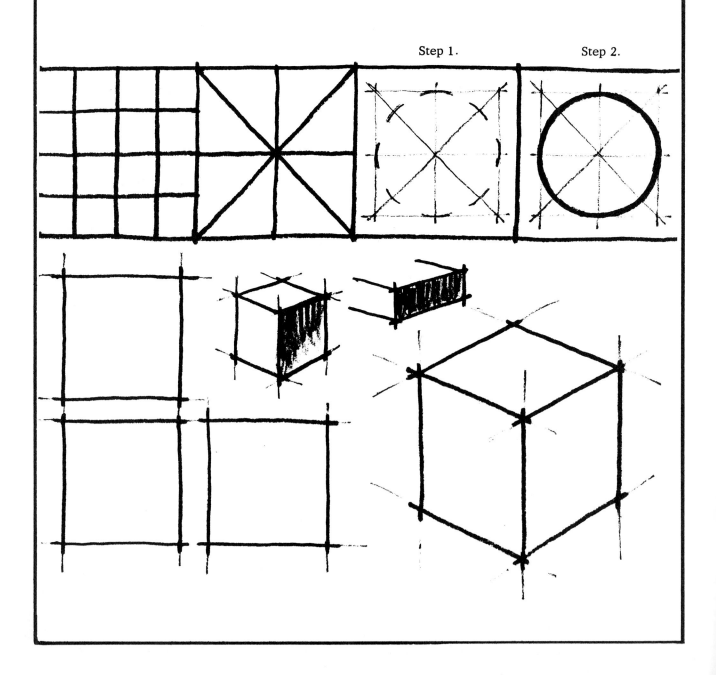

TYPE	CLASSIFICATION		PROJECTORS TO PICTURE PLANE	PROJECTORS TO EACH OTHER	RELATIONSHIP OF OBJECT TO THE PICTURE PLANE
ORTHOGRAPHIC (See Chapter 4.)	MULTI-VIEW		perpendicular	parallel	faces of a rectangular object are parallel to the picture planes
	AXONOMETRIC	ISOMETRIC	perpendicular	parallel	oblique the three axes make equal angles with picture plane
		DIMETRIC	perpendicular	parallel	oblique two axes make equal angles with picture plane
		TRIMETRIC	perpendicular	parallel	oblique all axes make different angles with picture plane
OBLIQUE (See Chapter 5.)	CAVALIER		oblique	parallel	one face parallel to the picture plane
	GENERAL		oblique any angle	parallel	one face parallel to the picture plane
	CABINET		oblique	parallel	one face parallel to the picture plane
PERSPECTIVE (See Chapter 11.)	ONE-POINT		various angles	converge to a point	one face parallel to the picture plane
	TWO-POINT		various angles	converge to a point	vertical faces oblique to the picture plane
	THREE-POINT		various angles	converge to a point	vertical faces oblique to the picture plane

TYPES OF PROJECTION DRAWING

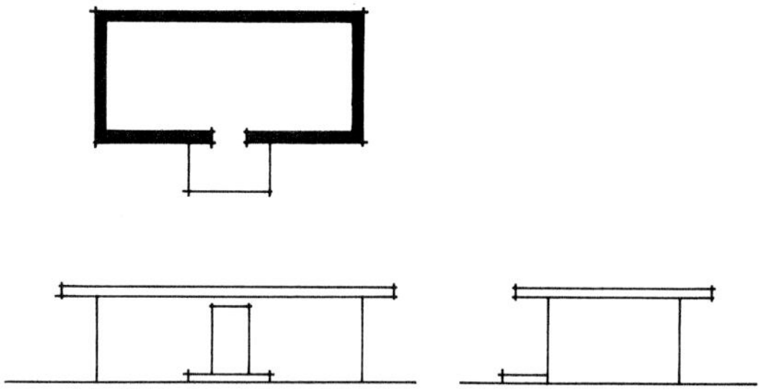

This is the most widely used type. Being the most easily dimensioned, it is used for most construction drawings.

Figure 1.   Multi-View (See Chapter 4.)

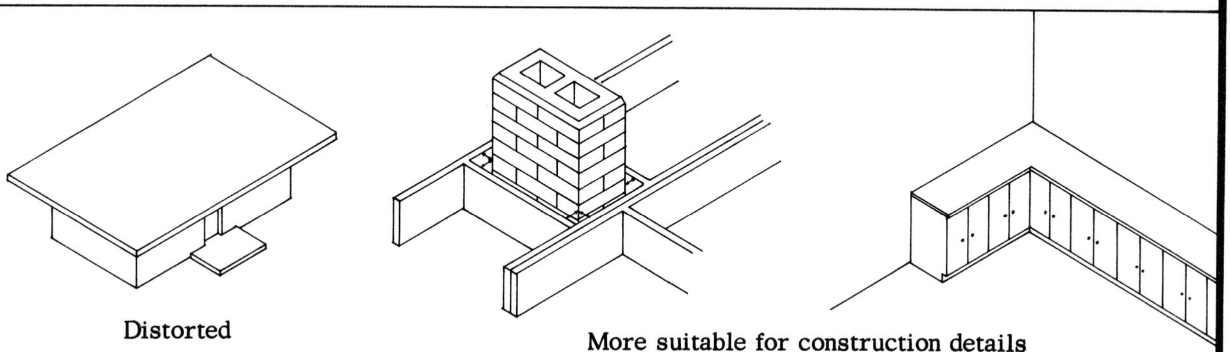

Distorted

More suitable for construction details

More easily understood than multi-view.

Figure 2.   Isometric (See Chapter 4.)

More suitable for objects of little depth, and when circles or arcs appear on front faces.

Figure 3.   Oblique (See Chapter 5.)

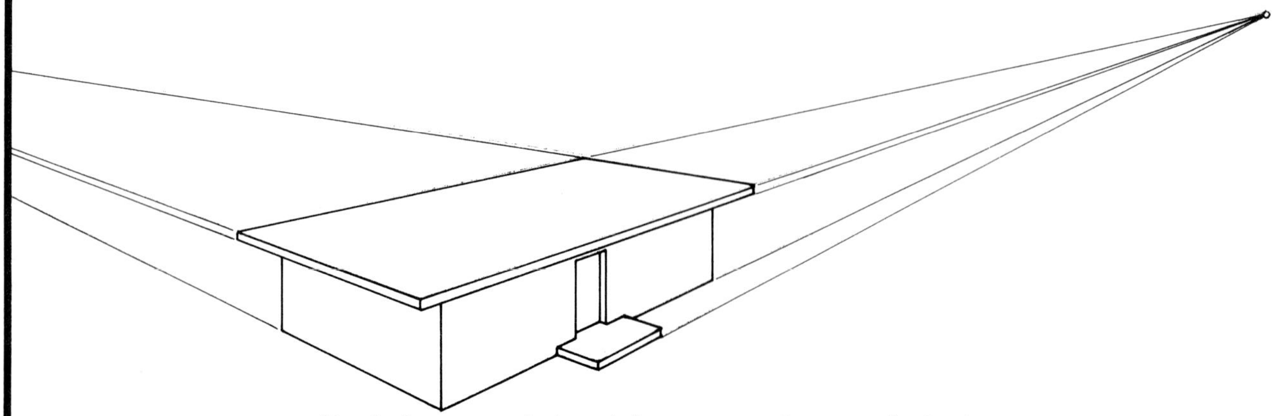

Used when natural pictorial representations are desired.

Figure 4.   Perspective (See Chapter 11.)

It is standard practice to make drawings on imaginary PICTURE PLANES. These PICTURE PLANES are considered transparent and placed between the observer and the object, to sort of "TAKE A PICTURE" of the object.

In PERSPECTIVE, as in photography, the lines of sight converge to the eye. The PICTURE is descriptive but difficult to measure. This type of drawing is used when a natural picture is the main objective.

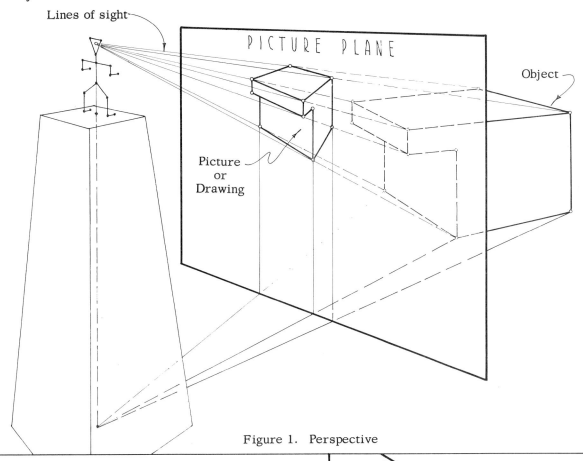

Figure 1. Perspective

To make a drawing that is easy to measure, consider all the LINES OF SIGHT PERPENDICULAR TO THE PICTURE PLANE. This is called ORTHOGRAPHIC PROJECTION.

This type of drawing is more practical for showing dimensions.

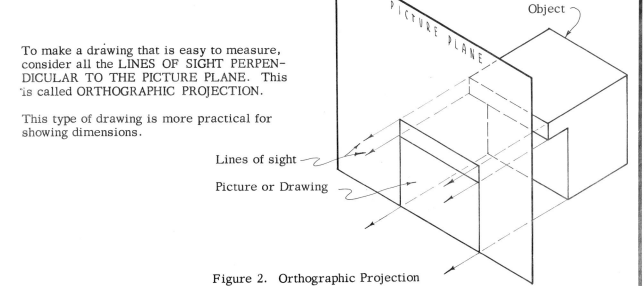

Figure 2. Orthographic Projection

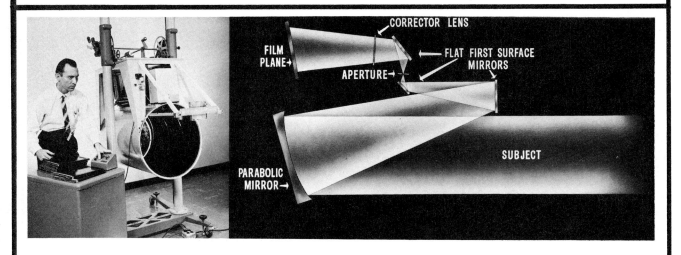

Figure 1.

Figure 2.

A unique camera, developed for use by the photographic department of Procter & Gamble in making photodrawings of scale models, virtually eliminates the effects of perspective. Pictures made with the unit are so orthographic that dimensions for plant construction could be read directly from the photograph.

The camera is shown in Figure 1. The optics of the lensless camera (Figure 2) are illustrated in the diagram. Critical in the system is the aperture, which is equivalent to about f/500. In conjunction with the parabolic first mirror, the aperture keeps non-parallel light from the subject from reaching the film and thereby prohibits the formation of a perspective image.

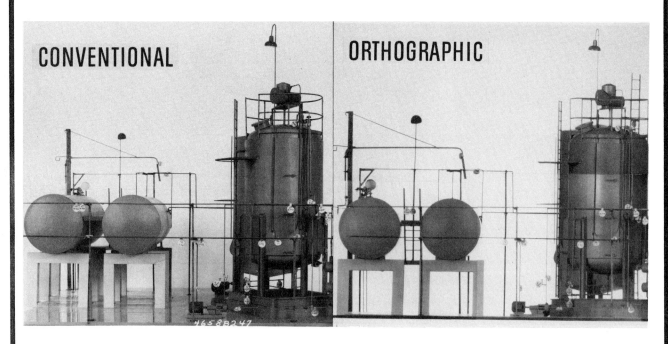

Figure 3.

A picture of apparatus taken with a conventional camera.

Figure 4.

A picture of the same apparatus taken with the NON-PERSPECTIVE camera.

Architects often make models of their building designs. Photographic equipment of this sort would aid in making studies as well as working drawings. Photographs, courtesy of Procter & Gamble.

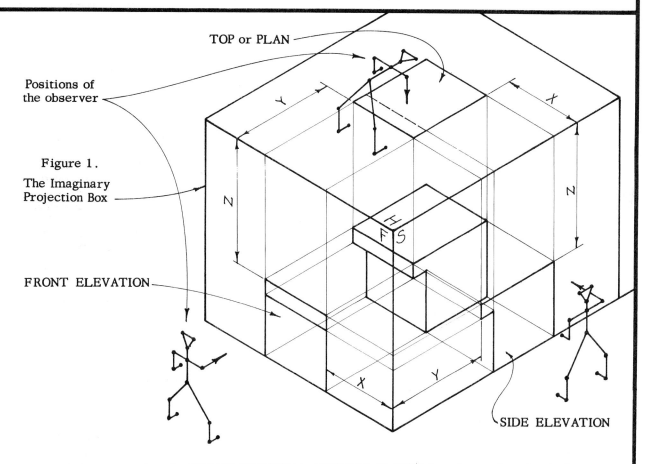

TOP or PLAN

Positions of
the observer

Figure 1.
The Imaginary
Projection Box

FRONT ELEVATION

SIDE ELEVATION

In orthographic projection the THREE PRINCIPAL PICTURE PLANES (or planes of projection) are HORIZONTAL, FRONT, and SIDE, arranged perpendicular to each other.

The illustration above shows the imaginary projection box and the imaginary positions of the observer in obtaining the PLAN, FRONT ELEVATION, and SIDE ELEVATION. ELEVATIONS are so named because there, heights or elevations can be measured.

The 3-view orthographic drawing (Figure 2) is MULTI-VIEW because more than one view is used and they are related by projection. H, F, and S are the picture planes.

The example on this page is very simple and presents no great problem of visualization. However in later problems it will be important to be able to visualize the distances X, Y, and Z. These represent the distances from the object to the picture plane. Note these distances on the pictorial drawing above and on the Multi-View drawing at the left.

RECOMMENDATION FOR BETTER VISUALIZATION: "Don't imagine the projection box unfolded, rather be able to imagine yourself in different positions and in only one at a time, when you look at a Multi-View drawing."

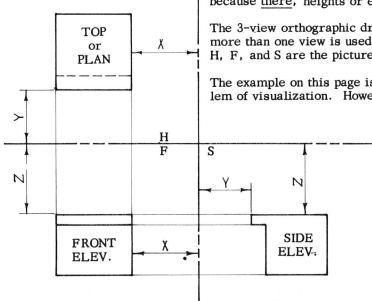

Figure 2. Multi-View Drawing

SYSTEMS OF ORTHOGRAPHIC PROJECTION

The system of projection used to obtain information about lines and planes shown on the following pages is the system used in almost all schools and offices today. It is called the DIRECT METHOD, or the AUXILIARY PLANE METHOD, or can be referred to as the PICTURE PLANE METHOD.

Though several methods or systems can often be used for solving the same problem, and one method may sometimes be better than another, it is considered advantageous to concentrate on mastering one method for solving many problems.

However, the system of projection by the REVOLUTION METHOD is shown in two recommended applications on pages 10 and 11 of this Chapter 4.

RECOMMENDATIONS FOR STUDY

1. Read the discussion and follow its references to the illustrated example.

2. Set up the same example shown in the text and work the problem by freehand sketching or with instruments, following the discussion in the text. This will often bring out points you may have missed in just reading the text.

3. Set up a similar problem or problems and check yourself again on the correct method before attempting a challenging problem of a more practical nature.

4. Learn the system of notations and terminology used in the text. It will help you understand the text as well as make it possible for you to discuss it with others. Notations and terminology are actually unnecessary except for discussion purposes.

5. It is important to be able to visualize the space relationships of lines and planes in space. After sketching or drawing the problems graphically, fold the paper to show the relationship between the different picture planes, similar to the pictorial drawings shown on pages 5, 6, and 7 of this Chapter 4. This procedure should be followed if the reader has any doubt at any time about the relationships of the distances objects are away from the picture planes.

ABBREVIATIONS: PP(picture plane), TL(true length), //(parallel),
                 H(horizontal PP), F(front PP), and P(profile or side PP).

CLASSIFICATION: HORIZONTAL LINE is one that is // to H.
                 FRONTAL LINE is one that is // to F.
                 PROFILE LINE is one that is // to P.
                 OBLIQUE LINE is one that is oblique to H, F and P.

DEFINITION OF A LINE IN SPACE:

BEARING is its direction or its deviation from north or south.
(Consider H as a map and read the deviation in degrees.)

TRUE LENGTH will appear on any PP that is // to the line. (Experiment with this fact by holding one of your triangles // to a pencil.)

INCLINATION is its deviation from horizontal. This is often expressed in degrees and can only be measured where the line appears in TL in an ELEVATION. An ELEVATION is a view obtained on any vertical PP. However, this true angle or deviation from horizontal can only be measured if the vertical PP is // to the line so the line appears in TL. Experiment with this fact by using your table top as H, a triangle as the vertical PP, and a pencil as the line.

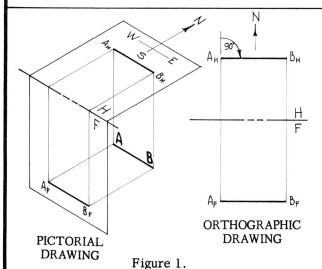

PICTORIAL
DRAWING

ORTHOGRAPHIC
DRAWING

BEARING of AB (from A to B) is N90°E.
BEARING of BA (from B to A) is N90°W.

TRUE LENGTH of AB appears on both the H and F because it is // to both.

INCLINATION of AB is 0° because it is // to H. It is a level line.

CLASSIFICATION: HORIZONTAL-FRONTAL because it is // to H and F.

(Check these facts about line AB with the DEFINITION OF A LINE IN SPACE above.)

Figure 1.

(The pictorial should be the mental picture suggested by the orthographic drawing.)

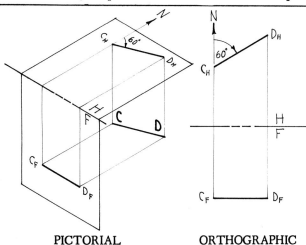

PICTORIAL   ORTHOGRAPHIC

BEARING of CD is N60°E. Bearing of DC is S60°W.

TRUE LENGTH of CD appears in H because CD is // to H.

INCLINATION of CD is also 0° because it is level (horizontal).

CLASSIFICATION: HORIZONTAL because it is // to H. This is evident in F.

(Check these facts about line CD with the DEFINITION OF A LINE IN SPACE above.)

Figure 2.

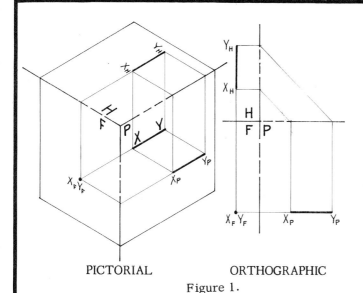

PICTORIAL   ORTHOGRAPHIC

Figure 1.

BEARING of XY is N 0° E.
BEARING of YX is S 0° E.

TRUE LENGTH of XY appears on both H and P.

INCLINATION of XY is 0° because it is level (horizontal).

CLASSIFICATION: HORIZONTAL-PROFILE because it is // to both H and P.

(Note: the PROFILE view would not be needed to describe this line. With two given views the third can be drawn by projection from the other two, if necessary. All the necessary information can be obtained from two.)

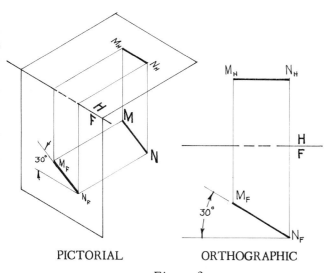

PICTORIAL   ORTHOGRAPHIC

Figure 2.

BEARING of MN is N 90° E.
BEARING of NM is N 90° W.

TRUE LENGTH of MN appears on F because it is // to F. This is evident in H.

INCLINATION of MN is -30°. (Minus because it sloped down from M to N.) Inclination of NM is +30°. (Plus because it slopes up from N to M.)

Note: the inclination of MN can be measured in F because it shows the TL of MN and is an ELEVATION. An ELEVATION is obtained with a vertical PP.

CLASSIFICATION: FRONTAL (// to F)

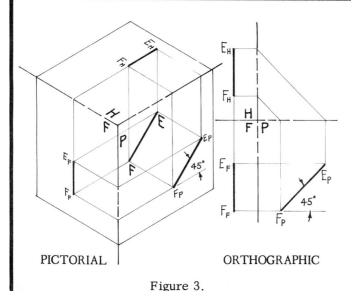

PICTORIAL   ORTHOGRAPHIC

Figure 3.

BEARING of EF is S 0° E.
BEARING of FE is N 0° E.

TRUE LENGTH of EF appears in P. This is evident in H and F where it shows that EF is // to P

INCLINATION of EF is -45°.
INCLINATION of FE is +45°.

Note: Inclination can be measured in P because EF shows in TL and P is an ELEVATION.

CLASSIFICATION: PROFILE

In the pictorial below, the notations on the projections
of the line AB have been omitted. They should now
be obvious.

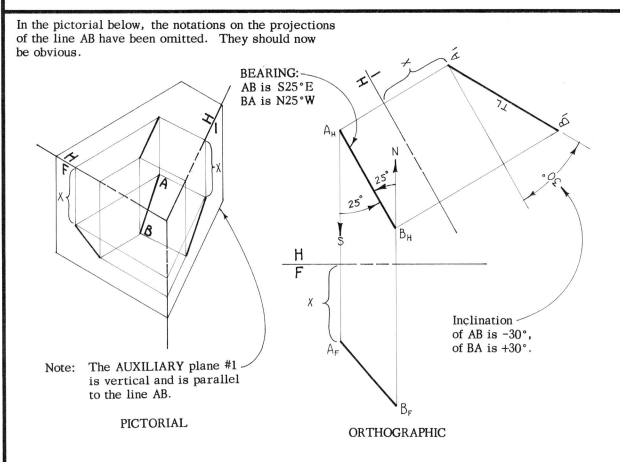

BEARING:
AB is S25°E
BA is N25°W

Inclination
of AB is −30°,
of BA is +30°.

Note: The AUXILIARY plane #1
is vertical and is parallel
to the line AB.

PICTORIAL

ORTHOGRAPHIC

PROBLEM

GIVEN: The Plan (H) and Front Elevation (F) of the OBLIQUE LINE AB.
REQUIRED: Determine the BEARING, TRUE LENGTH, and INCLINATION of the given line.

Observations to be made before the problem can be solved:

1. The H and F do not show TL or INCLINATION.

2. Since Inclination is always measured in a VERTICAL PP that shows TL of the line, a PP other
   than H, F, or P must be used.

3. Remember two views of the line are given and a third will be sufficient for the solution.

SOLUTION:

1. Place the third PP // to the line AB and in a vertical position. (PP's other than H, F, and P
   will be referred to as AUXILIARY picture planes.)

   Note: the AUXILIARY PP can be placed anywhere just so it is // to AB and is vertical.

2. Point A can be located on AUXILIARY PP "1" by measuring the distance "X" shown in F and
   laying it off on the AUXILIARY PP as shown on the drawing above.
   Remember, Orthographic Projection means PROJECTING PERPENDICULARLY TO THE
   PP; therefore, the distance "X" must be laid off on a line from A_H PERPENDICULAR to the
   AUXILIARY PP "1". The distance "X" represents the distance point "A" is below the H pic-
   ture plane, and should be the same in all ELEVATIONS.

3. Point "B" can similarly be located.

4. To determine the BEARING and measure the INCLINATION, review pages 5 and 6.

SUGGESTION: If you have the least difficulty in visualizing the above problem, sketch it on paper,
fold it into the 3 PP's, and observe the distance "X."

TRUE ANGLE WITH H, and
TRUE ANGLE WITH F.

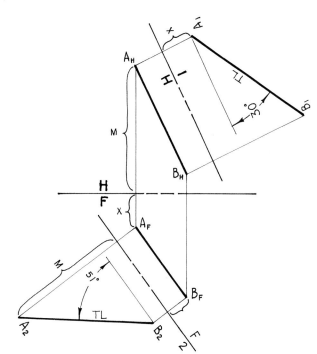

Figure 1.

The orthographic drawing at the left shows the problem on the preceding page, with AUXILIARY PLANE #2 added.

This Auxiliary PP is perpendicular to F and parallel to the line AB.

In addition to showing the TL of AB, it also shows the angle the line makes with F. This angle is often confused with INCLINATION, but cannot be inclination because the auxiliary PP #2 is not vertical and does not show elevation.

It is important to be able to visualize the space relationship of any THREE RELATED VIEWS. Three related or consecutive views can be better visualized by sketching this problem on paper and folding it into planes. It will then be easier to visualize the distances M and X, as well as the angle line AB makes with F.

LINE AS A POINT

Obtaining a view showing a line as a point is a necessary maneuver used to obtain INCLINATION AND TRUE SHAPE OF PLANE SURFACES. (See following pages.)

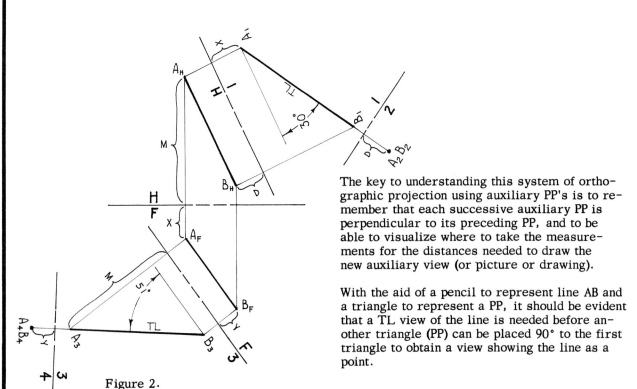

Figure 2.

The key to understanding this system of orthographic projection using auxiliary PP's is to remember that each successive auxiliary PP is perpendicular to its preceding PP, and to be able to visualize where to take the measurements for the distances needed to draw the new auxiliary view (or picture or drawing).

With the aid of a pencil to represent line AB and a triangle to represent a PP, it should be evident that a TL view of the line is needed before another triangle (PP) can be placed 90° to the first triangle to obtain a view showing the line as a point.

PROBLEM: Draw the Plan and Front Elevation of line AB, whose BEARING is N 30° W, INCLI-
NATION is -30°, and TRUE LENGTH is 1". (Given point A)

PROCEDURE: The procedure is shown in three illustrated steps below:

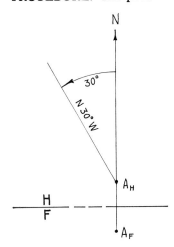

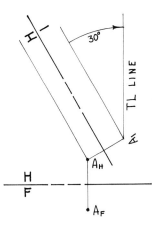

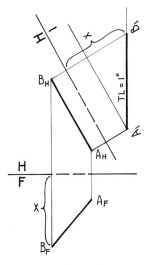

Step 1

Through point A draw the
BEARING: N 30 ° W.

Step 2

Place an auxiliary PP parallel to bearing. Then pro-
ject A to the auxiliary PP.
Draw the INCLINATION -30°

Step 3

Measure 1" on the TL
line to locate B.
Project point B to the
Plan and Front Elevation.

Figure 1.

PROBLEM: Draw the plan and front elevation of line MN, whose bearing is S45°E, inclination is
+60°, and TL is 3/4". (If point M or N is not given, one of them will have to be
assumed.) (Point M is assumed below.)

PROCEDURE: Follow the same procedure as in the problem of Figure 1 above, using the data of
this problem.

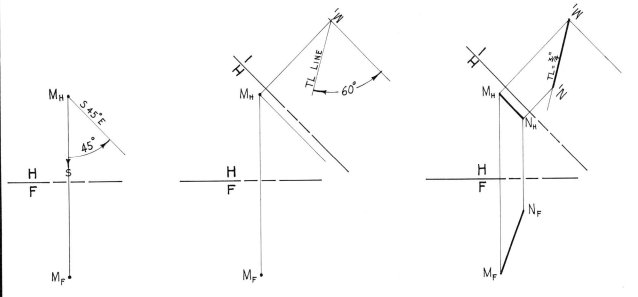

Figure 2 .

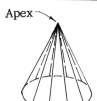

RIGHT CONE

Obviously all straight lines from the apex to the base of a <u>right cone</u> are equal in true length. In orthographic, the TL will appear as the <u>SLANT HEIGHT</u> of a right cone. (See below.)

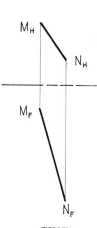

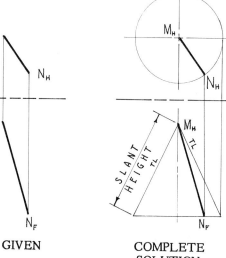

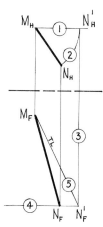

TL of MN by Revolution

Figure 1.

GIVEN

COMPLETE
SOLUTION
(A)

MINIMUM
CONSTRUCTION
(B)

PROBLEM: Given line MN. Find its TL by constructing a right cone containing the line.

SOLUTION: By constructing a complete cone as shown in (A), the TL of the line MN will be the slant height of the cone. (B) shows the minimum necessary construction for finding the TL.

THIS METHOD IS CALLED REVOLUTION since MN is <u>revolved</u> to a position that places it parallel to F. Therefore its new position $M_H N'_H$ and $M_F N'_F$ shows the $\overline{TL}$ of the line to be $M_F N'_F$. (The steps of construction are marked 1, 2, 3, 4, and 5.)

In the two solutions below, a different apex has been chosen. (Same TL results.)

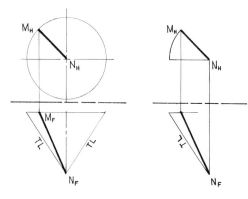

In this solution the cone is inverted.

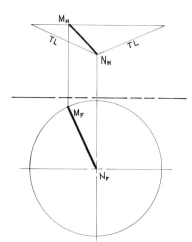

In this solution the base of the cone is parallel to F.

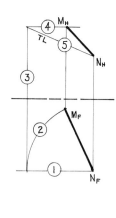

Figure 2. TL of MN by Revolution

A right cone can be defined as the locus (or path) of a line that is fixed at one end and makes a constant angle with a plane. The plane becomes the base of the cone, and the fixed point becomes the apex.

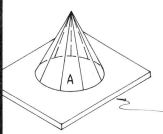

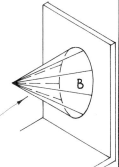

CONE LOCUS can conveniently be used to solve the follow-
                            ing problem:

PROBLEM: Construct a line that has an inclination of –30°
                 and at the same time makes an angle of 45°
                 with a vertical wall.

LOCUS of a line having constant inclination.
LOCUS of a line having constant angle with a wall.

PROBLEM ANALYSIS: The pictorial (below) of the solution, shows two cones having the same apex, the same slant height, and therefore with bases that intersect. A line from the apex to each of the intersection points of the bases will be the lines common to both cones. If each cone satisfies one of the requirements of the problem, then the lines common to both cones should satisfy both angle requirements of the problem.

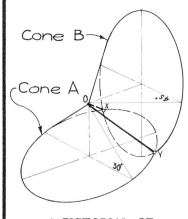

A PICTORIAL OF
THE SOLUTION

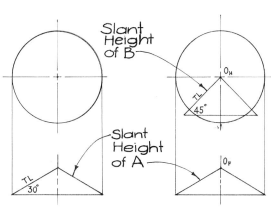

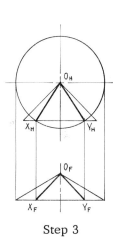

Step 1

Step 2

Step 3

SOLUTION

Step 1.   Draw the plan and front elevation of cone A having an inclination of 30°, and of any conven-
          ient slant height. Any line on this cone will satisfy the 30° requirement.

Step 2.   Through the same apex construct the plan view only, of cone B whose slant height is the same
          as the cone A and makes an angle of 45° with the Front PP. Any line on this cone satisfies the
          45° requirement. Note that the bases of the two cones intersect.

Step 3.   Connect the two intersection points of the bases, with the apex. Either line common to both
          cones, satisfies the two-angle requirement of the problem. (Either OX or OY.)

INCLINATION of LINES and PLANES is measured in a vertical plane. Although the different expressions of INCLINATION have particular applications, they are often interchanged. The drawings below show elevations only, of a LINE in TL, or a PLANE in EDGE VIEW.

1. SLOPE ANGLE

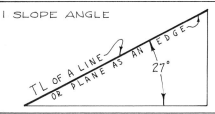

DEFINITION: The vertical angle. DIHEDRAL for planes.
EXPRESSION: Degrees (Angle with a horizontal plane).
APPLICATION: General production industry
EXAMPLE: 27°
(All examples on this page were drawn with the same inclination for all expressions, for comparison.)

2. SLOPE

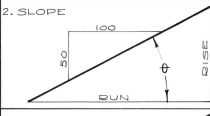

DEFINITION: RISE/RUN or TANGENT of angle θ
EXPRESSION: Decimal
APPLICATION: Drainage and pipe lines where slope is small
EXAMPLE: RISE/RUN = 50/100 = .5
(Measure RUN 100 on some convenient scale to avoid computations in arithmetic.)

3. GRADE

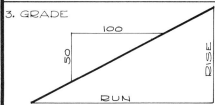

DEFINITION: RISE/RUN
EXPRESSION: Percent
APPLICATION: Plot grading and roadways where slope is small
EXAMPLE: RISE/RUN = 50/100 = 50%

4. SLOPE RATIO

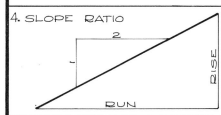

DEFINITION: RISE/RUN when run is greater than rise
EXPRESSION: Ratio of 1/RUN (RISE is always "1").
APPLICATION: Roofs and terraces
EXAMPLE: RISE/RUN = 1/2 (1 to 2 or 1 on 2)
C.E.'s often say 2 to 1 or 2 on 1. Though technically incorrect, it has become accepted practice through usage.

5. BATTER

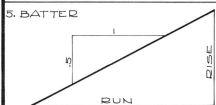

DEFINITION: RUN/RISE when rise is greater than run (RUN is always "1").
EXPRESSION: Ratio of 1/RISE
APPLICATION: Steep embankments
EXAMPLES: RUN/RISE = 1/.5 (Left ex.).
(More suitable) = 1/4 (Right ex.)

6. SLOPE RATIO

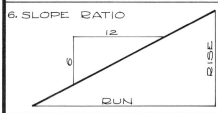

DEFINITION: RISE/RUN
EXPRESSION: Ratio with 12 for the longer, RISE or RUN
APPLICATION: Structural members and roofs and stairways
EXAMPLE: 6/12 (numerator should be in inches and fractions of inches).

7. PITCH

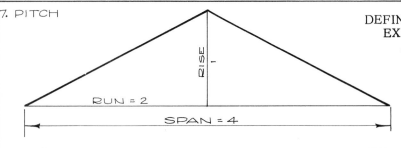

DEFINITION: RISE/SPAN (RISE always 1)
EXPRESSION: Ratio of 1/SPAN
APPLICATION: Roofs and trusses
EXAMPLE: RISE/SPAN = 1/4

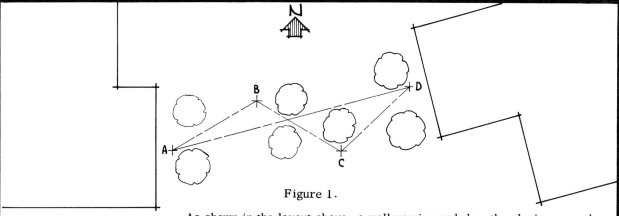

Figure 1.

Figure 2.

The above illustration may
help you visualize the
centerlines of the walks on
sloping ground.

As shown in the layout above, a walkway is needed on the sloping grounds
between two buildings, from point A to point D. The grounds slope uniformly due west. See Figure 2.

At this stage of planning, two schemes are being considered:

SCHEME I: A walk directly from A to D. Point D is 225' N 75° E of
             point A, at a grade of +20%.

SCHEME II: A winding walk from point A to B to C to D, which would have
             less inclination but greater length. Point B is 90' N 60° E
             of A. Point C is 90' S 60° E of B.

THE PROBLEM: How much longer is SCHEME II than SCHEME I?
               What is the slope of each leg of SCHEME II?

THE SOLUTION is shown below, in Figure 3.

SCHEME I can be drawn (only centerline shown) according to page 9 of Chapter 4.

SCHEME II can be drawn according to the same principles as was SCHEME I but a point "X" must be
assumed anywhere on the line AB. (The front view of line AD is also the edge view of the
plane of the sloping grounds, and contains all points, A, B, C, and D. See Figure 2.)

BC has the same slope and length as AB, and is different only in bearing.

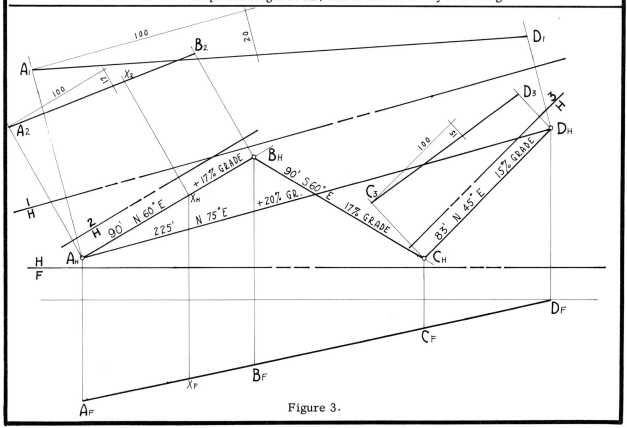

Figure 3.

A To look at the orthographic drawing of an object and be able to visualize the three dimensions is often difficult for a beginner. It becomes easier as his "experience" makes him more efficient.

It is a matter of mental trial and error to imagine the shape described by the orthographic views.

As a start consider the two-view drawing that shows an object as a square in the horizontal or top view and as a square in the front view. Below are shown 7 possible solutions. There are even more. The side view in orthographic is shown for each, as well as a pictorial showing the mental picture you should have as you see the three orthographic views of the object.

Since most working drawings are orthographic, the architect, the draftsman, the builder, and anyone needing to use them, need to be able to interpret them.

Add to your "experience" by noticing the two examples below. One shows one solution, but the other shows two.

Try sketching the side view that will satisfy each solution.

B

SOLUTION

ORTHOGRAPHIC
DRAWING

C

TWO SOLUTIONS

ORTHOGRAPHIC
DRAWING

D The example below shows a two-view orthographic drawing of a stack of blocks, some of which are wedges and some are cubes.

As a student it will benefit you to create and solve similar problems to add to your "experience," increasing your ability to interpret orthographic drawings.

SOLUTION

ORTHOGRAPHIC DRAWING

Two orthographic views of each object is given. Trace this page and sketch a third view and a pictorial for each as was done in Problem 1.

(A tip on #6: the circular portion represents a plane surface.)

1

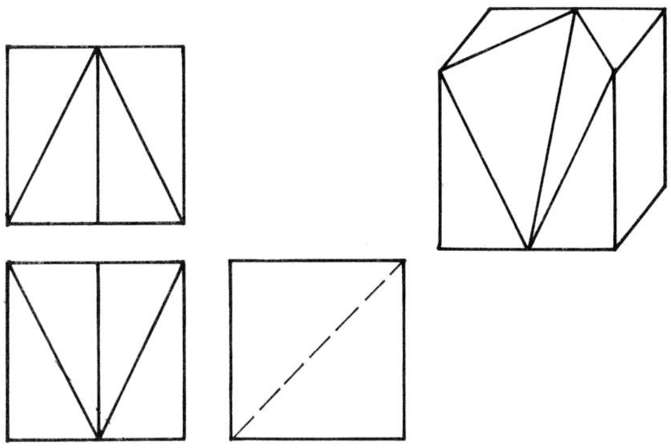

2

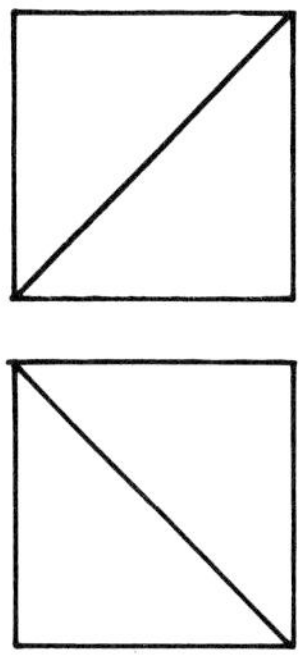

3

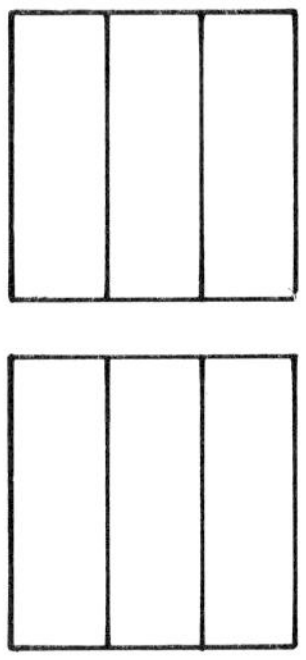

4

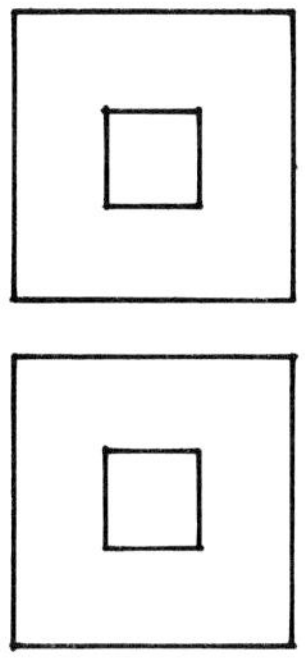

5

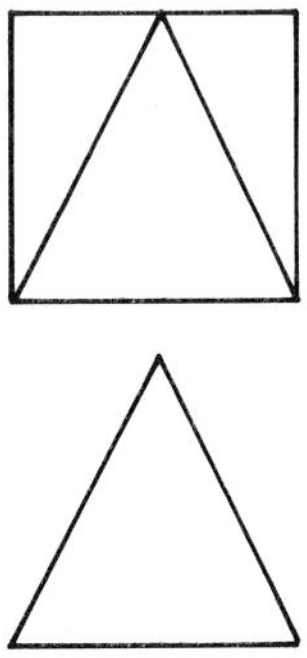

6

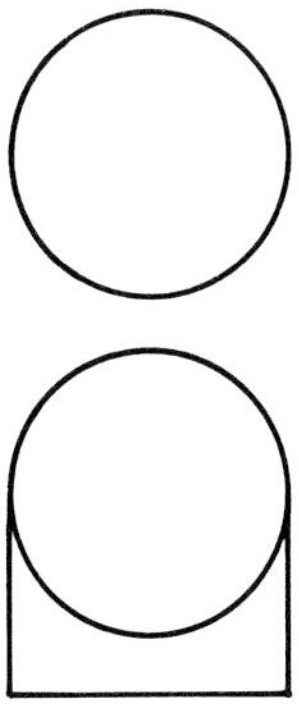

7

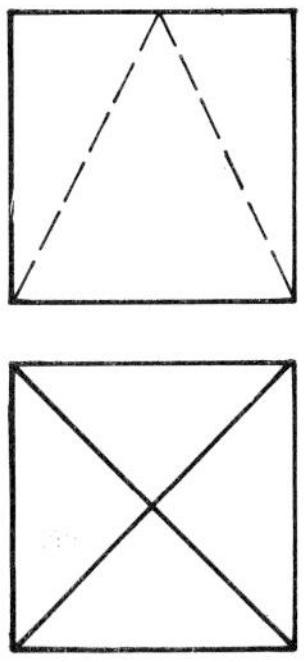

8

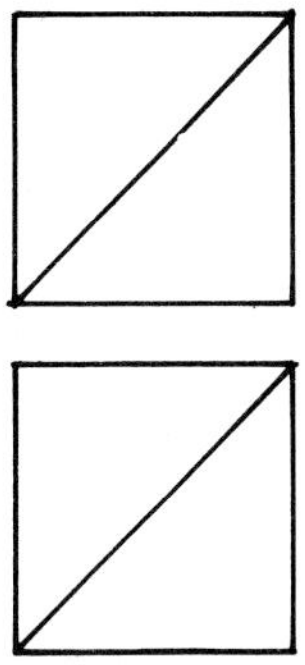

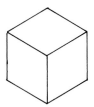

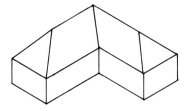

Figure 1. Figures Bounded by Plane Surfaces

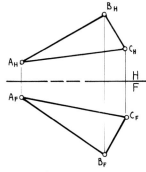

Figure 2.

MINIMUM REPRESENTATION OF A PLANE

Specifically, a minimum of three points not in a straight line, determine a plane.

For reasons of simplicity and expediency a plane represented by three points connected to form a triangle will be used for most of the typical demonstrations of orthographic projection of planes. (Three points not in a straight line or a point and a line would be minimum.)

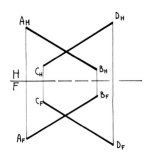

Figure 3.

INTERSECTING LINES DETERMINE A PLANE

In terms of geometry a plane surface is one on which it is possible to draw two intersecting lines. In other words TWO INTERSECTING STRAIGHT LINES DETERMINE A PLANE.

The two lines shown at the left do intersect because the apparent point of intersection in H is in projection with the apparent point of intersection in F. In other words the point exists so the lines do intersect, and therefore determine a plane.

TO DETERMINE IF A SURFACE IS A PLANE

Obviously a surface bounded by three straight lines is a plane. Surfaces bounded by 4 or more straight lines or by curved lines are not always obviously planes. Check by drawing intersecting lines on the plane in question.

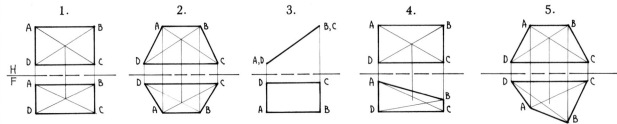

1 and 2 are planes because 2 intersecting lines can be drawn on them.
3 is obviously a plane, evident in H.

4 and 5 are not plane surfaces, because intersecting lines cannot be drawn on them. These surfaces are consequently warped.
(See WARPED SURFACES on page 4, Chapter 10.)

Figure 4.

SEVEN BASIC PROJECTIONS

Typical problems involving planes can usually be solved by being able to do the following projections:

1. Place a line on any plane in space and draw its projections.

2. Place a point on any plane in space and draw its projections.

3. Draw a line perpendicular to any plane in space.

4. Draw a line parallel to a plane or a plane parallel to a line.

5. Draw a plane parallel to another plane.

6. Pass a cutting plane through a given plane and find the line of intersection between the 2 planes.

7. Project a line until it shows as a point. (See Figure 2, Chapter 4, page 8.)

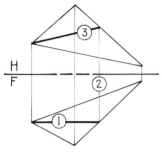

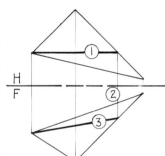

BASIC PROJECTION
1. PLACE A LINE ON ANY PLANE IN SPACE

A. PLACE A HORIZONTAL LINE ON A GIVEN PLANE

    1. Draw the Front Elevation of the line first, since there it must appear // to H to be horizontal.

    2. Project it to H.

    3. Draw the Plan of the line.

(The steps of construction are marked 1, 2, and 3 on the drawing.)

B. PLACE A FRONTAL LINE ON THE GIVEN PLANE

    1. Draw the Plan of the line first, since there it must appear // to F to be a frontal line.

    2. Project it to F.

    3. Draw the Front Elevation of the line.

(In a similar manner any straight line can be placed upon a given plane and projected to the required picture planes.)

Figure 1.

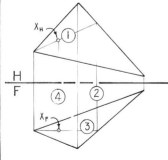

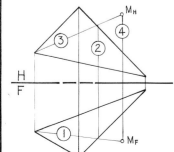

BASIC PROJECTION
2. PLACE A POINT ON ANY PLANE IN SPACE

A. FIND THE FRONT ELEVATION OF POINT X WHEN THE PLAN IS GIVEN

    1. Draw any line on the plane through the given point X_H.

    2. Project this line to the Front Elevation.

    3. Draw the Front Elevation of the line.

    4. Project X to the Front Elevation.

B. ASSUMING THAT THE TRINAGLE SHOWN REPRESENTS A POR-TION OF A PLANE OF LIMITLESS SIZE, FIND THE PLAN OF THE POINT M. (The Front Elevation of point M is given.)

    1. Draw any line on the plane through M_F.

    2. Project this line to the Plan.

    3. Draw the Plan of the line.

    4. Project M to the Plan.

Figure 2.

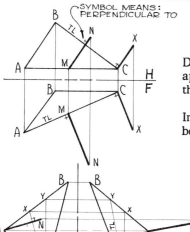

BASIC PROJECTION
3. DRAW A LINE PERPENDICULAR TO ANY PLANE IN SPACE

DIRECTION PRINCIPLE: If a line is perpendicular to a plane, it will appear (in any orthographic view) at right angles to any line on the plane that shows in TL in that view.

In the first example MN and CX are both perpendicular to the plane ABC because they show perpendicular to the TL views of BC and AC.

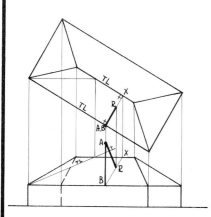

In the second example no given line appears in TL, therefore lines CX (a frontal line) and CY (a profile line) were placed on the plane ABC. AN is perpendicular to ABC because of the DIRECTION PRINCIPLE.
(Note F and P picture planes were used in this problem instead of the usual H and F.)

Figure 3.

AN APPLICATION OF THE DIRECTION PRINCIPLE

GIVEN: The building and the vertical pole AB.
REQUIRED: A brace from A perpendicular to the roof.
SOLUTION: In plan, AR will appear perpendicular to lines of the roof that appear TL in plan.

In elevation AR will appear perpendicular to lines of the roof that appear TL in elevation. Since no lines of the actual roof shape appear TL in elevation, it is necessary to place a line on the roof that will appear TL in elevation.

It is logical that point R will be somewhere on the line BX.

Figure 4.

BASIC PROJECTION
4. DRAW A LINE PARALLEL TO A PLANE OR A PLANE PARALLEL TO A LINE

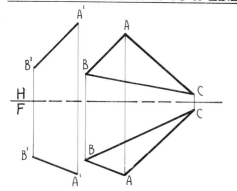

A'B' is // to ABC because it is // to a line on the plane (or vice versa).

Figure 4.

BASIC PROJECTION
5. DRAW A PLANE PARALLEL TO ANOTHER PLANE

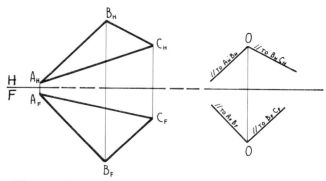

The two intersecting lines drawn through "O" form a plane that is // to ABC because each of the lines is // to ABC.

Figure 5.

BASIC PROJECTION

6. PASS A CUTTING PLANE THROUGH A GIVEN PLANE AND FIND THE LINE OF INTERSECTION BETWEEN THE 2 PLANES

This CUTTING PLANE is inserted as is done with AUXILLIARY PLANES. It is not used as a PP but only to cut the given plane at some determined place. (See application on pages 22 and 23, Chapter 4.)

The two examples at the left illustrate the steps necessary to find the line of intersection XY. Since these only illustrate the BASIC PROJECTION, the cutting planes were placed at random. (Again see applications on pages 22 and 23, Chapter 4.)

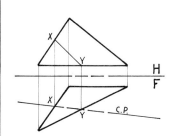

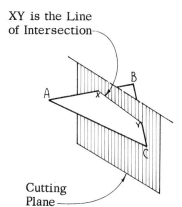

XY is the Line of Intersection

Cutting Plane

7. PROJECT A LINE UNTIL IT SHOWS AS A POINT
   (See Figure 2, Chapter 4, page 8.)

SEVEN TYPICAL PROBLEMS

The SEVEN BASIC PROJECTIONS should be adequate to solve the following SEVEN TYPICAL PROBLEMS involving planes. (The number "seven" has no matching significance between projections and problems.)

The challenging part of each typical problem is to be able to choose and execute the BASIC PROJECTIONS necessary for the solutions of the TYPICAL PROBLEMS.

1. Find the inclination of a plane.

2. Find the True Shape of a plane.

3. Find the Dihedral Angle between two planes.

4. Find the angle between a line and a plane.

5. Locate the piercing point of a line and a plane.

6. Find the line of intersection between any two planes.

7. Determine clearances between non-parallel non-intersecting lines.

TYPICAL PROBLEM 1. FIND THE INCLINATION OF A PLANE

INCLINATION of a plane is expressed in various ways. See page 12, Chapter 4. Measurement must be made where the plane shows as an edge in elevation.

Often the inclination of a roof is easily measured because the front or side elevations of the building will show the edge view.

To become proficient in handling planes that are not so conveniently located, it is necessary to be able to project any plane into such a position that the inclination can be measured.

A plane will appear as an edge WHERE ANY LINE ON THAT PLANE SHOWS AS A POINT, but for inclination to be measured it must appear as an edge in elevation.

PROBLEM: Given the Plan and Front Elevation of ABC and MNOP. Find the inclination of each.

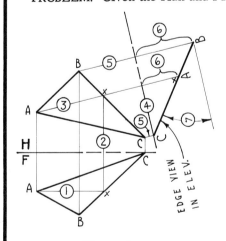

Figure 1.

SOLUTION: Steps 1, 2, and 3 place a horizontal line AX on ABC. Plane MNOP already has horizontal lines (MN and OP).

Step 4 places a vertical Auxiliary PP to see AX as a point. The Front Elevation of MNOP already has point views of MN and OP.

Steps 5 and 6 project ABC and X to the Auxiliary PP. AX shows as a point, therefore the plane ABC shows as an edge.
The Front Elevation of MNOP already shows as an edge.

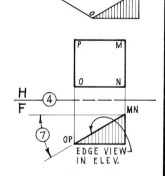

Figure 2.

Step 7 measures the inclination of each plane. (See page 12, Chapter 4.)

The unit of measurement used or chosen for determining the inclination depends on the circumstances of the problem in its application.

TYPICAL PROBLEM 2. FIND THE TRUE SHAPE OF A PLANE

GIVEN: The H and F views of a plane, in Figures 1 and 2.
SOLUTION: True shape will appear on a PP that is // to the given plane. Note: The edge view of a given plane is needed before a PP can be placed // to the given plane.

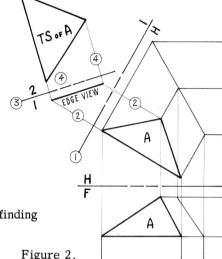

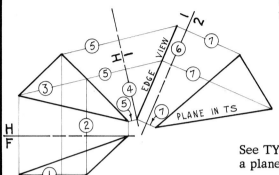

See TYPICAL PROBLEM 1 for finding a plane as an edge.

Figure 1.

Figure 2.

TYPICAL PROBLEM 3. FIND THE DIHEDRAL ANGLE BE-TWEEN TWO PLANES

GIVEN: The H and F views of planes A and B in Figures 3 and 4.
SOLUTION: The Dihedral angle can be measured in a PP that shows both planes as edges. This is possible by finding the line of intersection XY as a point. (Note: only one extra point from each roof, in addition to XY need be projected to PP's #1 and #2.

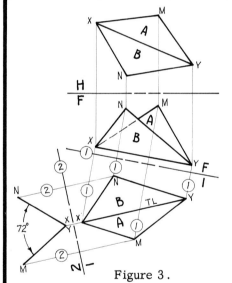

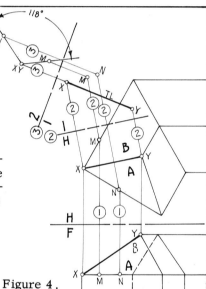

Figure 3.

Figure 4.

TYPICAL PROBLEM 4. FIND THE ANGLE BETWEEN A LINE AND A PLANE

GIVEN: The H and F views of a line and a plane.
SOLUTION: The angle can be measured where the line shows in TL and the plane shows as an edge. Since any view off of True Shape will again show edge view, view #3 must be chosen to show the line in TL. PP #3 will then show the true size of the required angle because XY shows in TL and the plane shows as an edge.

Figure 5.

The builder would need to know the ANGLE BETWEEN A LINE AND A PLANE to build this tower of the First Methodist Church in North Little Rock, Arkansas. Architects: Brueggeman, Swaim and Allen.

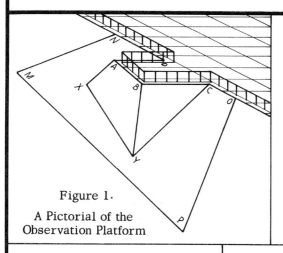

Figure 1.

A Pictorial of the
Observation Platform

TYPICAL PROBLEM 5. LOCATE THE PIERCING POINT
OF A LINE AND A PLANE

PROBLEM: Draw the OBSERVATION PLATFORM in
orthographic.

GIVEN: Embankment MNOP, Platform ABCD, and the requirement that a BATTER for all sides be 1:3.

PROBLEM ANALYSIS: To locate X and Y, find where the
lines AX and BY pierce the plane MNOP.

METHODS: Any one of the three basic methods for finding where a LINE PIERCES A PLANE shown below can
be used for solving the above problem.

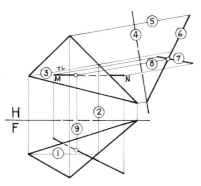

Figure 2. Method 1

A view of the line and the
plane, where the plane is
shown as an edge.
(See Figure 1, page 20)

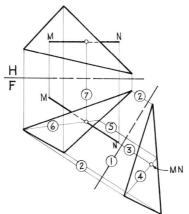

Figure 3. Method 2

A view of the line and the
plane, where the line is
shown as a point.
(See Figure 2, page 8.)

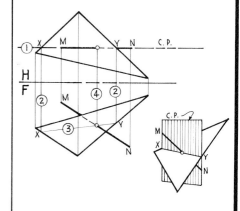

Figure 4. Method 3

Pass a CUTTING PLANE through
the line. The line of intersection XY will show the P.P.
(See page 19.)

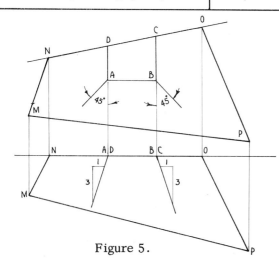

Figure 5.

SOLUTION
using
Method 3

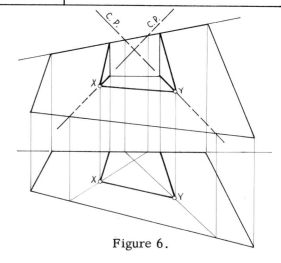

Figure 6.

Figure 5 shows the given planes MNOP and ABCD. Since the BATTER is 1:3 for all sides ADX, ABYX,
and BCY, lines AX and BY can be drawn at 45° in plan; and since ADX and BCY show as edges in the
Front Elevation, the BATTER can be drawn in elevation. The drawing at the right shows CUTTING
PLANES used to find the PIERCING POINTS X and Y. Once they are located the orthographic drawing
can be completed.

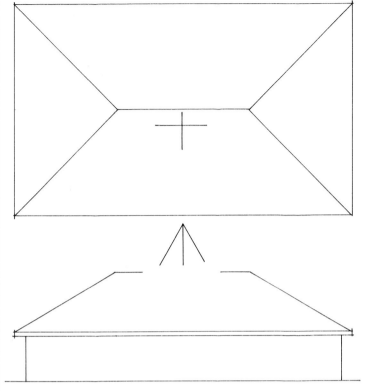

Figure 1 shows the Plan, Front Elevation, and Side Elevation of a building. The drawing is not completed. To complete it requires the knowledge of how to determine where a LINE PIERCES A PLANE. Figure 2 shows the drawing completed.

Figure 1.

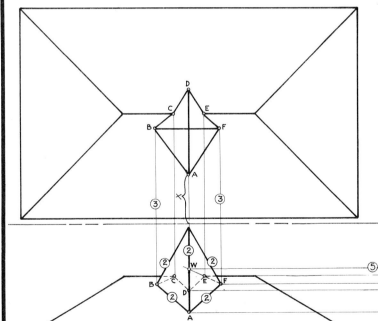

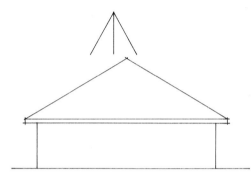

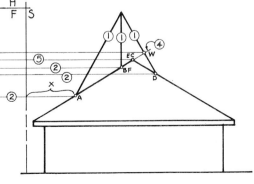

The LINE (ridge of the roof) pierces the PLANES (the two back sides of the pyramidal spire) at points E and C.

Familiarity with Method 2 on page 22 is sufficient to complete the drawing. Construction lines in Figure 2 on this page are numbered in order, for your convenience.

Line 4 is placed ON the plane of the pyramid and projected to the Front Elevation to locate point E.

Figure 2.

TYPICAL PROBLEM 6. <u>FIND THE LINE OF INTERSECTION BETWEEN ANY TWO PLANES</u>

THREE METHODS

When the LINE OF INTERSECTION BETWEEN TWO PLANES is not shown, it can be found by three different methods: (This step may be necessary in order to find the DIHEDRAL angle.)

1. PLANE AS AN EDGE METHOD: A view of both planes showing one plane as an edge will show the line of intersection between the two planes. (See Figure 1 on page 20 on how to find the edge view of a plane.)

2. PIERCING POINT METHOD: By placing a line on one of the planes (Figure 1, page 17), and finding where this line pierces the other plane (Figures 2, 3, and 4; page 22), will locate one point on the line of intersection between the two planes. By repeating the above procedure another point can be located. A line through these two points will be the line of intersection between the two planes.

3. CUTTING PLANE METHOD: By passing a cutting plane through both of the given planes, the two lines of intersection will intersect to locate one point on the line of intersection between the two given planes. By passing another cutting plane through both of the given planes, another point can be located. A line through these two points will be the line of intersection between the two given planes.

CUTTING PLANE METHOD

GIVEN: Two planes ABC and RST.

REQUIRED: The line of intersection (L of I) be-
                tween the two given planes.

SOLUTION: THE CUTTING PLANE METHOD
                was used as shown below.

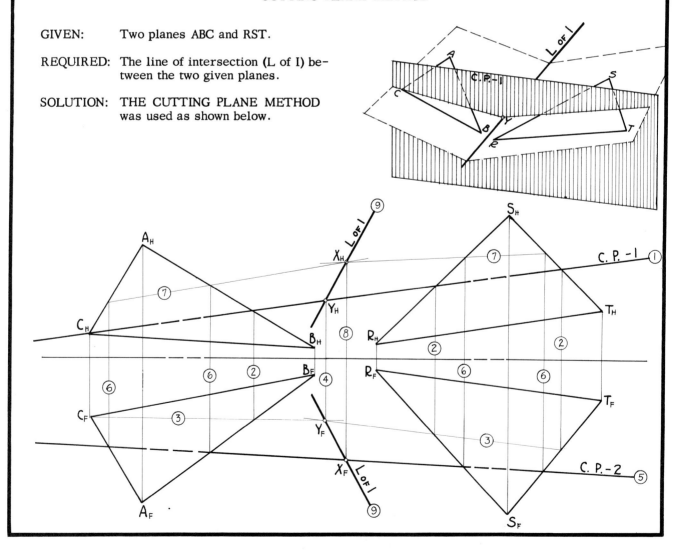

CLEARANCES (shortest distances) between (a) a point and a plane, (b) a plane and a line parallel to the plane, (c) two parallel planes, and (d) a plane and a sphere, can be determined by being able to find a plane as an edge.

TYPICAL PROBLEM 7.   DETERMINE CLEARANCES BETWEEN NON-PARALLEL NON-INTERSECT-
                     ING LINES

Other clearances can usually be resolved into SHORTEST DISTANCES or SHORTEST CONNECTORS between non-parallel non-intersecting lines. The suitability of the word CLEARANCE, DISTANCE, or CONNECTOR depends on its particular application in a problem.

When two lines are not parallel and are not intersecting, there is only one other condition possible. The geometric description of this condition is NON-PARALLEL NON-INTERSECTING. These lines are often referred to as SKEW LINES. Technically this is not correct because the lines are more than skew, they also do not intersect. The term SKEW LINES is sort of an "expression of the trade," "trade" meaning DESCRIPTIVE GEOMETRY. For convenience of using a shorter term, SKEW will be used in the following discussion to mean NON-PARALLEL NON-INTERSECTING.

Before studying examples or attempting to work any problems involving CONNECTORS between SKEW lines, it is important to be able to visualize them in space. The solution of the problems involves no new basic projections or maneuvers, but merely a choice of basic projections or maneuvers to obtain the desired results.

Holding two pencils in a skew position with one hand and with the other hand placing a third pencil in each of the following situations will help visualization of the connectors and the maneuvers required to locate and measure them:

1. SHORTEST CONNECTOR: Note that it will be perpendicular to each of the skew lines, and that it will appear in true length when one of the skew lines appears as a point, or where the two skew lines appear parallel.

2. SHORTEST HORIZONTAL (level) CONNECTOR: Its true length and the fact that it is level, will appear in an elevation where the two skew lines appear parallel.

3. SHORTEST CONNECTOR HAVING A SPECIFIED INCLINATION: Again, its inclination and true length will be evident in an elevation where the two skew lines appear parallel.

4. VERTICAL CONNECTOR: Plan view shows this connector as a point, and its true length appears in any elevation.

5. The edge view of a plane containing one of the lines and being parallel to the other line, will make the two skew lines appear parallel. Hold a triangle against one of the lines and make this triangle (plane) parallel to the other line (pencil). When the plane is viewed as an edge, the two skew lines will appear parallel. This view will show the true length of the SHORTEST CONNECTOR, and if it is an elevation it will show the true length of all four of the connectors mentioned above.

(It is important to be able to visualize the above "set-ups" before problems are attempted graphically. If difficulty is encountered when graphic solutions are attempted, making a space set-up again, is often helpful.)

TYPICAL PROBLEM 7. DETERMINE CLEARANCES BETWEEN NON-PARALLEL NON-INTERSECTING LINES.

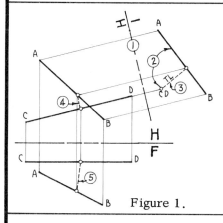

Figure 1.

SHORTEST CONNECTOR
(Given H and F)

GEOMETRY OF TWO PERPENDICULAR LINES: If two lines are perpendicular to each other, they will appear perpendicular to each other when at least one of them is shown in true length.

Steps 1 and 2 maneuver line CD to show as a point.
Step 3 shows the SHORTEST CONNECTOR (or clearance) in TL, therefore it is drawn perpendicular to CD.
Step 4 shows the connector perpendicular to CD because CD is shown there, in TL. Also line 4 must be // to H-1 since 3 is TL in auxiliary plane 1.

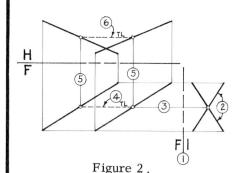

Figure 2.

SHORTEST HORIZONTAL CONNECTOR
(Given H and F)

PROBLEM ANALYSIS: Because the skew lines appear // in F, a preliminary conclusion requires the front elevation of the connector to be TL and // to H. Therefore the plan of the connector must also show in TL.

Steps 1 and 2 locate the connector as a point.
Steps 3, 4, 5, and 6 show the connector in the front elevation and plan.

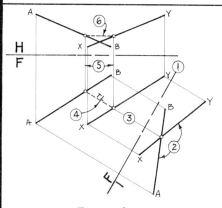

Figure 3.

SHORTEST CONNECTOR HAVING
A SPECIFIED INCLINATION

Required: Show the shortest connector sloping -30° from AB to XY.

Because the skew lines appear // in F, the front elevation must show the TL and true inclination of the connector. Since that conclusion indicates its direction, which shall be -30° from AB to XY.

Steps 1 and 2 locate the connector, and
Steps 3, 4, 5, and 6 show it in elevation and plan.

Should the requirement have been +30° from AB to XY, an attempt to construct it would prove it to be impossible, and such a connector could not exist.

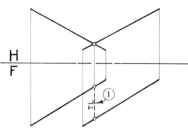

Figure 4.

VERTICAL CONNECTOR
(Given H and F)

Since a vertical line must show as a point in plan, the plan view of the skew lines locates the connector, and its TL appears in the front elevation or any elevation view of the skew lines. On page 27, lines 21 and 22 show the TL of the Vertical Connector. It could also have been drawn in view 1.

It is well to observe that under certain circumstances these connectors cannot exist. Their existance depends on the relative length and position of the given lines.

GIVEN: Skew lines AB and CD as shown in H and F.
REQUIRED: Find the SHORTEST CONNECTOR by two different methods, the SHORTEST HORIZON-
           TAL CONNECTOR, the SHORTEST CONNECTOR HAVING A SPECIFIED INCLINATION,
           and the VERTICAL CONNECTOR.

SHORTEST CONNECTOR

1. LINE AS A POINT METHOD: Since neither line shows as TL in H or F, auxiliary PP's #1 and #2
   were necessary to find line CD as a point. Steps 1 through 7 illustrate the procedure. Refer to
   Figure 1, page 26.
2. PLANE AS AN EDGE METHOD: Utilizing the statement 5 from page 25, a plane CDX was constructed parallel to the line AB by Steps 8, 9, and 10. 8: is CX parallel to AB in H and F. 9 and 10:
   Completes plane CDX with DX as a horizontal line with TL in H. Step 11 positions the auxiliary PP
   #3 to see plane CDX as an edge, producing a view in which the skew lines appear //. Steps 13 and
   14 locate the SHORTEST CONNECTOR using auxiliary PP #4. Note, it projects back to coincide with
   Steps 6 and 7 from the first method.

SHORTEST HORIZONTAL CONNECTOR

Anticipating the direction of this connector, Step 15
positions the auxiliary PP #5, Steps 16, 17, and 18
locate it, and Steps 19 and 20 show it projected back
to the plan and front elevation.

SHORTEST CONNECTOR HAVING
A SPECIFIED INCLINATION

This connector can be located off from PP #3 in a
manner similar to Figure 3, page 26.
Note, PP #3 shows the skew lines // in elevation
as does F in Figure 3. To avoid congestion it
is not shown in the solution on this page.

VERTICAL CONNECTOR

This connector can be located as shown in
Figure 4, page 26, in H and F; and could
also be shown in PP #3 in TL because
PP #3 shows elevation (Steps 21 and 22).

NOTE: If all 4 CONNECTORS were shown
in PP #3, they would all appear to cross
through the same point.

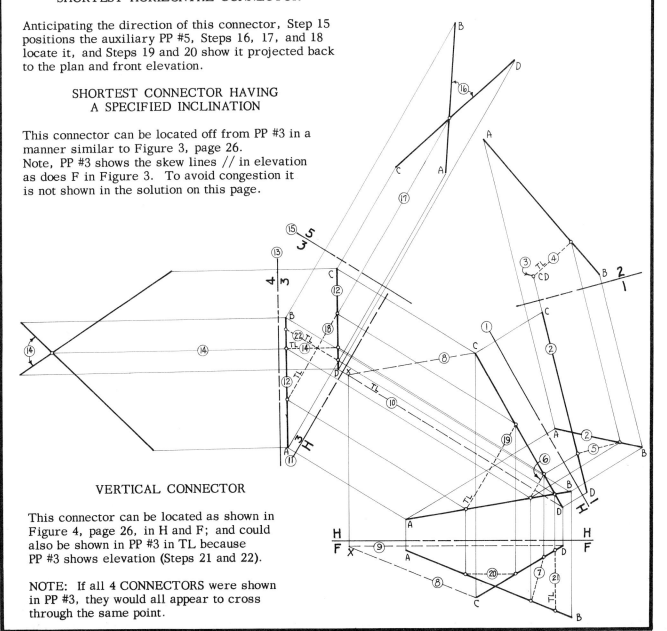

AXONOMETRIC

AXONOMETRIC includes: ISOMETRIC, DIMETRIC, AND TRIMETRIC. (See Chapter 3, page 1.)

In axonometric (a form of pictorial drawing) three faces of a rectangular object will show in one orthographic view.

Whether the "picture" becomes ISOMETRIC, DIMETRIC, or TRIMETRIC depends on how the object is turned or tilted to emphasize certain sides.

Axonometric can best be explained by using a cube as a basic object, because all faces are theoretically the same size and their relative emphasis can more easily be demonstrated.

ISOMETRIC

In Isometric the object is turned or tilted in such a position that all 3 faces appear equal. It is tilted in such a way that the diagonal of the cube is seen as a point.

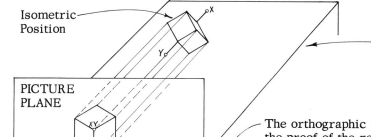

Isometric Position

PICTURE PLANE

The pictorial view at the left shows the projectors perpendicular to the picture plane and // to each other, which makes it ORTHOGRAPHIC PROJECTION.

The orthographic projection drawing at the lower left is the proof of the resulting ISOMETRIC PROJECTION. Note that the edges measure 0.816 inches instead of the original 1 inch.

It is customary procedure, in the interest of time and convenience, to make an ISOMETRIC DRAWING (shown below) directly without other projections. The edges are measured a full 1" in the direction of the Isometric axes.

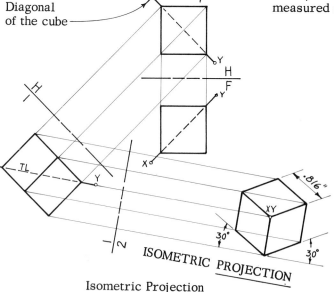

Diagonal of the cube

ISOMETRIC PROJECTION

Isometric Projection

Figure 1.

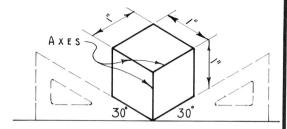

AXES

30°   30°

Figure 2. ISOMETRIC DRAWING

The Isometric Drawing is slightly larger than the true PROJECTION, but is executed with more ease and serves its purpose as well.

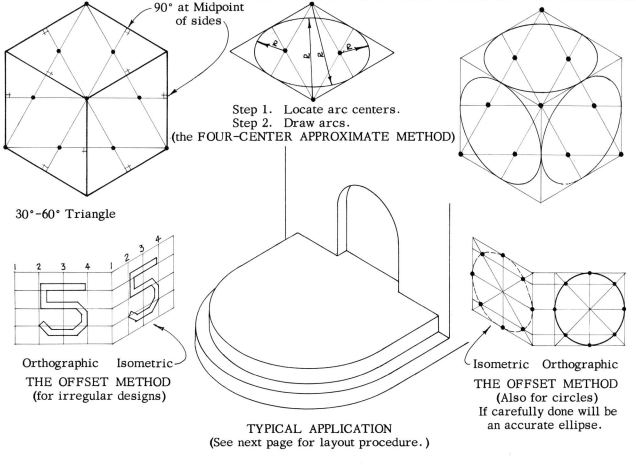

Isometric Axes

Looking Down   Looking Up

Figure 1.   Choosing Position for Axes

Locate both ends of a non-isometric line by measuring along isometric axes.

Figure 2.   Non-Isometric Lines

90° at Midpoint
of sides

Step 1.   Locate arc centers.
Step 2.   Draw arcs.
(the FOUR-CENTER APPROXIMATE METHOD)

30°-60° Triangle

Orthographic   Isometric
THE OFFSET METHOD
(for irregular designs)

TYPICAL APPLICATION
(See next page for layout procedure.)

Isometric   Orthographic
THE OFFSET METHOD
(Also for circles)
If carefully done will be
an accurate ellipse.

Figure 3.   Circles and Designs in Isometric

PROCEDURE FOR ISOMETRIC DRAWING INVOLVING ARCS (Circular).

Lines marked 1 block out the basic shape of the object before the centers for the arcs are located.

Line 2 blocks out a rhombus, which is a square in isometric, similar to one side of the cube in isometric. See Figure 3, page 29.

Lines marked 3 are drawn with the 30-60 triangle and T-sq, to locate the centers for the arcs.

Lines marked 4, 5, and 6 are the arcs needed for this portion of the drawing.

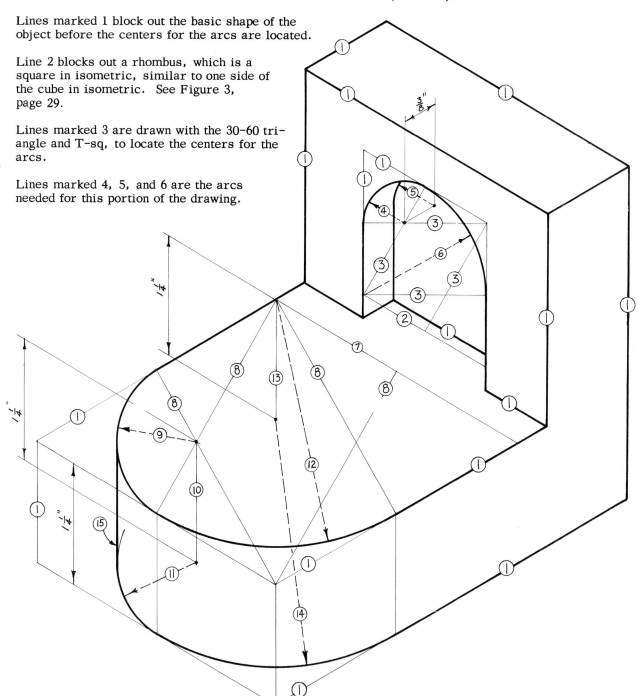

SEMI-CIRCLES IN ISOMETRIC

Similar to the above procedure, the line marked 7 makes a rhombus in which lines marked 8 will locate the centers for the arcs 9 and 12, and tangent points.

Line 10 is drawn vertically down to the bottom side of the block to locate the center for arc 11. This is easier than repeating the procedure of lines 7 and 8 for the bottom side of the block. 15 is drawn tangent to arcs 9 and 11.

Similarly line 13 locates the center for arc 14. (Also note the 3/8" dimension for the upright portion of the object locates the center for the back arc.)

DIMETRIC DRAWING

DIMETRIC PROJECTION can be "proven" similar to the illustration for Isometric Projection shown on page 28 in Figure 1, but the discussion here will be devoted only to DIMETRIC DRAWING.

DIMETRIC DRAWING uses two scales and various angles.   Therefore it takes longer to draw, but is often more desirable than ISOMETRIC because:

1. One of the faces can be emphasized or subordinated to better suit the purpose of the drawing.

2. Some "predicaments" arising in Isometric can be avoided in Dimetric.

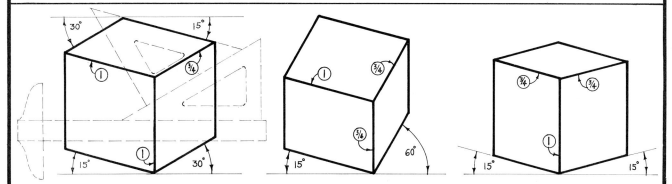

Figure 1.   The numbers indicate the ratio of scales used (1" = 1' - 0", 3/4" = 1' - 0" etc.) The angles are not exact for Dimetric but ones convenient with ordinary triangles.   (These are only a few of the possible dimetric positions.)

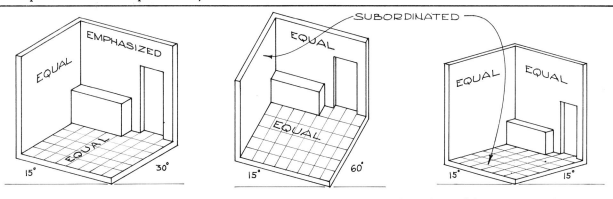

Figure 2.   Interiors are typical applications.   Similar effects can be achieved for exterior views.

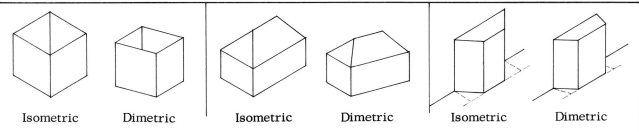

Figure 3.   The 3 comparisons above show "predicaments" in Isometric overcome by using Dimetric.

TRIMETRIC DRAWING

TRIMETRIC PROJECTION can be "proven" similar to Isometric and Dimetric projection.   It differs from Isometric and Dimetric in that no two faces appear equal.   The scales and angles become more involved, to a point where PERSPECTIVE would be a wiser choice for presentation.   Perspective will be discussed in a later chapter.

In review, ORTHOGRAPHIC PROJECTION including AXONOMETRIC PROJECTION uses parallel projectors <u>perpendicular</u> to the picture plane.

OBLIQUE PROJECTION uses parallel projectors, not perpendicular to the picture plane but <u>OBLIQUE</u> to the picture plane, thereby making it possible to see three faces of a rectangular object in one pictorial view when the front face of the object is parallel to the picture plane as in multi-view orthographic. Therefore the front face of the pictorial will often be exactly the same as the front view in multi-view orthographic. Application is the most practical when intricate detail or contour appear in the front face.

OBLIQUE <u>DRAWING</u>, as in axonometric, is a direct procedure omitting projections.

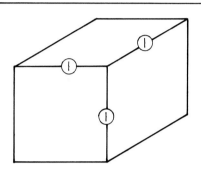

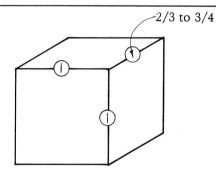

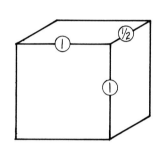

CAVALIER OBLIQUE DRAWING
Used when distortion is not an objection. Quickest to draw because of only 1 scale.

GENERAL OBLIQUE DRAWING
Used when distortion <u>is</u> objectionable.

CABINET OBLIQUE DRAWING
Most widely used but appears a little too short.

Figure 1. Types of Oblique Drawing

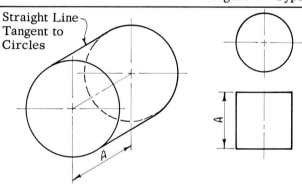

Straight Line Tangent to Circles

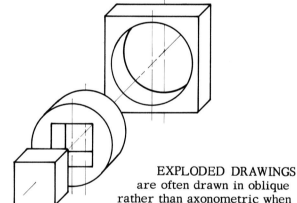

The greatest advantage of oblique drawing is that circles and arcs can be drawn with a compass if they are <u>on</u> or <u>parallel</u> to the front face.

EXPLODED DRAWINGS are often drawn in oblique rather than axonometric when circles or arcs are involved.

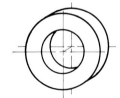

Oblique drawing is suitable for letters, objects of little depth, and objects whose intricate contour appear in only one face or direction.

Figure 2. Applications of Oblique Drawing

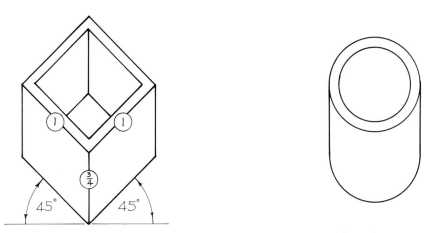

This is actually the same as the GENERAL OBLIQUE DRAWING, only it is turned to make the true shape face appear as the top and plan.

Figure 1. Theory of the True-Shape-Plan Method

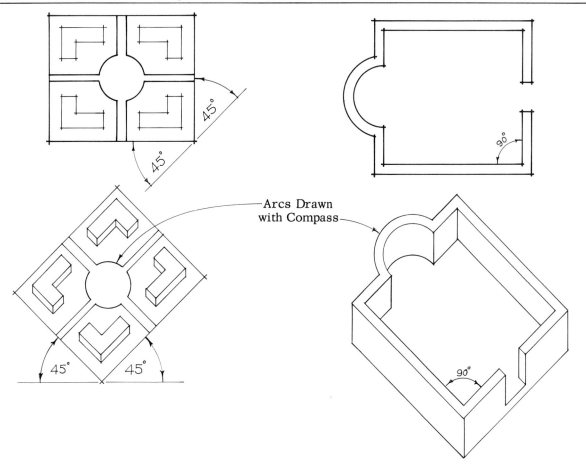

Arcs Drawn
with Compass

In this method, if a plan of a layout or a building is available, it can simply be traced and the third vertical dimension easily added to make it pictorial. It is versatile in its application. Room partitions and furniture or equipment can also be shown. This method is suitable when slight distortion is not objectionable.

Figure 2. Applications of the True-Shape-Plan Method

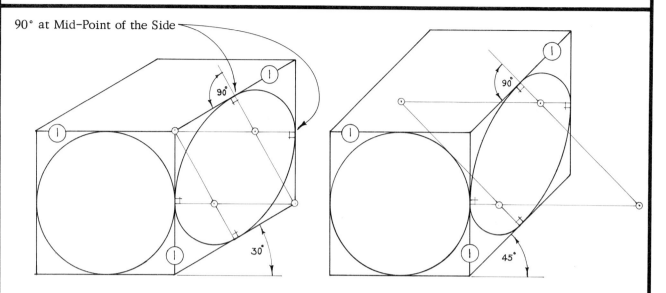

When CAVALIER OBLIQUE DRAWING is drawn with receding lines at 30°, the receding face will have circles constructed in the same manner as for circles in isometric, approximate method.

When CAVALIER OBLIQUE DRAWING is drawn with receding lines at some angle other than 30°, the location of the 4 centers for the circle are theoretically the same as for isometric, but the centers for the larger arcs will not fall on the corners of the rhombus. (Note the receding face must be a rhombus.)

Figure 1. Circles on the Receding Face for Oblique Drawing

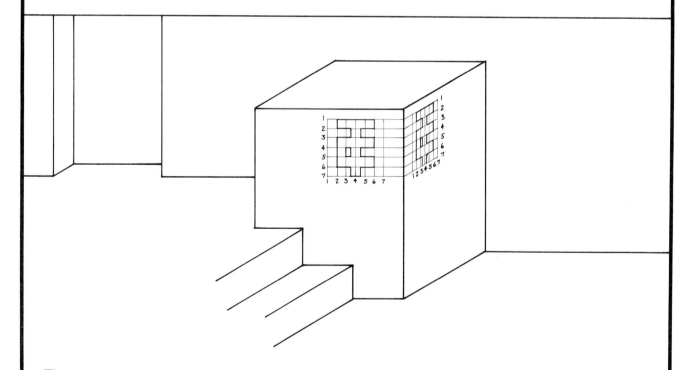

This method is also used for circles when the receding faces are not rhombuses. (Also see Figure 3, page 29; Chapter 4.)

Figure 2. Offset Method for Designs on the Receding Face in Oblique Drawing

SECTIONS are drawn to show the interior of an object when it is confusing to use hidden lines. Often hidden lines for one part of the interior overlap hidden lines for another part and make it difficult to interpret the drawing. Several sections may be needed to fully explain the interior. The examples shown here are so simple that actually no sections would be required, but they are purposely simple only to illustrate the types of sections.

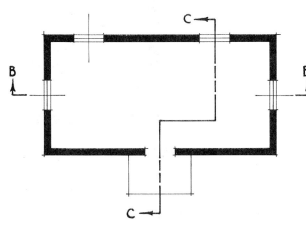

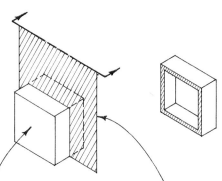

FLOOR PLAN (SECTION A-A) This is actually a HORIZONTAL SECTION placed high enough to locate the windows. It is not customary to show this cutting plane line.

An imaginary cutting plane is passed through the object. Theoretically this part is removed and the remainder viewed in the direction of the arrows. Note the cutting plane lines identified by A-A, B-B, and C-C. When it is obvious where the cutting plane would be located it may be omitted.

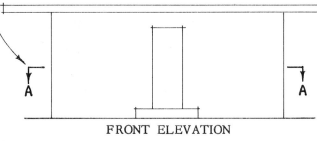

FRONT ELEVATION

SIDE ELEVATION

SECTION B-B

SECTION C-C

This FULL SECTION is called a LONGITUDINAL section because it is taken lengthwise through the building or object. Note the cutting plane line on the plan above. It can be drawn through the entire floor plan if needed but is usually drawn as shown to avoid unnecessary lines across the drawing.

This FULL SECTION is called a CROSS section or TRANSVERSE section because it is taken across the width of the building or object. Note the cutting-plane-line on the plan above. This cutting plane is OFFSET in order to include the window as well as the door without drawing an extra section.

FULL SECTIONS

Figures 1 and 2 on this page show two different types of sections of the same building and having the same cutting plane. The difference in the two types is in the purpose of drawing the section.

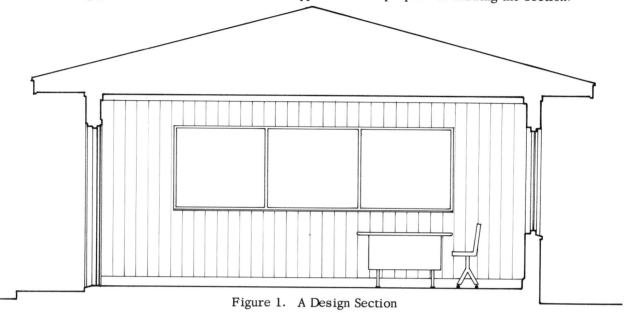

Figure 1. A Design Section

The purpose of a DESIGN SECTION is to describe the interior of the building; the space occupied by the structural elements are usually only outlines. The criteria is to emphasize the design of the interior by making the structural space as inconspicuously as possible. Footings are never shown in DESIGN SECTIONS.

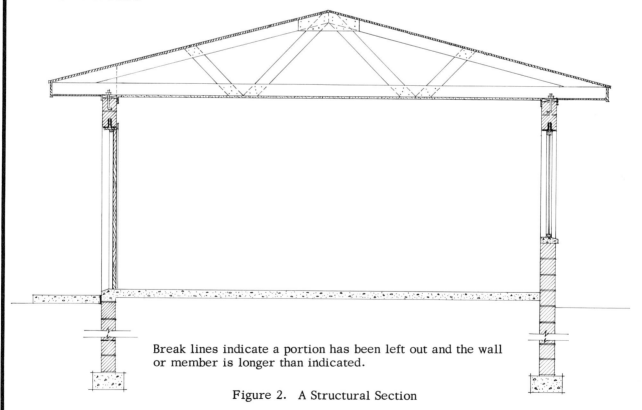

Break lines indicate a portion has been left out and the wall or member is longer than indicated.

Figure 2. A Structural Section

A structural section shows the building construction. In large buildings, when the scale of the drawing prevents showing construction parts clearly in a full section, DETAIL SECTIONS are shown separately for the various parts of the entire building. (See Figure 2, page 4, Chapter 6 and, pages 3, 4 and 6, Chapter 7.)

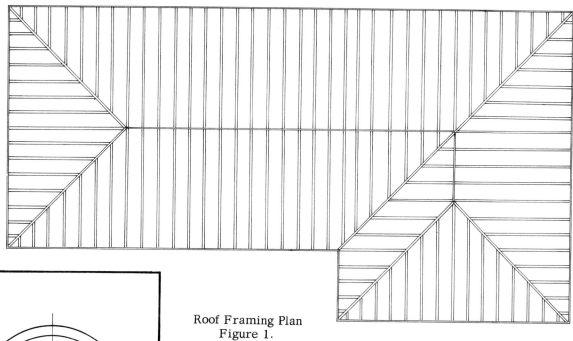

Roof Framing Plan
Figure 1.

The roof framing plan above shows the position of all the rafters
for a hip roof.

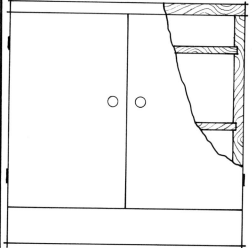

A FLOWER POT

Figure 2. Half Section

Half Sections are used when the
object is symmetrical and when
it is desirable to show the
inside and the outside in only
one view. Avoid hidden lines.

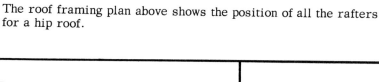

A STORAGE CABINET

Figure 3. Partial or Broken-Out Section

A partial section shows a special
feature without showing an extra view.

The wall is shown
in phantom section

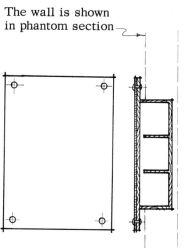

A MEDICINE CABINET

Figure 4. A Phantom Section

A phantom section clarifies
the installation of an object,
or its relation to other parts.

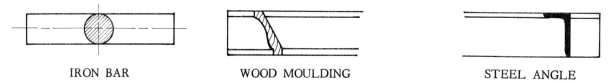

IRON BAR   WOOD MOULDING   STEEL ANGLE

A revolved section often explains the shape of parts to an advantage besides eliminating an extra view.

Figure 1.   Revolved Sections

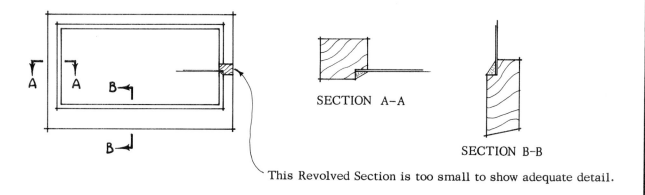

SECTION A-A

SECTION B-B

This Revolved Section is too small to show adequate detail.

The front elevation of the window is not drawn at a large enough scale to make revolved sections practical. DETAIL SECTION A-A and B-B can then be drawn removed and at a larger scale.

Figure 2.   Detail or Removed Sections

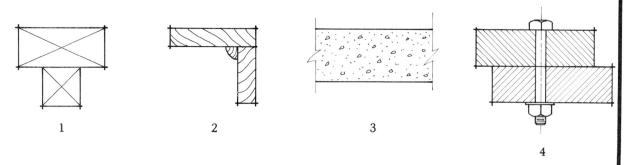

1   2   3   4

1. An "X" is standard identification for framing members or rough lumber members in cross section.

2. The grain of wood is usually drawn in section to indicate "finish" lumber.

3. Shows the standard symbol for poured concrete in section.

4. When two sectioned parts are next to each other it is customary to crosshatch them in different directions for clarity. This crosshatch symbol is used when material designation is not important.
   See Architectural Graphics Standards for a complete list of symbols.

Figure 3.   A Few Standard Section Symbols

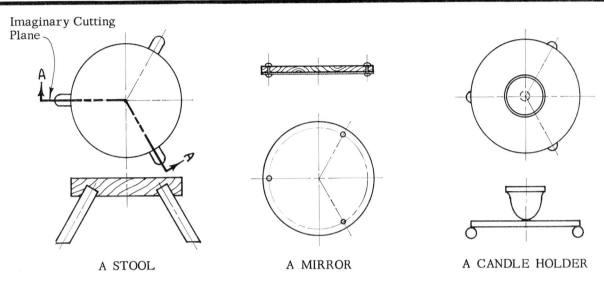

A STOOL   A MIRROR   A CANDLE HOLDER

The above are examples of conventional violations in orthographic projection as recommended by the AMERICAN STANDARDS ASSOCIATION for the purpose of making it easier to draw and interpret drawings. Note the position of the legs of the stool and the holes in the mirror when sectioned. This recommendation is also followed when the object is not sectioned, as shown in the drawing of the candle holder.

Figure 1.   Conventional Violations

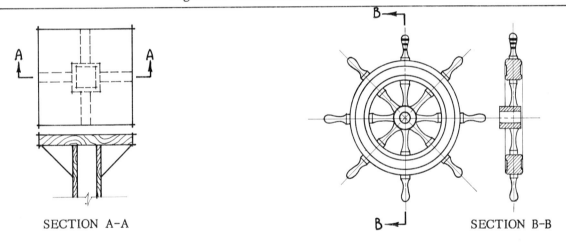

SECTION A-A   SECTION B-B

Sections A-A and B-B show that ribs and spokes are not sectioned even if the cutting plane passes through them. The sectioned view is easier to interpret when those members are not sectioned.

Figure 2.   Unsectioned Members

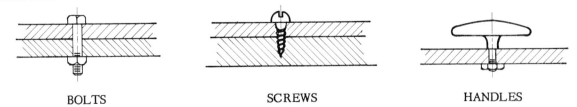

BOLTS   SCREWS   HANDLES

It is conventional practice not to section bolts, screws, rivets, shafts, rods, handles, etc. The criteria being: these parts are better explained when they are not sectioned.

Figure 3.   Unsectioned Parts

A good architect is familiar with available materials and existing good practices in building construction. He knows the criteria (1) for selection of good material, and (2) for designing good building construction. He uses his knowledge of materials and building construction to design a functional building with a desired aesthetic expression.

CRITERIA FOR CHOOSING MATERIALS

Materials on the outside of a building are exposed to the weather and must withstand the elements such as wind, rain, snow, hail, high and low temperatures, vibrations, and others. Materials on the interior of buildings must withstand various forms of wear and perform various functions depending on their location in the building. Geographical location and availability of materials are also factors affecting a choice.

Depending on its function and location in a building, a <u>material</u> is chosen on the basis of the following criteria:

1. Strength to withstand its intended load.
2. Durability to withstand wear, shock, denting, scratching, etc.
3. Appearance, including color and texture.
4. Cost, including material and labor.
5. Ease of handling, placing, fastening, etc.
6. Ease of finishing, cleaning or refinishing.
7. Resistance to rust, rot, dampness, warping or shrinking.
8. Absence of objectionable odors.
9. Resistance to heat, heat transmission and fire.
10. Ability to absorb or reflect sound.

SPECIFICATIONS are given for materials describing their qualities and characteristics on the basis of their function and the above criteria.

Some of the most common types of building materials are stone, wood, brick, blocks of various compositions, tile, glass, concrete, sheet metal, steel, plaster, stucco, and numerous others including many forms of plastics.

The ARCHITECTURAL GRAPHIC STANDARDS gives standard sizes of materials and information about their application and placing.

Catalogs such as SWEET'S FILE furnish information about available materials and the industrial firms that produce them. Each firm will acclaim its material by emphasizing its outstanding specifications and support their statements with results of laboratory tests or a list of satisfied users, and will furnish samples. The architect must use his judgment in choosing them.

The NATIONAL BUREAU OF STANDARDS tests many materials and publishes reports on their results. This is valuable unbiased information to use, especially in choosing new or untried materials.

NATIONAL BOARD OF FIRE UNDERWRITERS rates materials with respect to their resistance to fire. This information is published and is available in libraries.

CRITERIA FOR CHOOSING TYPES OF BUILDING CONSTRUCTION

The geographical location of a building has perhaps more influence on the type of construction used than on the material chosen. Depending on the geographical location and the function of the building, its construction is designed on the basis of the following criteria:

1. Strength to withstand loads imposed by its own weight, occupancy of the building, wind, snow, and even cyclones, tornadoes, earthquakes, and coastal hurricanes.

2. Waterproof protection against rain and snow.

3. Airtightness against wind, dust, snow, and dampness.

4. Resistance to heat transmission in hot or cold weather.

5. Protection against vermin.

6. Protection against rot.

7. Protection against fire and the spreading of fire within a building.

8. Insulation against noise from outside the building and against the transmission of noise from one room to another.

9. Ease of construction.

10. Cost, including labor, material, and equipment.

SPECIFICATIONS for a building includes, in addition to specifications for the materials, instructions for complete erection of the building on the basis of the above criteria including minimum workmanship requirements. "Specs" are written by the architect.

The ARCHITECTURAL GRAPHIC STANDARDS shows many types of construction in detail, including the materials used and useful information about many standard practices.

In SWEET'S FILE the firms' recommendations for their materials are often accompanied by the types of construction recommended for obtaining the best results.

The NATIONAL BUREAU OF STANDARDS also furnishes bulletins of information on the results of their tests on numerous types of construction.

BUILDING CODES, national and local, spell out minimums of construction and regulations concerning safety, convenience and health.

The NATIONAL BOARD OF FIRE UNDERWRITERS have building code standards as suggestions for inclusion in national and local building codes. They consist of official recommendations and test results for materials and equipment for buildings.

The purpose of the illustrations and notes on the following pages on building construction is (1) to familiarize the reader with the most common types of standard construction by comparing their features on the basis of the above criteria, and (2) to define the standard architectural terminology for proper identification of materials and parts of structures.

The following general types of construction will be briefly considered on the following pages:

1. Wood Frame Construction

2. Masonry Construction

3. Concrete Frame Construction

4. Steel Frame Construction

5. Post and Lintel

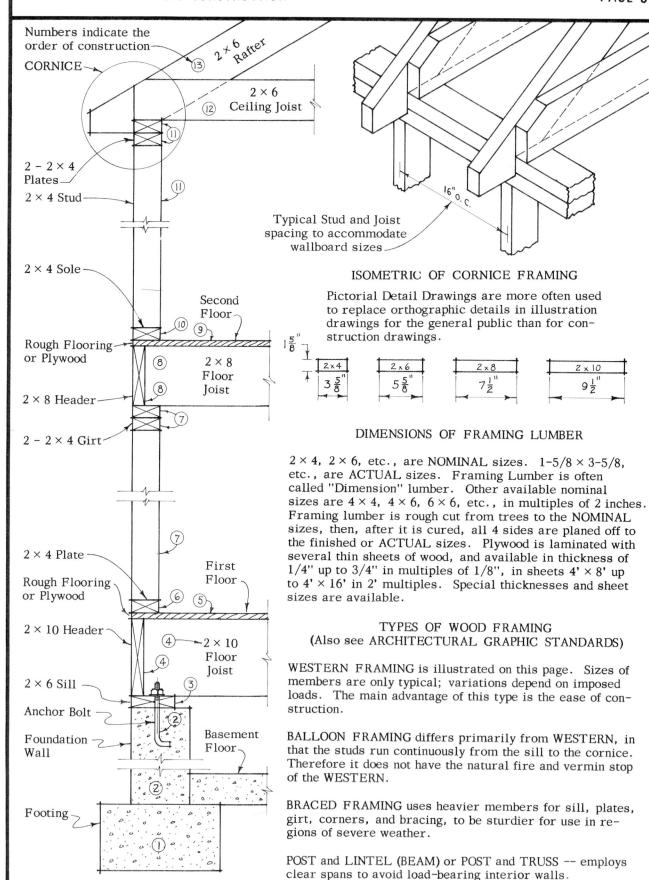

Numbers indicate the order of construction

CORNICE

⑬ 2 × 6 Rafter

⑫ 2 × 6 Ceiling Joist

2 – 2 × 4 Plates

2 × 4 Stud

⑪

2 × 4 Sole

Second Floor

⑩ ⑨

Rough Flooring or Plywood

⑧

2 × 8 Floor Joist

1 5/8"

⑧ 2 × 8 Header

⑦ 2 – 2 × 4 Girt

2 × 4 Plate

First Floor

⑥ ⑤

Rough Flooring or Plywood

2 × 10 Header

④ 2 × 10 Floor Joist

④

2 × 6 Sill

③

Anchor Bolt

②

Foundation Wall

Basement Floor

②

Footing

①

WESTERN FRAMING

Typical Stud and Joist spacing to accommodate wallboard sizes

16" O.C.

ISOMETRIC OF CORNICE FRAMING

Pictorial Detail Drawings are more often used to replace orthographic details in illustration drawings for the general public than for construction drawings.

2 × 4	2 × 6	2 × 8	2 × 10
3 5/8"	5 5/8"	7 1/2"	9 1/2"

DIMENSIONS OF FRAMING LUMBER

2 × 4, 2 × 6, etc., are NOMINAL sizes. 1-5/8 × 3-5/8, etc., are ACTUAL sizes. Framing Lumber is often called "Dimension" lumber. Other available nominal sizes are 4 × 4, 4 × 6, 6 × 6, etc., in multiples of 2 inches. Framing lumber is rough cut from trees to the NOMINAL sizes, then, after it is cured, all 4 sides are planed off to the finished or ACTUAL sizes. Plywood is laminated with several thin sheets of wood, and available in thickness of 1/4" up to 3/4" in multiples of 1/8", in sheets 4' × 8' up to 4' × 16' in 2' multiples. Special thicknesses and sheet sizes are available.

TYPES OF WOOD FRAMING
(Also see ARCHITECTURAL GRAPHIC STANDARDS)

WESTERN FRAMING is illustrated on this page. Sizes of members are only typical; variations depend on imposed loads. The main advantage of this type is the ease of construction.

BALLOON FRAMING differs primarily from WESTERN, in that the studs run continuously from the sill to the cornice. Therefore it does not have the natural fire and vermin stop of the WESTERN.

BRACED FRAMING uses heavier members for sill, plates, girt, corners, and bracing, to be sturdier for use in regions of severe weather.

POST and LINTEL (BEAM) or POST and TRUSS -- employs clear spans to avoid load-bearing interior walls.

The wall section below shows the typical materials (and their terms of identification) needed to complete a typical frame building after the framing has been erected as shown on the preceding page.

ROOF SHEATHING braces the roof rafters and serves as a solid base on which thinner and more expensive roofing materials can be placed.

BUILDING PAPER makes the roof more airtight.

ROOFING should be waterproof and preferably fireproof. Types vary especially with respect to whether the roof is sloped or flat.

FASCIA helps box in the cornice, and its protruding lower edge serves as a drip edge to prevent water from creeping up to the underside of the cornice.

SOFFIT completes the box cornice and seals off the attic space. Ventilation openings are needed if there are no attic windows or if roof is flat.

COVE MOULDING makes the corner more weathertight.

FRIEZE makes a square corner for the cove moulding, not possible with beveled siding.

SIDING is beveled to permit lapping for more weathertight construction.

WALL SHEATHING braces the wall construction and makes a solid base for siding.

BUILDING PAPER makes the wall more weathertight.

FURRING BLOCK makes it possible for the first siding board to have the same slope as the others.

INSULATION reduces heat transmission.

LATH and PLASTER, or plasterboard, or panel boards provide a standard wall surface.

BASEBOARD covers the edge of the plaster.

BASE SHOE protects the baseboard and makes a better fitting corner.

SUB-FLOOR serves as a support for the finish floor.

INSULATION

LATH & PLASTER

BASEBOARD

BASE SHOE

FINISH FLOOR

SUBFLOOR

PLASTER GROUND

FINISH GRADE

TYPICAL COMPLETE
WOOD FRAME WALL SECTION

The architect may use any materials he chooses for the desired aesthetic effect provided they satisfy the necessary criteria of good building materials and construction. Consult the ARCHITECTURAL GRAPHIC STANDARDS and SWEET'S FILE for other standard practices.

PURPOSE OF A WINDOW

A window is designed to provide light, ventilation, a view to the outdoors or a view between rooms, to admit sunlight, to shed water, and add beauty to the structure.

CONSTRUCTION REQUIREMENTS OF A WINDOW

A well-designed window is weathertight, easy to install, easy to operate, and is so constructed that sash and glass can be removed or replaced.

PURPOSE OF THIS STUDY

The purpose of the following disucssion and illustration is to point out the features necessary for a window to function properly, and to acquaint the reader with the terminology for proper identification of the various parts of the construction.

An architect needs to satisfy these construction requirements in designing a window area as well as in evaluating and specifying prefabricated window units that can be purchased ready for installation.

GENERAL TYPES OF PREFABRICATED WOOD OR METAL WINDOWS

1. DOUBLE HUNG WINDOW is the type illustrated on the following page. This type was chosen because it includes the functional parts common to most of the other types.

2. CASEMENT WINDOWS open and close like a door. They are mounted either vertically or horizontally. When mounted horizontally they are sometimes referred to as AWNING windows.

3. PIVOT WINDOWS are similar to casement but pivot on vertical pins in centers of top and bottom sash rails. (See identification of sash rails on page 6 of this chapter.)

4. GLIDING WINDOWS open and close by sliding horizontally.

5. STATIONARY WINDOWS are designed not to open, and are used when ventilation is provided elsewhere or not needed.

RECOMMENDATIONS FOR STUDYING WINDOWS

1. Compare the drawings on the following page with a double hung window in an existing building or with a cut-away model of a double hung window.

2. Consult the ARCHITECTURAL GRAPHIC STANDARDS and SWEET'S FILE for information on other available types of windows, noting their similarities and differences in design and construction.

3. Consult BUILDING CODES for minimum area requirements for light and ventilation for types of rooms and buildings.

4. Obtain price lists and specifications of several window units from building material suppliers and try to evaluate their different features.

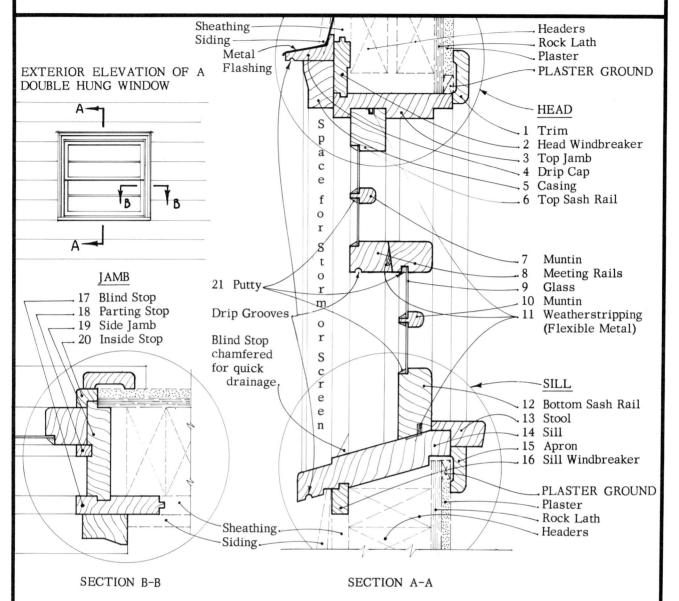

EXTERIOR ELEVATION OF A
DOUBLE HUNG WINDOW

Sheathing
Siding
Metal
Flashing

Headers
Rock Lath
Plaster
PLASTER GROUND

HEAD

1 Trim
2 Head Windbreaker
3 Top Jamb
4 Drip Cap
5 Casing
6 Top Sash Rail

Space for Storm or Screen

7 Muntin
8 Meeting Rails
9 Glass
10 Muntin
11 Weatherstripping
(Flexible Metal)

JAMB

17 Blind Stop
18 Parting Stop
19 Side Jamb
20 Inside Stop

21 Putty

Drip Grooves

Blind Stop
chamfered
for quick
drainage

SILL

12 Bottom Sash Rail
13 Stool
14 Sill
15 Apron
16 Sill Windbreaker

PLASTER GROUND
Plaster
Rock Lath
Headers

Sheathing
Siding

SECTION B-B   SECTION A-A

DOUBLE HUNG WINDOW

FUNCTIONS OF THE VARIOUS PARTS OF A DOUBLE HUNG WINDOW

A. Note that the parts exposed to the weather are so shaped and arranged to permit quick drainage from rain or melting snow. Note the DRIP GROOVES are designed to cause the water to drip down instead of permitting it to creep back in between the parts of the construction.

B. TRIM (1), APRON (15), and CASING (5), are designed to cover the joints between the window and the plaster or siding or other wall covering.

C. WEATHERSTRIPPING (11) makes the window more airtight against dust and heat loss.

D. STORM WINDOWS or DOUBLE GLAZING (not shown here) creates a dead air space to provide insulation in hot or cold weather, and to prevent moisture condensation on the inside surface of the glass in cold weather. Windows between rooms are often double or triple glazed against sound transmission.

E. Screens (not shown here) are removable like storms, but some window units have provisions for self-storing storms and screens.

F. Headers are part of the rough framing for windows. Rock lath and plaster are merely one of many possible wall coverings.

1. This model of the Civic Center for Tallahassee, Florida by Architect Walter Adolf Gropius and Architects Collaborative shows this roof structure of reinforced concrete, employing BARREL VAULTS.

2. A spired New England STEEPLE (early 1800), SPIRE may be conical or pyramidal.

3. A HIP ROOF with GABLE DORMERS and CUPOLA cover the Mount Vernon home of George Washington.

4. A Colonial GAMBREL ROOF (early 1700).

5. A New England SALT-BOX house (1700's).

Except for the civic center shown above, the roof shapes shown on this page are the most common of those found in this country. Chapter 10 shows applications of geometry to some of the more recently developed roof shapes.

All except illustrations 1 and 8 are courtesy of the editors of LOOK AT THE U.S.A.

6. This Kentucky stable for thoroughbreds has a GABLE ROOF with PYRAMIDAL roofed CUPOLAS.

7. On the Tanglewood Estate, the home of the Berkshire Music Festival are many rehearsal buildings like this, which has a GABLE ROOF and a lean-to with a SHED ROOF.

8. One of the first office and laboratory buildings on the Iowa State University campus has a MANSARD ROOF.

9. The DOMED United States Capitol (1793). Architects: Thornton, Latrobe and others. PARAPET ROOF is over entrance wing.

Stones, bricks, tiles, and blocks of various compositions, laid up with mortar between the joints to form a wall, is called masonry construction. These materials are manufactured in various sizes and shapes, designed to be suitable for various types of walls. Three typical masonry units and four typical wall constructions are shown below.

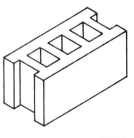

CONCRETE BLOCK

BRICK

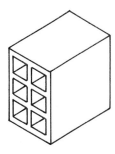

HOLLOW TILE

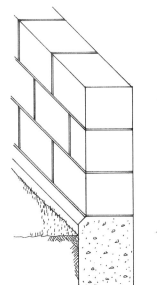

SOLID MASONRY WALL
concrete block
(1)

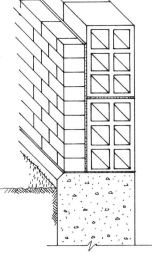

SOLID MASONRY WALL
brick and hollow tile
(2)

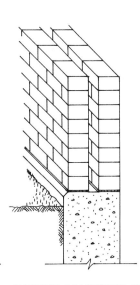

CAVITY MASONRY WALL
brick with 2" cavity
(3)

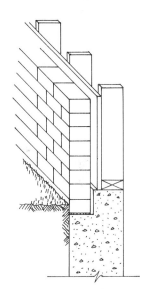

MASONRY VENEER
brick and frame
(4)

Four typical masonry wall constructions are shown above. Wall thickness requirements vary with the height of the wall and the imposed loads.

When a building has to be heated in cold weather, moisture will tend to condense on the inside surface of the wall making it wet, unless it is insulated in some way. The air space in a hollow wall as shown in (3) and (4) or the air spaces in the masonry units themselves often are sufficient to prevent condensation depending on the severity of the temperature. Special insulating material can be added in (4) in between the studs, to further insulate against heat transmission.

MASONRY WALLS

Steel reinforced concrete construction is used mostly for office buildings and other commercial and industrial buildings. In addition to being fireproof, its outstanding features are strength and durability. With the use of steel bars, the concrete is reinforced to withstand loads making it practical as a building material.

DENISON PARKING, INC., Indianapolis, Indiana. Architects: D. A. Bohlen & Son. This structure with cantilevered floors is of monolithic concrete. (Cantilevered beams or floors extend out beyond the column or wall supporting them. Monolithic means continuous pour.)

UNIVERSITY APARTMENTS
Chicago, Illinois
Architects: Loewenberg & Loewenberg
(Monolithic Concrete Skeleton Frame)

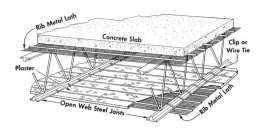

Combination Construction, using CONCRETE FLOOR SLAB and OPEN WEB STEEL JOISTS.

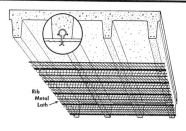

MONOLITHIC CONCRETE COMBINATION of floor and joists provides economy of material and reduced weight over the SINGLE SLAB construction. The spaces between joists provide convenient space for utility piping and wiring.

Steel Reinforcing Bars

A SINGLE SLAB of reinforced concrete is often used for floors and roofs of small buildings where spans are comparatively short.

Steel Reinforcing Bars

Steel H-Column

CONCRETE COLUMNS are reinforced with round steel bars or with structural steel.

STANDARD STRUCTURAL STEEL SHAPES

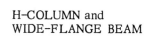

H-COLUMN and
WIDE-FLANGE BEAM

Flange

BETHLEHEM
I-BEAM

Web

STANDARD CHANNEL

STANDARD I-BEAM

EQUAL LEG ANGLE

Legs

UNEQUAL LEG ANGLE

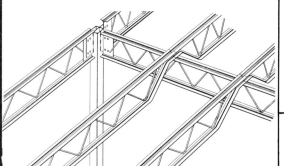

OPEN-WEB STEEL JOISTS
The above design is made by the American Bridge Division of U.S. Steel Corp.

The structural steel COLUMNS, BEAMS,
CHANNELS, and ANGLES are so shaped,
1. To resist bending in two directions, and
2. To provide better adaptation to the
   various parts of a structure.

Steel members are RIVETED, BOLTED, or
WELDED to each other in framing a structure.

Consult structural steel handbooks and the
Architectural Graphic Standards for sizes,
weights and other design data of the various steel shapes.

STATE MUTUAL LIFE ASSUR-
ANCE COMPANY, Worcester,
Mass. Architects--Engineers:
Cram & Ferguson. Photos:
Courtesy of American Bridge
Division of the United States
Steel Corporation.

PAN AMERICAN TERMINAL BUILDING, Idlewild Airport
Architects--Engineers: Tippetts-Abbett-McCarthy-Stratton
Associate Architects: Turano & Gardner

UPJOHN COMPANY, Kalamazoo, Michigan
Architects: Skidmore, Owings & Merrill
This structure illustrates the use of the
SPACE FRAME.

Dimensioning practices vary in the different fields such as BUILDING CONSTRUCTION, MANUFAC-TURING, and LAND MEASUREMENTS. The necessary dimensions for any working drawing are simply those necessary for constructing a building, manufacturing an article, or fully describing a piece of land. Therefore the architect must have a knowledge of building construction to furnish the necessary dimensions for the construction of the building; the engineer must have a knowledge of manufacturing methods in order to supply the necessary dimensions for the manufacture of the article; and the land surveyor must know the methods of obtaining, and the legal requirements for, the de-scription of a piece of land.

The architect needs to understand drawings and descriptions of the land on which the building is to be built, and obtain information from drawings of the manufactured equipment that will be incorporated in the building.

DIMENSIONS FOR BUILDING CONSTRUCTION

For building construction, dimensions are given in feet and inches and fractions of an inch. Gener-ally, accuracy to the nearest 1/16 inch is adequate, and it is understood that a tolerance (permitted variation) of plus or minus 1/16 inch is permitted unless otherwise specified. 12" is expressed as 1'-0". Larger dimensions are given as 1'-6", 2'-3 1/2", 30'-6 1/4", etc. It is standard practice to give fractions with denominators of 2, 4, 8, 16, and of 32, 64, 128, etc., if accuracy requires it. Typical fractions are 15/16, 7/8, 13/16, 3/4, 11/16, 5/8, 9/16, 1/2, 7/16, 3/8, 5/16, 1/4, 3/16, 1/8, 1/16, and in 32's or 64's or more accurate if necessary.

CONVENTIONS IN DIMENSIONING FOR BUILDING CONSTRUCTION

1. Neatness, legibility, size of letters and numerals, spacing the dimension lines to avoid crowding, placing the dimension nearest the part for which it is describing, keeping dimensions off the inte-rior part of the drawing if possible, and any other rules that could be made concerning the place-ment of dimensions, are all prompted by the consideration to make the drawing easy to read and pleasing in appearance.

2. Numerals are placed above the dimension line in all structural drawings. This is only an estab-lished practice and has little other significance. In production drawing the dimension line is broken |←——— 32" ———→|. Placing the dimension above the dimension line is quicker, but breaking the dimension line takes less room.

3. The use of arrowheads is a universal practice although some architectural offices use other sym-bols.

4. The use of foot marks (') and inch marks (") varies in practice. Some structural drawings show only the foot marks (') and omit the inch marks ("). General practice seems to favor omitting the inch marks (").

5. Some dimensioning practices are shown below. Leaders to holes point to the center of the holes. Radii of arcs originate or point to their centers. Dimensions for angles are arcs whose centers are at the vertex of the angles.

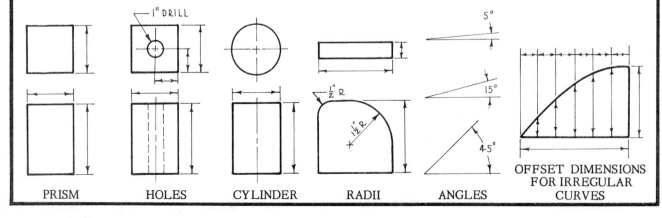

PRISM   HOLES   CYLINDER   RADII   ANGLES   OFFSET DIMENSIONS FOR IRREGULAR CURVES

6. Other conventions, if they may be called that, are based on the actual procedure in constructing the building and therefore are the necessary dimensions. On the partial plans for masonry and frame construction shown below note:

   a. The difference in locating doors, windows, and partitions in the two types of construction. In masonry construction the dimension for the masonry openings for doors or windows are needed while the wall is being laid up, but in the frame construction the frame for the entire wall is erected before the window opening is cut. In locating partitions, the masonry wall is dimensioned to its faces while the frame partition is located to its center (or to the stud sill). The thickness of the masonry partition is shown but the thickness of a frame partition is shown only in detail drawings, where its details of construction can best be shown at a larger scale.

   b. The overall dimensions on frame construction are given to the outside of the stud frame because that dimension is used first, before the sheathing and other wall covering is applied. Even in masonry veneer on wood frame construction, the overall dimension is for the stud frame because the frame is constructed before the veneer is laid up. An overall dimension including the veneer would indicate how much space the building would occupy but would not be a dimension necessary for construction as long as a detail were shown explaining the wall section.

   c. The "X" dimension (in masonry construction) is for plaster, tile, etc.

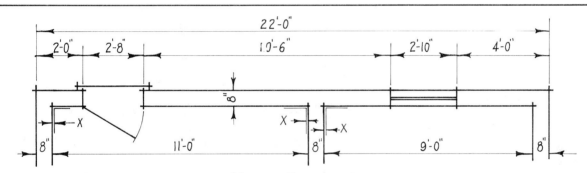

Masonry Construction

Figure 1.

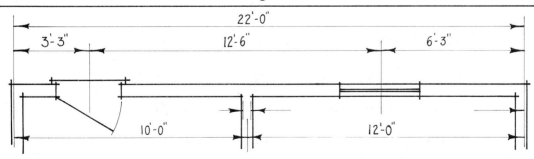

Frame Construction

Figure 2.

7. DESIGN DRAWINGS, or preliminary drawings as they are often called, have only approximate dimensions of the overall size of the building and the sizes of the interior rooms. These dimensions are subject to adjustments when the working drawings are made, depending on the wall thicknesses required for structural strength and types of wall finishes. The purpose of design drawings is to show the approximate interior space and exterior mass relationships rather than details of construction.

MODULAR DIMENSIONING avoids the use of fractions. It is based on modular design, consisting of a grid system where each square is, for example, 4 inches. Then the overall dimensions of the building, the sizes and location of openings such as doors and windows, thicknesses of walls, sizes of columns, etc., are 4 inches or multiples of 4 inches. To make the system effective requires the co-operation of the architect, the manufacturer, and the construction contractor. The architect designs on the modular system; the manufacturer supplies building materials and equipment, as well as window and door units that will fit modular spaces and openings; and the construction contractor must interpret the dimensions on the drawings as modular and not exact dimensions and build accordingly.

The drawing shown below is the floor plan of a simple masonry building shown here to illustrate the comparison of EXACT and MODULAR dimensioning. The masonry unit used here is a modular concrete block whose modular size is 8" × 8" × 16" and whose exact size is 7 5/8" × 7 5/8" × 15 5/8". This implies that the mortar joint must be 3/8" thick to conform to the obvious 8" module for which this block was designed. Note that the modular dimensions are without fractions. On drawings for larger buildings having many partitions, columns, etc., the absence of fractions makes it possible to check dimensions more quickly. The absence of fractions is likewise advantageous during the construction of the building.

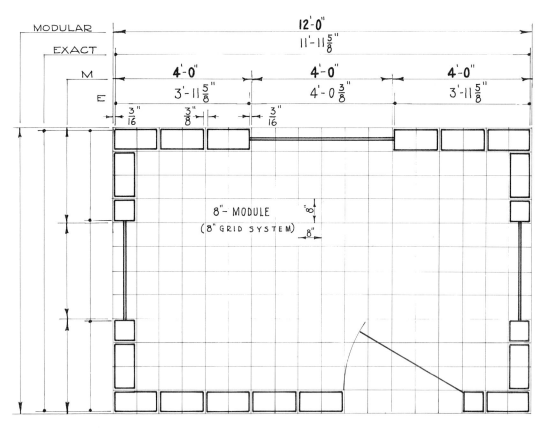

The remaining dimensions are left for the reader to complete.

Vertical modular dimensions are worked out on the same principles as the above horizontal dimensions.

MODULAR DIMENSIONING

The floor plan on this page is the same as the one on page 3. The one shown below is dimensioned with MODULAR DIMENSIONS. The exact dimensions are not shown, but the builder will build the building using the modular dimensions. When he finishes, the building will measure exactly according to the dimensions shown on page 3 as EXACT DIMENSIONS.

The building block to be used will be described in the SPECIFICATIONS written by the architect. If the builder used the MODULAR BLOCK and the specified mortar joint size, the building will be built correctly and as intended.

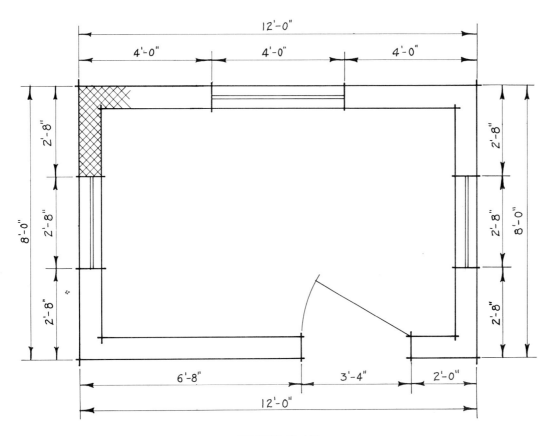

FLOOR PLAN
(Modular Dimensions)
Scale: 3/8" = 1'-0"

THE FIVE

FUNDAMENTALS

OF

MODULAR DRAFTING

This pamphlet was prepared in 1955 by William Demarest Jr., as an aid for architects, structural engineers and draftsmen beginning to use Modular Measure. Single copies obtainable free from:

MODULAR BUILDING STANDARDS ASSOCIATION
2029 K STREET, N.W.
WASHINGTON, D.C.

The FIVE Fundamentals of MODULAR DRAFTING

IT IS HARD TO REALIZE how simple the change to Modular drafting can be until you have done it yourself. Once they have begun dimensioning their drawings by Modular Measure, architects and draftsmen are surprised to find that there was nothing at all to the conversion from traditional procedure. There are just five fundamental practices which must be followed in order to produce Modular drawings; they are illustrated on the next few pages.

You will quickly discover, after you have started to dimension working drawings and details by Modular Measure, that this system encourages two things.-- Drafting short-cuts, to help you produce the drawings, and clarity of presentation, which will not only be helpful to those in the drafting room, but will also assist the contractor and his men to get the job built in strict accordance with the architect's intentions. It is undoubtedly for these reasons that one hears architects who have been using Modular Measure state flatly that they would never consider going back to haphazard dimensioning, even if Modular-size materials were no longer available.

Riding a bike looks tricky only to those who haven't learned. This is the case, too, with Modular drafting; the only way to learn is just to start doing it. Once practised, Modular dimensioning (like bike-riding) turns out to be so simple that it quickly becomes second-nature. It is soon unbelievable that the whole idea once seemed difficult. To "just start doing it", follow the rules numbered 1 through 5 on the succeeding pages. THEY ARE ALL THAT YOU NEED KNOW about Modular drafting. Once acquainted with these simple requirements, you can take it from there yourself.

Before you are well into your second set of Modular drawings, you will have begun to profit from the countless advantages offered by orderly dimensioning through Modular Measure.

THE FIRST THING you will want answered about Modular drafting is "Where do I begin? When does it come into the picture? For you, in the role of the designer working up preliminary sketches, Modular Measure has no effect other than this one point.-- If you make use of one or more design-modules in laying out the building, be sure that they are multiples of four inches, such as 16", 40", 7'-8, 20'-0 and so on. That is Rule Number One. Any 4-inch multiple whatsoever will do, the idea being simply to make it easier for the draftsman, later on, to convert your preliminary sketches into scale-drawings dimensioned in multiples of the basic 4-inch Module.

* * * * * * * *

Of course, good design entails more than merely sketching small-scale plans, sections and elevations. Certain significant details need to be developed by means of rough sketches, since the solutions to these details will have a direct bearing on the design process itself - how the various elements of the structure are to be brought together, how much a particular detail is to count visually, and so on. It is not for a primer such as this to demonstrate how the Modular grid facilitates this part of the architectural process. It will quickly become apparent to you in actual practice. But for a basic rule which you must follow from the outset, turn the next page to Rule Number Two which applies to even the roughest sketch-details.

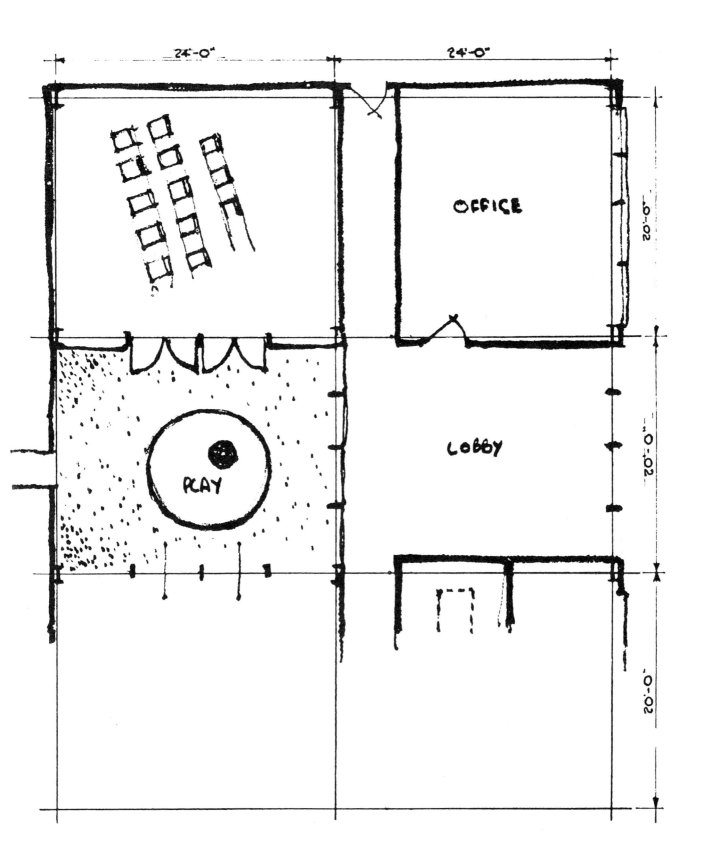

A DETAIL BEGINS WITH THE GRIDLINES. As a detailer, you must set them down
first whenever you do a detail-drawing of any kind. This has to be an in-
violate rule for any drafting team which intends to produce Modular drawings.
There are no exceptions; even hasty freehand sketches of only part of a detail, jotted down during discussion or study of a problem, must all start
with an indication of the 4-inch Modular grid. An underlay showing the grid
will not do, although it can be useful as a guide for drawing in the gridlines.

When you are going to work up any detail-drawing with T-square and triangle,
rather than freehand, it is helpful to rule the gridlines in ink or on the
back of the tracing paper. Then they cannot be erased as changes are made,
since it is necessary that they appear on the blueprints. (One major architectural firm even tried having the grid printed in ink on tracing paper for
final working drawings, but found the expense was not justified. It takes a
draftsman only a moment to rule in the gridlines, at the proper scale, just
where the detail will be located.) When you put dimensions on a Modular detail, locate the surfaces of parts, centerlines, etc. by dimensions to the
gridlines shown, not to points elsewhere in the building. Because of the 4-
inch grid, a Modular detail needs fewer small, fractional dimensions than does
a detail drawn the old way. Remember to show only those dimensions that will
actually help the builder.

(The distinction between detail-drawings and small-scale drawings is thought
of here as being at the scale of 3/4" = 1'-0. Smaller scales are too fine to
show the 4-inch grid; all drawings at larger scales must start with the gridlines.)

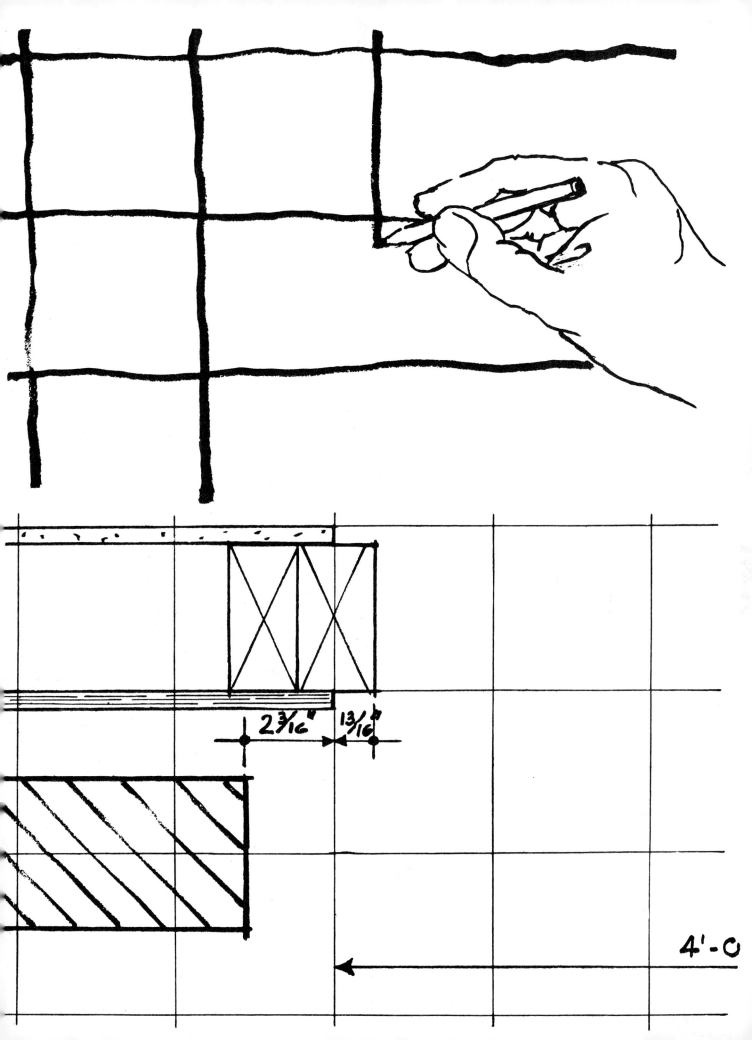

2³⁄₁₆" 13⁄₁₆"

4'-0

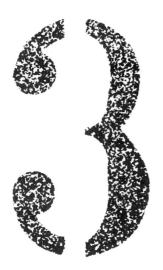

SMALL-SCALE LAYOUT DRAWINGS -- plans, sections and elevations -- give nominal, or "grid", dimensions. As draftsman, you must realize that the grid is still there, even though it has to be invisible when the building is drawn at such scales. These drawings show nominal surfaces: nominal walls and partitions, nominal finished-floor, etc. This will mean that, for the most part, lines indicating such surfaces will coincide with the invisible gridlines. Thus, the distance between the arrow at one end of a dimension-line and the arrow at the other end will be some multiple of 4 inches.

Do not interpret this to mean that such things as nominal 6" stud partitions and nominal 10" cavity walls should be increased arbitrarily to 8" and 12". Use the nominal dimensions as originally intended. And, although nominal finished-floors must be located on gridlines, floor thicknesses need not be 4-inch multiples; Modular Measure introduces no requirements as to ceiling heights.

On small-scale plans for houses of conventional wood-frame construction, such as the example opposite, a single arrow is commonly used to indicate the actual face of wall- or partition-studs, coinciding with a gridline.

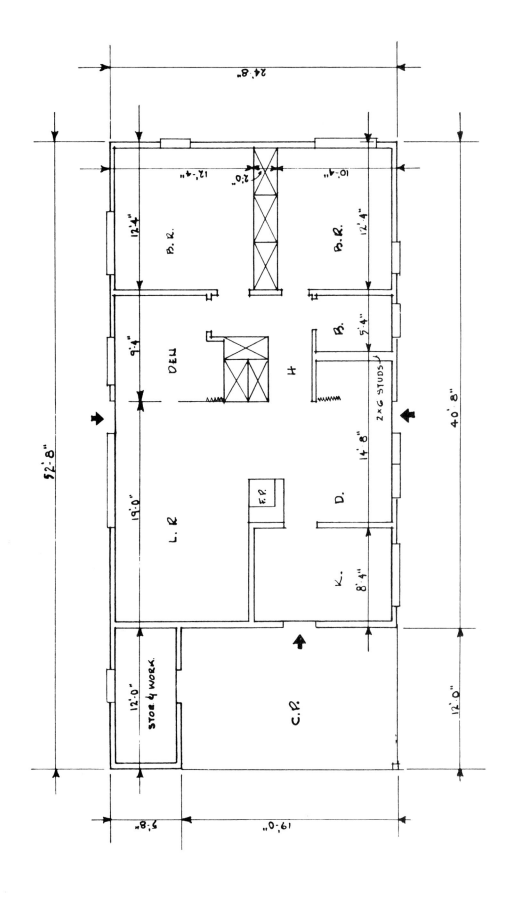

DOTS and ARROWS at the ends of dimension-lines have a definite significance
on Modular drawings. This results from the fact that you do not show the
4-inch Modular grid on small-scale plans, sections and elevations. In re-
ferring back and forth between these layout drawings and the large-scale
detail drawings, it is important to know exactly where any particular detail
fits into the building as a whole. The Modular grid makes this clear and
simple, even when the same detail occurs at several different locations.

This is possible only because the grids appearing on the various detail-
drawings actually represent small portions of the three-dimensional over-all
building grid, already described in connection with Rule Number Three. A
great many of the lines to which you dimension on the small-scale layout drawings will coincide with the building grid   In other words, they will be gridlines; it is therefore important that you identify them as such. Rule Number
Four requires that a dimension taken to a gridline be indicated by an **arrow;**
but where a dimension-line terminates off the grid, a dot must be used instead.

Using a specific example, when the nominal jamb of a window is located on a
small-scale plan by a dimension arrow, it is evident that this dimension is to
a gridline. On the window detail, that gridline is part of the regular 4-inch
Modular grid which always appears on large-scale drawings. Recognizing the
same gridline appearing on both the plan and the detail, the construction man
readily sees just exactly where the designer intended that jamb to be located.

--Whether at large scale or small, whether the grid is drawn in or not, always
use an ARROW when dimensioning to a gridline; when dimensioning to a point off
the grid, use a DOT.

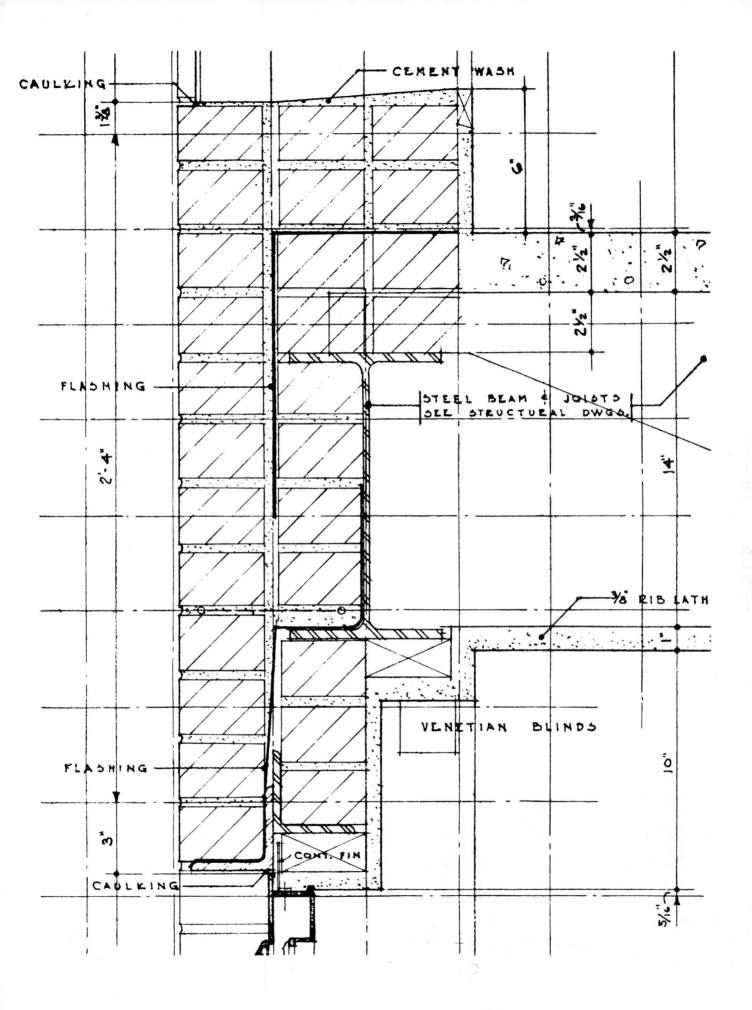

CAULKING

CEMENT WASH

FLASHING

2'-4"

STEEL BEAM & JOISTS
SEE STRUCTURAL DWGS.

⅜" RIB LATH

VENETIAN BLINDS

FLASHING

3"

CONT. FIN

CAULKING

VERTICAL DIMENSIONS are coordinated by the final rule of Modular drafting,
which fixes floor heights as follows:

Nominal finished floor is a gridline; actual finished floor is located 1/8"
below a gridline, with one exception. --

       In wood-frame construction, the top of the sub-floor or

       of slab-on-ground coincides with a gridline.

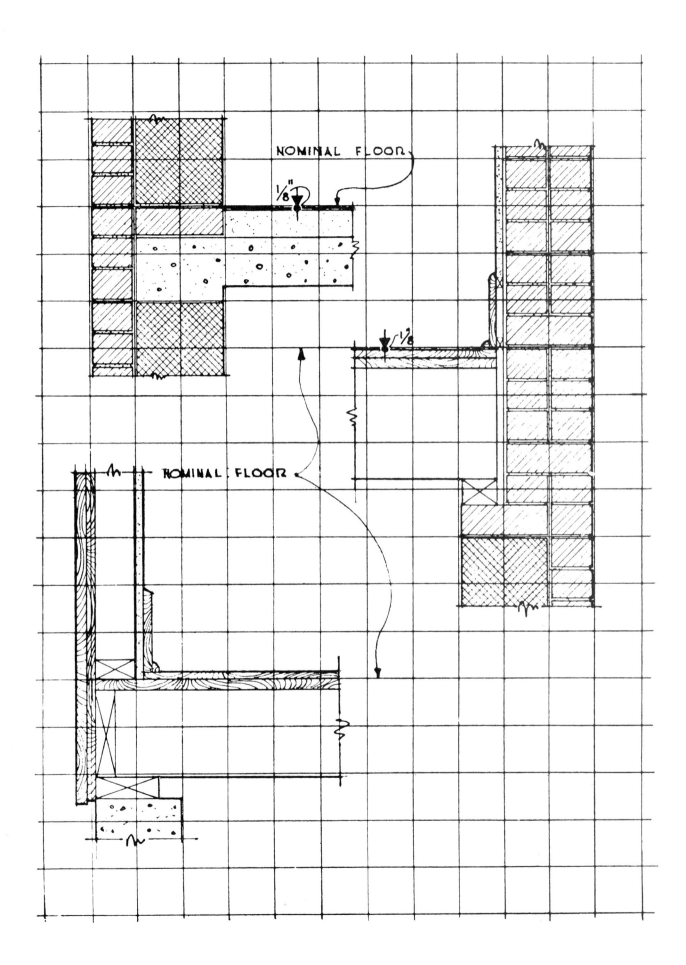

NOMINAL FLOOR

$\frac{1}{8}''$

$\frac{1}{8}$

NOMINAL FLOOR

NOMINAL FLOOR

"The gridlines make everything fit."

HOW MODULAR MEASURE WORKS is pretty well indicated by the five fundamental requirements of Modular drafting, enumerated on the preceding pages. The principle is almost too obvious for some people; they had been expecting it to be far more complicated.

Modular Measure makes possible orderly, systematic dimensioning by introducing an "egg-crate" of reference planes which are everywhere throughout the space which the building will occupy. The egg-crate consists of series of parallel planes, each using a 4-inch spacing, of course. -- That's the Module. And, on paper, they appear as lines making a grid of 4-inch squares -- the gridlines.

It's a very simple concept, although it just took 57 words to describe it. It would not be too serious an oversimplification to say that the building is laid out, drawn up and finally constructed by "filling up" certain of the 4-inch cubes in the egg-crate.

Once the draftsman has formed the habit of thinking primarily in terms of this "3-D" egg-crate, instead of "1-D" dimension-lines, he has made the change to Modular Measure. He will then need no coaching from anyone in order to achieve more orderly, more accurate drafting of working drawings and details.

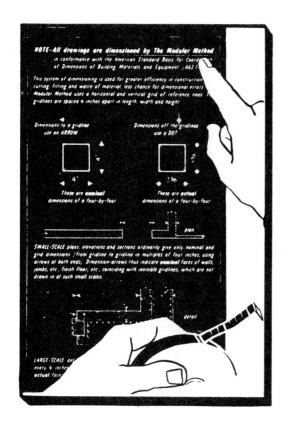

STATE THAT THE DRAWINGS ARE MODULAR

A set of working drawings dimensioned by Modular Measure looks only slightly different from the old, traditional drawings. Failure to state that the drawings are Modular may therefore waste the time of contractor and subcontractors. A conspicuous general-note making this clear should appear on one of the first drawings of the set. Such a note has been prepared by the AIA Modular Coordinator and is recommended by the authoritative Modular Measure Committee of the American Standards Association. This group emphasizes the importance of uniformity in the appearance of all architects' general-notes covering Modular dimensioning.

In order to make it easier to put this note on working drawings, it has been made up as a "Stanpat" for direct, permanent application to tracing paper or linen. ("Stanpat" is the trade name of a thin, translucent material upon which standard notes, title-blocks, North-arrows or the like can be printed. It is affixed by a pressure-sensitive adhesive to the tracing itself; whatever is on it shows clearly on the blueprint.) Use of the Stanpat note makes possible completely uniform appearance of general-notes on Modular dimensioning, no matter whose drawings carry them. For construction men, it serves as a sort of trademark for quick and sure identification of Modular drawings. Half a dozen Stanpat notes on Modular Measure, with illustrated instructions for application, can be obtained for a dollar by writing to: STANPAT COMPANY, 150-42 12TH ROAD, WHITESTONE 57, NEW YORK.

SPECIFY MODULAR-SIZE MATERIALS

Although Modular Measure helps the draftsman to produce concise working drawings and generally simplifies job layout for the contractor, the real pay-off -- in terms of construction economies -- requires Modular drawings plus Modular building materials. Unit sizes are then automatically coordinated with the dimensions of the building. As well as reducing material waste, specifying Modular products will simplify the work of everyone -- estimator, engineer, superintendent and foreman.

MODULAR DIMENSIONING COORDINATION

The purpose of the modular coordination between designer, manufacturer, and contractor is to bring about more efficient and economical building. The aim is to conserve materials and manpower, and to permit fast and efficient operations in the building industry.

The American Institute of Architects and the Producers' Council have undertaken jointly an educational program to speed adoption of the method of coordination. The A.I.A. has prepared and published a booklet, "Building Better from Modular Drawings" for the Housing and Home Finance Agency. The booklet was designed to show job superintendents and foremen why modular drawings differ from the blueprints to which they have been accustomed.

DIMENSIONING FOR MANUFACTURING

In manufacturing, dimensions are also given in feet, inches, and fractions of an inch. They are often given in inches up to 6 feet, such as 48", 54", 71 1/2", then in dimensions over 6 feet they would be given as 6'-1", 8'-4 1/2", etc. In precision manufacturing such as in the automotive industry and building equipment manufacturing, when mating parts require great accuracy to guarantee movement or non-movement between parts, dimensions are given in decimals, often as accurate as to 10,000ths of an inch. For example, a dimension might read 2.8485 inches with a tolerance (permitted variation in accuracy) of plus or minus 0.0002 inches. The architect seldom encounters the need for such accurate dimensioning but must appreciate the fact that accuracy is used where required and that it should always be called for to the extent that it is functionally desirable. Usually the greater the requirement of accuracy the higher the cost.

DIMENSIONING FOR LAND MEASUREMENTS

The architect needs maps of building sites in order that he may establish the location of the building and elevations of floor lines, walkways, driveways, etc. Consequently it is information that must be considered even before the building is designed.

Linear land measurements describing the boundaries of a tract of land are generally given in feet and decimals of a foot to two places beyond the decimal point (100ths of a foot), such as 125.87', 4634.64', etc. These dimensions are given with bearings such as N 64° 15'45" E, etc. The location of any tract is usually referred to a section corner established by the U.S. Geological Survey.

Other units of standard linear land measurements used can be obtained from mathematical tables available in handbooks, textbooks, and in the Architectural Graphic Standards.

A plat drawing of a tract of land including its legal description is on file in the county auditor's office and is similar to the one shown below.

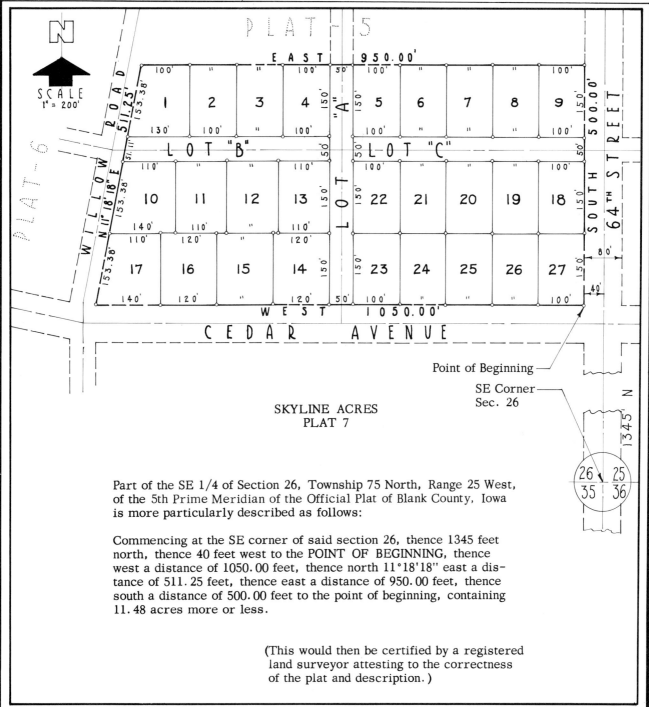

SKYLINE ACRES
PLAT 7

Part of the SE 1/4 of Section 26, Township 75 North, Range 25 West, of the 5th Prime Meridian of the Official Plat of Blank County, Iowa is more particularly described as follows:

Commencing at the SE corner of said section 26, thence 1345 feet north, thence 40 feet west to the POINT OF BEGINNING, thence west a distance of 1050.00 feet, thence north 11°18'18" east a distance of 511.25 feet, thence east a distance of 950.00 feet, thence south a distance of 500.00 feet to the point of beginning, containing 11.48 acres more or less.

(This would then be certified by a registered land surveyor attesting to the correctness of the plat and description.)

PLAT DRAWING

Vertical dimensions expressing the slope of the land is expressed with contour lines (shown on the following pages) indicating elevations above some existing datum. The U.S. Geological Survey usually shows elevations above sea level. When elevations are referred to some datum other than sea level, they usually refer to some nearby existing BENCH MARK. This bench mark may be on any permanent structure such as a fire hydrant, the foundation of a building, water tower, etc.

107.0	105.0	103.0	102.0	101.5	100.5	99.5
104.0	102.5	101.5	101.0	100.0	99.0	98.0
101.0	100.5	99.5	99.0	98.00	97.0	95.0
98.5	98.0	97.0	98.0	98.0	97.0	93.0

Figure 1.   Land Elevations Furnished by a Land Surveyor

Scale: 1" = 10'

The surveyor will often take level readings on a grid system as shown above. From these readings a contour map can be made. The contour map below was made from the above data. Each number on the grid above represents the land elevation at that point on the grid. (Study Suggestion: Study the contour map and discussion below. Then place tracing paper over the above data, sketch the contour lines, then superimpose them on the map below for comparison.)

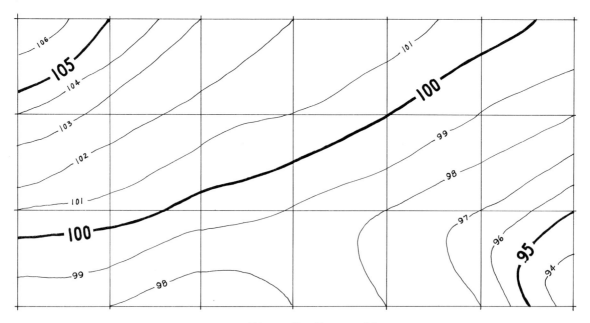

Figure 2.   Contour Map

Each contour line is plotted to represent the same elevation along the entire line. On the above map, contours were drawn for every one-foot interval. This is done by interpolating between the readings to establish points at which the contours will cross the grid lines of the survey. This interpolation may be done by eye or by calculation.

(One-foot INTERVAL means a one-foot CHANGE IN ELEVATION.)

PROBLEM: Using the contour map from the preceding page make a plot plan showing the necessary grading for the location of a building.
SPECIFICATIONS FOR THE SITE: Level a space 22' × 17' at elevation 100'. Grade the cuts and fills to a slope of 1:2.

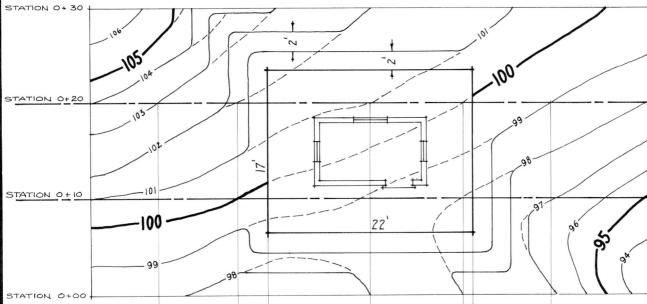

Since the grading is to be done on a slope of 1:2, and since each contour represents 1 ft. change in elevation, the horizontal distance between the new contours will be 2 ft. Note the dotted lines show which contour lines were changed.

Figure 1. Plot Plan (Scale: 1" = 10')

CROSS SECTIONS are used in estimating the amount of dirt to be moved and to aid in determining the footings necessary for the building. Below are shown only two such sections to explain how they are to be drawn and interpreted.

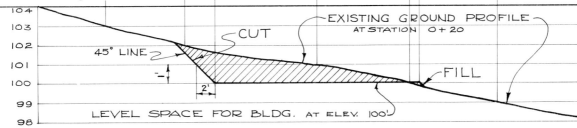

Note the vertical scale of the cross section (1" = 5') is greater than the map scale. This is standard practice in order to exaggerate the surface irregularities. Often the irregularities are slight and are necessarily exaggerated to make calculations easier. Since the vertical scale is twice the horizontal scale the CUT and FILL slope-lines can be drawn at 45°.

Figure 2. Cross Section at Station 0 + 20

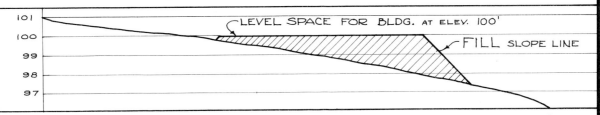

PROCEDURE for drawing a CROSS SECTION: (1) draw the existing ground profile by projecting down from the plan (map); (2) draw the level line at Elev. 100; and (3) draw the FILL and/or CUT lines.

Figure 3. Cross Section at Station 0 + 10

The TRAPAZOIDAL METHOD is used in estimating the amount of earth to be CUT or FILLED in grading a plot of land.

Page 22 shows the PLAN of a typical plot of land and two typical CROSS SECTIONS. The Cross Sections are used in determining the amount of earth to be moved.

The TRAPAZOIDAL METHOD is simply finding the volume of a trapazoid.

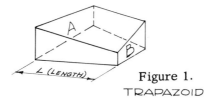

Figure 1.
TRAPAZOID

FORMULA:

Average area of two parallel opposite sides multiplied by the length between them.

In Figure 1:   Volume $= \dfrac{\text{Area A } + \text{ Area B}}{2} \times$ Length

Figure 2 shows how this would be applied to a series of cross sections to determine the total volume for a larger area. The oftener or closer together the cross sections are taken, the more accurate the final result will be. The assumption is made that the slope from one cross section to the next is uniform. In most cases this is not true and an approximation results. However, this approximation becomes practicably accurate.

The area of each cross section is usually computed with the aid of a PLANIMETER, an instrument capable of computing the area of an irregular shape without the use of mathematics.

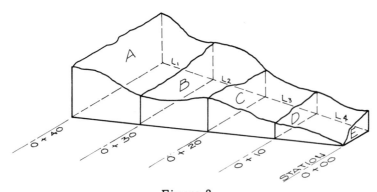

Figure 2.

Total VOLUME $= \dfrac{A + B}{2} (L_1) + \dfrac{B + C}{2} (L_2) + \dfrac{C + D}{2} (L_3) + \dfrac{D + E}{2} (L_4)$

Computations would be kept separately for CUT and FILL. Ideal conditions exist when CUT and FILL balance (are equal), that is, when no earth needs to be hauled away from the site nor does any have to be hauled in.

ENGINEERING DATA AN ARCHITECT OBTAINS FROM CONTOUR MAPS AND CROSS SECTIONS

1. Cross sections are used to estimate the amount of dirt to be moved in preparation of the building site.

   In order to estimate the quantity of dirt to be moved and to determine if dirt will have to be hauled away or "borrowed" from elsewhere, cross sections will have to be "taken" at enough stations to make an accurate estimate possible.

   The area of a cross section of cut and fill is usually computed on cross section drawings with the aid of a planimeter. The areas of two successive cross sections are averaged and multiplied by the distance between them to determine the volume. This is repeated until the entire site surface affected is covered. The results are tabulated and the total volume determined.

2. Data about soil conditions will be used by the architect to determine the practical angle for cuts and fills, the necessity for retaining walls, or the advisability of terracing.

3. Test holes may have to be drilled to furnish data affecting the depth required for footings of the building.

4. Contour maps are also used for studying the drainage of the surrounding area in order to determine the floor elevations and locations for driveways.

5. Cross sections and profiles of existing storm drainage systems and sanitary sewer systems need to be studied for efficient coordination with the entire building project.

I. PRELIMINARY DRAWINGS

    1. Site plan.

    2. Floor plans and elevations partially dimensioned.

    3. Perspective drawing of the building or a model.

    4. Cost estimate.

II. FINAL PLANS AND SPECIFICATIONS

    1. Site plan (contour drawings) showing building location and finished contours.

    2. Elevations.

    3. Sections including longitudinal and transverse as necessary.

    4. Details, including detail sections, partial pictorials, typical wall, window, and door details, and numerous other details of every part of construction.

    5. Door and window schedules showing their type and locations.

    6. Electrical wiring layouts and diagrams, with lighting fixture schedules.

    7. Plumbing, heating, ventilating and air conditioning drawings.

    8. Specifications covering all materials, all equipment performance, workmanship, painting, decorating and finishing.

    9. Construction progress schedules.

    10. All drawings, dimensions, specifications, schedules and costs constitute the complete LEGAL CONTRACT between the owner and the builder.

Architecture should be aesthetically pleasing as well as structurally sound, capable of withstanding the forces to which it is subjected. In designing a building the architect must specify the material to be used and calculate the sizes of the structural members, keeping in mind that the choice of both types and sizes of the material will often influence the beauty of the structure.

The architect generally makes preliminary studies of his design before any structural analysis is considered. After the preliminary design is completed, a structural analysis may be made on the basis of the tentative materials and dimensions. This analysis may lead to certain changes being made in the design and in the selection of materials. After these changes, the design will be restudied until a satisfactory architectural solution has been achieved.

It is the purpose of this chapter to present a method of determining forces GRAPHICALLY, that is, without the use of mathematics. This method is called GRAPHICAL VECTOR ANALYSIS.

While structural problems in architecture are most often solved algebraically, the solution of the problems by graphical means will enable the designer to better visualize these forces than by algebraic solutions alone.

PARALLELOGRAM LAW

This system of VECTOR ANALYSIS is GRAPHICAL because:

1. The DIRECTION of a force is represented by the direction of a line, and

2. The MAGNITUDE of the force in pounds is represented by the measured length of this line, as 1" = 20# or 1" = 60# on the Engineer's scale.

3. The SENSE of the force is represented by an arrowhead.

In Figure 1 the forces AB (40 lbs.) and AC (60 lbs.) acting at point A are drawn to a scale of 1" = 100#.

According to the PARALLELOGRAM LAW a parallelogram can be constructed on these two forces and the diagonal AD of the parallelogram ABCD is equivalent to AB and AC in action on the point A and therefore could replace the two forces AB and AC. This force AD is called the RESULTANT of the two forces AB and AC. See Figure 2.

If the body on which these forces act, is to remain in EQUILIBRIUM (STATIC -- without motion), the EQUILIBRANT AX, which is equal in magnitude and direction but opposite in sense to the RESULTANT, will hold the body in equilibrium, as shown in Figure 3. Figure 4 expresses the same relationship of the forces and is proven by the parallelogram law.

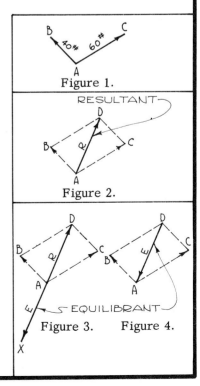

Figure 1.

Figure 2.

Figure 3.   Figure 4.

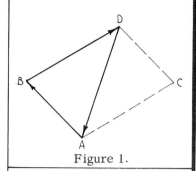

Figure 1.

Furthermore, according to the PARALLELOGRAM LAW, force AC = BD and force AB = CD. Then as shown in Figure 1, the forces AB and BD and the EQUILIBRANT DA form a VECTOR DIAGRAM of the force system. In systems in EQUILIBRIUM (static) the VECTOR DIAGRAM (often called the FORCE POLYGON) is a closed figure. The arrows indicating the sense of the forces will show the continuous chain of forces closing at a point of beginning, proving the system is in equilibrium.

A VECTOR DIAGRAM showing a system of only 3 forces in equilibrium constitutes a triangle and this portion of the parallelogram law can be called the TRIANGLE LAW. The TRIANGLE LAW can be used to solve problems as follows:

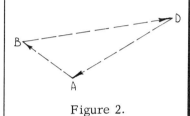

Figure 2.

1. If any two forces are known (magnitude, sense and direction), the third force can be drawn to close the triangle (polygon). See Figure 2. Since these forces are all in the same plane, they appear in true length; and the equilibrant, the unknown force, can be measured at the same scale.

2. If one force is known (magnitude, direction and sense), and the directions of the other two are known, the magnitude and sense of each of the other two can be determined by the TRIANGLE LAW in a VECTOR DIAGRAM. See Figure 3.

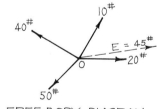

Figure 3.

A VECTOR DIAGRAM can also be used to determine the RESULTANT or EQUILIBRANT of any number of known forces.

Figure 4 shows a FREE-BODY DIAGRAM which shows graphically the direction and sense of each force acting at point 0. For convenience the magnitudes are only indicated numerically and not drawn to scale.

The VECTOR DIAGRAM may be drawn (See Figure 5.) as a continuous chain taking the forces in any order. Each link or line of this chain is drawn to the same scale in pounds and with the same direction and sense as shown on the FREE-BODY DIAGRAM, in Figure 4.

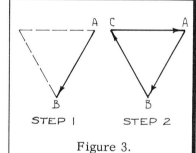

FREE-BODY DIAGRAM

Figure 4.

When all the forces have been drawn (See Figure 5.) the line needed to close the resulting "gap" of the polygon is the EQUILIBRANT or the RESULTANT and can be transferred to the FREE-BODY DIAGRAM to represent its position relative to the original forces.

Figure 4 shows the Free Body Diagram of a COPLANAR CONCURRENT FORCE SYSTEM. This system is further explained on pages 3, 4, and 5 following.

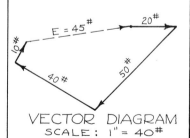

VECTOR DIAGRAM
SCALE: 1" = 40#

Figure 5.

PROBLEM: Find the magnitude of the stresses in the cables due to the 100 lb. weight.

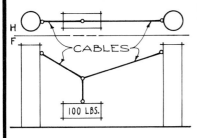

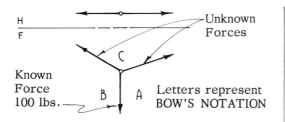

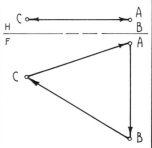

SPACE DIAGRAM

An orthographic drawing of the structural set-up shows the origin of the problem. This problem involves a COPLANAR CONCURRENT FORCE SYSTEM. Coplanar because the cables are all in the same plane and concurrent because they all meet at a common point.

FREE-BODY DIAGRAM

This is sort of a problem analysis. It shows the known and unknown forces in the cables drawn in the same direction as shown in the space diagram.

The letters A, B, and C are placed clockwise between the forces to aid in a systematic solution of the problem. Such a system is called BOW'S NOTATION. (It is hardly needed in this simple problem, but serves as an introduction to its use.)

VECTOR DIAGRAM

This is the final drawing in the solution of the problem. Here the magnitudes of the unknown forces are determined.

The 4 steps shown below illustrate the procedure for drawing the VECTOR DIAGRAM.

PROCEDURE FOR DRAWING THE VECTOR DIAGRAM:

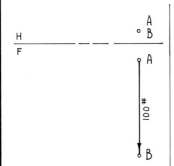

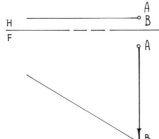

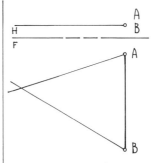

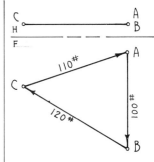

Step 1

Draw the line of action of the known force AB. Since it is a vertical force its true magnitude can be laid off in the front elevation. A scale of 1" = 100 lbs. will be used for this diagram. Place the arrowhead at B because the pull is downward.

Step 2

The VECTOR DIAGRAM is a continuous chain, one force beginning where the other ends. Beginning at B, draw the line of action of force BC. Its magnitude is unknown, therefore C cannot be located in this step.

Step 3

These forces are STATIC, having no motion. Therefore the system is in EQUILIBRIUM and the diagram must close at A. The line of action of force CA can be drawn back from point A.

Step 4

The intersection of the lines of action of the unknown forces automatically fixes point C. Now the magnitude of forces BC and CA can be measured in the front elevation since there the vectors show in their true length. The DIRECTION of the forces can be verified in this diagram. They form a continuous chain from A to B to C to A.

The above problem demonstrates the basic procedure for the solution of COPLANAR CONCURRENT FORCE SYSTEMS with two unknown forces.

The ELEVATION on page 5 shows how a truss can carry a roof load. In addition to the dead load, including roofing, sheathing, rafters, purlins and the truss itself, wind load is included in determining the total loading.

The SPACE DIAGRAM shows only the truss gage lines (centerlines of the rivets). The estimated loading is pro-rated to the purlins according to the area of the roof that would be carried at each point or joint of the truss. The total loading cannot be exactly determined until the analysis has been made. The analysis determines the stresses in the truss members according to the estimated load. When the stresses are determined, the sizes of the truss members can be determined. The sizes of the members are usually slightly different than the assumed weight of the truss before the analysis is made. If the variation is great, a second vector analysis needs to be made.

The exterior forces acting down on the truss total 4000#, therefore, since the truss design is symmetrical each reaction will be 2000# carried by the walls of the building under the truss.

Bow's notations ABCDEFG are placed between all external forces, and 12345 are placed between the members of the truss.

(The stresses 3000#, 2500#, etc., shown on the SPACE DIAGRAM cannot be placed there until the VECTOR DIAGRAM has been drawn to determine them.)

DRAWING THE VECTOR DIAGRAM (or FORCE DIAGRAM)

In order to understand this diagram you must be familiar with the one shown on page 3. The one on page 3 shows only one point of concurrance, with one known force and two unknown forces. Each joint of the truss on page 5 is a point of concurrance where 4 or more forces meet at one point. It is possible to solve for these forces provided only two are unknown.

In examining the SPACE DIAGRAM it is obvious that only three joints need to be solved, since they involve half of the members of the truss and the other half is the same. It is further obvious that the first joint has two unknowns, the second has 3 unknowns and the third has all 4 components unknown.

Beginning with the first joint which has the known 2000# and 500# you can begin the drawing of the VECTOR DIAGRAM. Follow Bow's notations clockwise around the joint. (It is immaterial whether the procedure is followed CLOCKWISE or COUNTERCLOCKWISE, provided the same procedure is followed throughout the analysis of the entire truss.)

1. Draw from A to B measuring 2000#, in the direction of the known 2000#.

2. Draw B to C measuring 500# in the known direction.

3. Draw the direction only of the force between the notations C and 1.

4. Since 1 cannot yet be determined on the VECTOR DIAGRAM, you can draw the direction of the force between 1 and A since you know it has to end at A to complete the closing of the Vector Diagram of a static force system.

5. This locates point 1 on the Vector Diagram, where C-1 and A-1 cross.

6. The two unknown forces can now be measured. This makes it possible to begin the solution of the forces at the second joint with the 1000# known force, since now it does not have three unknown forces, but only two unknown because one was resolved in our diagram for the first joint.

The forces acting at the third joint can in turn be determined when only two unknown remain. The VECTOR DIAGRAM can be continuous until all forces are determined.

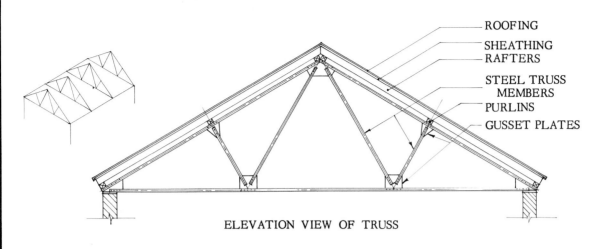

ELEVATION VIEW OF TRUSS

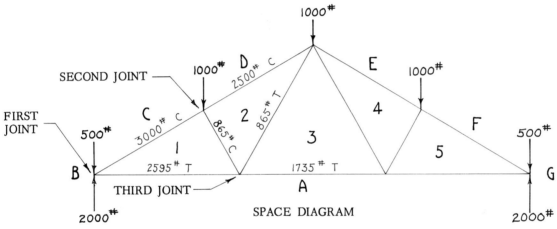

SPACE DIAGRAM

INTERPRETING THE VECTOR DIAGRAM AFTER IT IS DRAWN

To determine whether the stresses in each member are in TENSION or COMPRESSION the SPACE DIAGRAM and the VECTOR DIAGRAM must both be followed.

Considering the first joint where Bow's notations read clockwise from A to B to C to 1 to A. The unknown force C-1 reads from C to 1 (not 1 to C) when reading clockwise around the joint in the SPACE DIAGRAM. Therefore on the VECTOR DIAGRAM the arrowhead (sense) would be at 1. Now if you imagine you take the line C-1 from the VECTOR DIAGRAM and place it on the SPACE DIAGRAM, the line would be pointing toward the first joint, therefore, the member C-1 is in the COMPRESSION. If it pointed away from the joint, it would be in TENSION.

At the second joint, the Bow's notations read in the order of C to D to 2 to 1 to C. Now, from the VECTOR DIAGRAM the 3000# force reads from 1 to C which places the arrowhead at C. Imagining this line is placed on the SPACE DIAGRAM, it would point towards the second joint, signifying, again that it is in compression. Naturally, if a member is in compression it will be compression for its entire length, likewise for one in tension.

Since the determination of the sizes of the truss members and the sizes and number of rivets, etc., are not determined graphically, that phase of structural design will not be considered in this text.

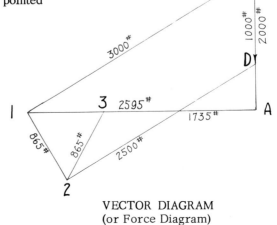

VECTOR DIAGRAM
(or Force Diagram)

Scale: 1" = 1000#

PROBLEM: Find the stresses in the three supports due to the 1200 lb. weight.

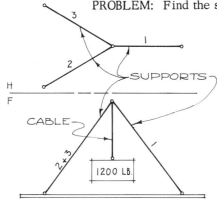

SPACE DIAGRAM

A problem involving 3 unknown forces can be solved if the lines of action of 2 of them are shown as one in one orthographic view. In this problem supports 2 and 3 were made to appear as one in the front elevation. (It is well to note also that supports 2 and 3 form a plane whose edge view shows in the front elevation.)

This problem is typical of a NONCOPLANAR CONCURRENT FORCE SYSTEM. Noncoplanar because all the forces are not in the same plane and concurrent because they all meet at a common point.

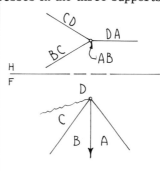

FREE-BODY DIAGRAM (FBD)

Bow's Notation, which has previously been explained, can be placed in any view, but is usually more convenient if placed on the view in which 2 forces appear as one. Therefore place Bow's Notation A, B, C, and D on the front elevation, after representing the 4th force with a wavy line. Complete the identification of the forces by marking them (AB), (BC), (CD), and (DA) in the plan view.

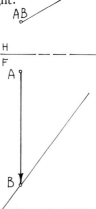

Step 1 of the VECTOR DIAGRAM

Draw the 1200 lb. Vector AB to some scale. In this problem 1" = 1000 lbs. will be used. Its direction is obviously down. It is the only one theoretically obvious. The others can be positively determined in Step 6 of VD.

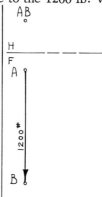

Step 2 of VD

Continue by drawing the line of action of the Vector BC. Point C cannot be located in this step because the magnitude of BC is not known. In the front view this line of action also represents CD.

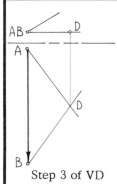

Step 3 of VD

Locate point D by drawing the line of action of Vector DA back from point A. Where it crosses BC and CD lines of action locates point D in the front elevation. Project it to plan.

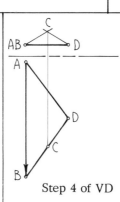

Step 4 of VD

Locate point C by drawing the line of action of force CD back from point D in the plan view. Where this line of action crosses BC line of action locates point C. Project it to front elevation.

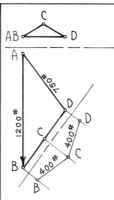

Step 5 of VD

Determine the MAGNITUDE of the forces by treating the Vectors as lines and finding their true lengths. Scale the TL's with the same scale used in Step 1 of VD.

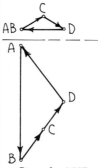

Step 6 of VD

To determine whether the structural members are in TENSION or COMPRESSION first draw arrows on the VD to form a continuous chain from A to B to C to D to A.

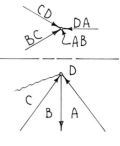

Step 7 of VD

Transfer these arrows to the FBD. If the arrow points toward the point of concurrence the member is in COMPRESSION. If it points away from the point of concurrence, it is in TENSION.

SPIRAL STAIRWAY
Iowa State Capitol, Des Moines
Photo: Courtesy, Des Moines Tribune

S T R A I G H T   L I N E S

Figure 1.   Straight Line   Right   Acute   Obtuse

ANGLES

C U R V E D   L I N E S

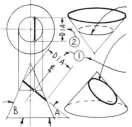

CIRCLE: A Conic Section // to the base.

ELLIPSE: A conic section with angle "A" less than angle "B." To construct an ellipse, draw the circles 1 and 2 = to major and minor diameters 1 and 2 respectively. Then locate points on the curve as shown in steps 3, 4, and 5 for "X."

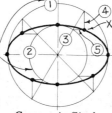

Concentric Circle Method

Figure 2.

PARABOLA: A conic section with angle "A" equal to angle "B." To construct a parabola, choose rise and span. When half of span equals 4, then rise equals 16. To locate points on the curve: $3^2 = 9$, $2^2 = 4$, and $1^2 = 1$. (The St. Louis arch is a CATENERY CURVE which is almost parabolic.)

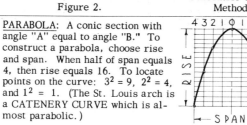

Offset Method

Figure 3.

HYPERBOLA: A conic section // to the cone's axis. Method of construction shown is orthographic. This method can also be used for constructing the other conic sections. All conic sections are plane curves.

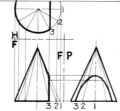

Orthographic Projection Method

Figure 4.

HELIX: The cylindrical, conical and spherical helices are space curves. The CYLINDRICAL HELIX is a curve of uniform slope limited by a cylinder.

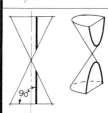

360° Cylindrical Helix

Development of the Helix

RUN = πD

The helix applies to circular stairways and ramps.

Figure 5.

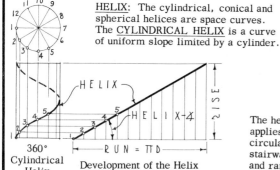

The plan of a conical helix is the Spiral of Archimedes, which is a plane curve.

12 elements with 12 vertical spaces will produce a 360° helix; 8 elements with 4 vertical spaces produces a helix of 180°.

Conical Helix of 360°   (These two helices have non-uniform slope.)   Spherical Helix of 180°

Figure 6.   Figure 7.

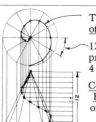

The CYCLOID and the INVOLUTE are plane curves seldom encountered in architecture. Consult other references for their construction.

MILWAUKEE WAR MEMORIAL
Eero Saarinen - Architect
Milwaukee Journal Photo

U.S. EXPOSITION
At Brussels World's Fair
Edward Stone - Architect
Louis Checkman Photo

JEFFERSON NATIONAL MEMORIAL
St. Louis, Missouri
Eero Saarinen - Architect

CIRCULAR STAIRWAY
General Motors Research Staff
Administration Building
Eero Saarinen - Architect

"HORTONSPHEROID"
Chicago Bridge and Iron Company

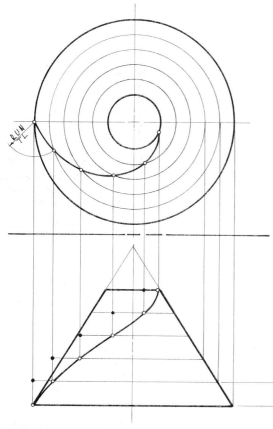

Figure 8.

Figure 8 shows a CONICAL HELIX of uniform slope. The uniform slope is desirable when the helix is used for the shape of a ramp or stairway on a conical surface.

GRAPHICAL CONSTRUCTION:

1. Divide the cone vertically into sections equal to the RISE of the desired slope.

2. Project these concentric circles to the plan view.

3. Locate points on the helix by striking arcs equal to the RUN of the desired slope, as shown in the plan view.

4. These points can then be projected to the elevation view.

5. The curve of the helix can then be drawn with a French curve. (More points on the helix will reduce the slight error.)

6. Once the HELIX is determined, it can be developed into a ramp or stairway as the requirement may be.

RUN
RISE

SLOPE OF THE HELIX

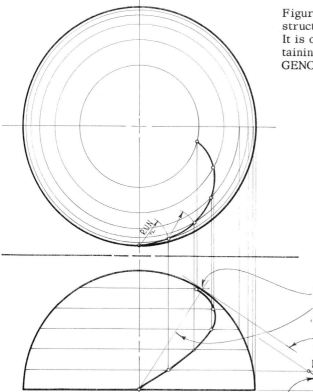

Figure 9.

Figure 9 shows the similar procedure for constructing a SPHERICAL HELIX of uniform slope. It is obvious to conclude the impossibility of maintaining a uniform slope beyond the POINT OF TANGENCY of the slope line on the spherical surface.

POINT OF TANGENCY

PERPENDICULAR TO THE TANGENT LINE THROUGH THE SPHERICAL CENTER

TANGENT LINE HAS SAME SLOPE AS THE HELIX

RUN
RISE

SLOPE OF THE HELIX

PLANE SURFACES

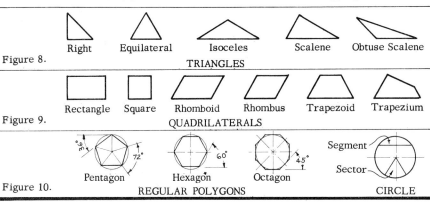

Figure 8.

Right   Equilateral   Isoceles   Scalene   Obtuse Scalene

TRIANGLES

Figure 9.

Rectangle   Square   Rhomboid   Rhombus   Trapezoid   Trapezium

QUADRILATERALS

Figure 10.

Pentagon   Hexagon   Octagon

REGULAR POLYGONS   CIRCLE

Segment

Sector

RULED SURFACES

SINGLE CURVED SURFACES

Cylinders   Cones

The surfaces of cones and cylinders are generated by a straight line whose successive positions are either // or intersecting. These surfaces are developable (see p. 6).

Figure 11.   Right   Oblique   Right   Oblique

WARPED SURFACES

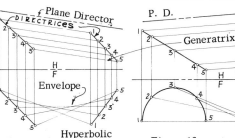
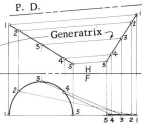
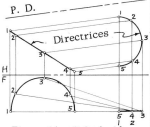

Figure 12. Hyperbolic Paraboloid   Figure 13.   Conoid   Figure 14.   Cylindroid

HYPERBOLIC PARABOLOID is a surface generated by a straight line Generatrix whose successive positions remain // to a Plane Director and skew to each other as its path is guided by two skew straight line Directrices. Its envelope is parabolic and the curves from a section cutting both directrices would be hyperbolic.

CONOIDS and CYLINDROIDS differ from the hyperbolic paraboloid only in the shape of the line directrices.

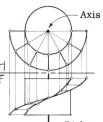
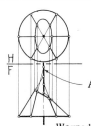
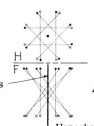
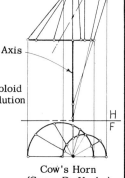

Line joining the centers of the curves

Figure 15. Right Helicoid   Figure 16. Warped Cone   Figure 17 Hyperboloid of Revolution

RIGHT HELICOID: Generatrix intersects a helix and its axis and remains perpendicular to the axis.

WARPED CONE: Generatrix intersects 2 non-// curves and an axis that passes through the centers of the curves.

HYPERBOLOID OF REVOLUTION: Generatrix revolves about an axis that is skew with the generatrix.

COW'S HORN: Generatrix intersects 2 similar and // curves and an axis that is ⊥ to the plane of the curves and passes through the center of a line joining the centers of the curves.

Cow's Horn (Corne De Vache)

Figure 18.

DOUBLE CURVED SURFACES   (See Figure 21 page 5.)

CHATEAU DE CHAUMONT IN FRANCE
Rene'-Jacques Photo in "Air France"
PLANE AND SINGLE-CURVED SURFACES

MUNICIPAL AIRPORT TERMINAL BUILDING
At Lambert Field, St. Louis
Architects-
Hellmuth, Yamasaki and Leinweber
CYLINDERS

VICKERS SERVICE STATION
In Haysville, Kansas
Architect – Architects Associated of Wichita, Kansas
HYPERBOLIC PARABOLOID

A SKATING RINK FOR YALE
Architect – Eero Saarinen
(Courtesy, NEWSWEEK)
CYLINDROID

P O L Y H E D R A

Cube Tetrahedron Octahedron Icosahedron Dodecahedron

CUBE: 6 equal square faces
TETRAHEDRON: 4 equilateral triangular faces
OCTAHEDRON: 8 equilateral triangular faces
ICOSAHEDRON: 20 equilateral triangular faces
DODECAHEDRON: 12 regular pentagonal faces

Figure 19a.   REGULAR POLYHEDRA

Square Prism

Triangular Prism

Oblique Prism

Right Pyramid

Oblique Pyramid

Figure 19b.   IRREGULAR POLYHEDRA

S O L I D S   O F   R E V O L U T I O N

Right Cylinder

Oblique Cylinder

Right Cone

Oblique Cone

Figure 20.   BY REVOLVING A STRAIGHT LINE

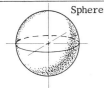 Sphere

 Torus

 Serpentine

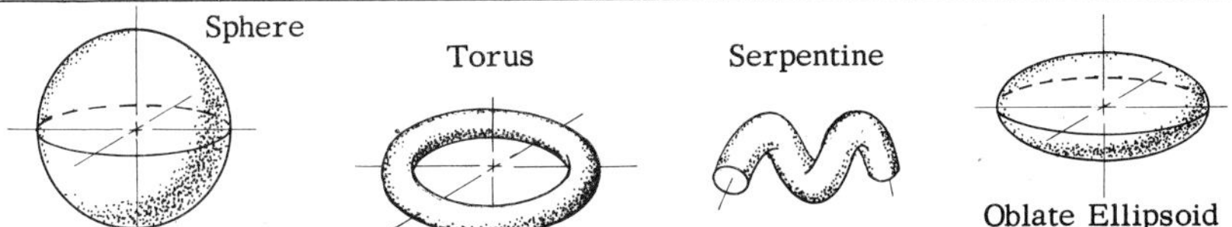

 Oblate Ellipsoid

SPHERE: A circle is revolved about its diameter.
TORUS: (Circular) A circle is revolved about an axis that is outside the circle and parallel to the plane of the circle.
SERPENTINE: A circle is rotated in the path of a helix.
OBLATE ELLIPSOID: An ellipse is revolved about its minor axis.

  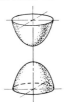

Prolate Ellipsoid

Paraboloid

Hyperboloid

Ovoid

Figure 21.   BY REVOLVING A CURVED LINED

SOLIDS BOUNDED BY WARPED SURFACES

For Examples of Solids Bounded by Warped Surfaces See Page 4.

UNITED STATES
AIR FORCE CHAPEL
Skidmor, Owings, & Merrill, Architects.
The Model of a Portion of the Chapel
Illustrates the Irregular Tetrahedron

M. I. T. AUDITORIUM
Cambridge, Massachusetts
Architect – Eero Saarinen
Illustrates the Sphere

FIRST CHRISTIAN CHURCH
Oklahoma City
Architect – R. Duane Connors
Illustrates the Paraboloid

Figure 22.

        Illustrating surfaces of solids that can be "rolled out" into a pattern. The graphical determination of these "roll-outs" is called DEVELOPMENTS

The surfaces of solids can be DEVELOPED or "rolled out" into a pattern. Solids bounded by plane surfaces or single curved surfaces (except oblique cones) can be developed exactly. All other surfaces can be developed approximately. The amount of error in the approximate developments can be reduced by dividing the surface into smaller ELEMENTS or by using material that is plastic or that can be slightly stretched.

An architect employs these principles in the design and construction of buildings. Their feasibility and ease and economy of construction are often dependent upon the effective application of these principles.

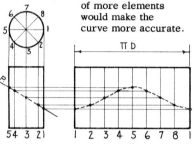

Cutting Plane

The dash lines on the development show where the C.P. has truncated the prism.

Figure 23. Prism (Exact Development)

Note that the TL's of the truncated element lines can be projected directly from the front elevation to the development. The use of more elements would make the curve more accurate.

Figure 24. Cylinder (Exact)

The angle "ϕ" can be computed by using the formula: $\phi = R/S \times 360°$. Note the TL's of the truncated element lines.

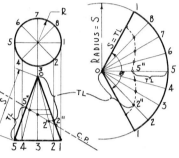

Figure 25. Right Cone (Exact)

The development of a right pyramid can be done similar to that of a right cone, except that the angle need not be computed.

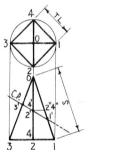

Figure 26. Right Pyramid (Exact Development)

TRIANGULATION (Constructing a triangle with a compass) is the method used to develop an oblique pyramid. The steps of construction are numbered 1 to 5.

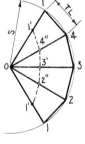
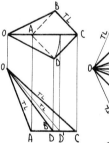

Figure 27. Oblique Pyramid (Exact Development)

Divide the surface into triangles to use triangulation. Use chord TL's to triangulate. Using a french curve to connect the points will partially rectify the curve.

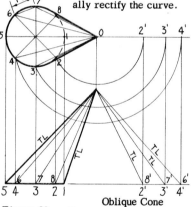

Figure 28. Oblique Cone (Approximate Development)

Divide the surface into triangles and triangulate for the development. This example shows a surface transition from a circle to a rectangle.

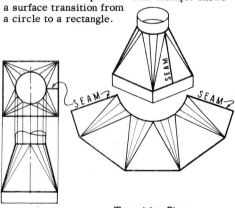

Figure 29. Transition Piece (Approximate & Exact)

This method of developing a sphere is called the SEGMENT method or the Polycylindrical method. It is often referred to as the "Orange Peel" method.

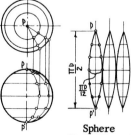
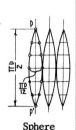

Figure 30. Sphere (Approximate Development)

A second method of developing a sphere is the ZONE (or cone) method shown below.

A third method not shown here, consists of a large number of nearly rectangular pieces which are pressed into a spherical shape and trimmed to fit a patchwork pattern.

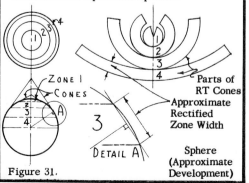

Parts of RT Cones

Approximate Rectified Zone Width

DETAIL A

Figure 31. Sphere (Approximate Development)

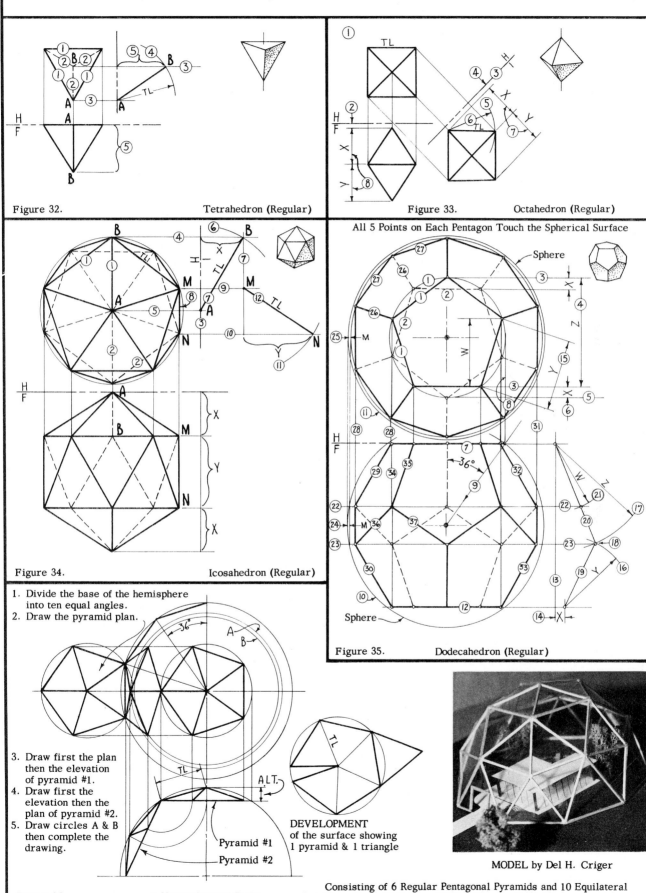

Figure 32.   Tetrahedron (Regular)

Figure 33.   Octahedron (Regular)

Figure 34.   Icosahedron (Regular)

All 5 Points on Each Pentagon Touch the Spherical Surface

Figure 35.   Dodecahedron (Regular)

1. Divide the base of the hemisphere into ten equal angles.
2. Draw the pyramid plan.

3. Draw first the plan then the elevation of pyramid #1.
4. Draw first the elevation then the plan of pyramid #2.
5. Draw circles A & B then complete the drawing.

Pyramid #1
Pyramid #2

DEVELOPMENT
of the surface showing
1 pyramid & 1 triangle

Figure 36.   A Hemispherical Dome

MODEL by Del H. Criger

Consisting of 6 Regular Pentagonal Pyramids and 10 Equilateral
Triangles, All Points of Which Touch a Hemisphere.

The intersection of two prisms can most easily be determind by the PIERCING POINT method when one of the orthographic views shows the involved planes as edges. In Figure 37, "Y" is the piercing point of line XY on the plane ABCD. This is evident in the plan view where ABCD shows as an edge.

In Figure 38 the PIERCING POINT method is again illustrated. The "lines" piercing the plane ABCD are "element" lines drawn on the surface of the cylinder. Accuracy of the curved line of intersection can be increased with the addition of more element lines.

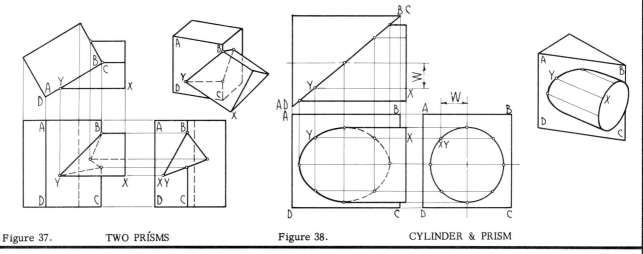

Figure 37.   TWO PRISMS

Figure 38.   CYLINDER & PRISM

CUTTING PLANES

The system of using cutting planes to determine the line of intersection is an all-around method effective in most all cases. The illustrations on this page show cutting planes cutting basic geometric solids. Figures 39, 40, 41, 42, and 43 show positions of the cutting planes placed in such a way that the resulting "cuts" are either circles or straight lines, which are easily and rapidly drawn by the draftsman. Avoid positions illustrated in Figures 44 and 45 where the resulting "cuts" are curves less easily drawn.

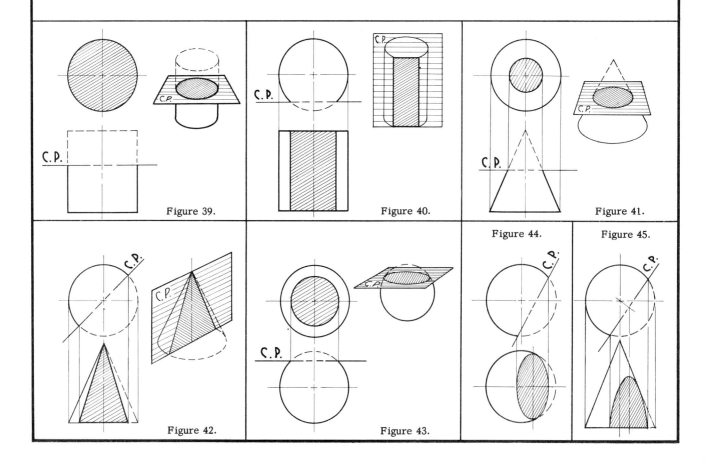

Figure 39.

Figure 40.

Figure 41.

Figure 44.

Figure 45.

Figure 42.

Figure 43.

Each horizontal cutting plane cuts 2 circles, 1 on the cone and 1 on the cylinder. The intersection of the circles locates points on the line of intersection.

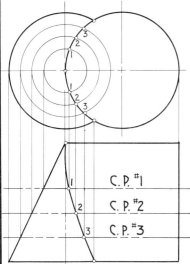

C.P. #1
C.P. #2
C.P. #3

Cone and Cylinder

Figure 46.

Each horizontal cutting plane cuts a circle on the cone and a square on the pyramid.

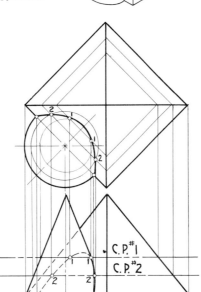

C.P. #1
C.P. #2

Cone and Pyramid

Figure 47.

INTERSECTION OF
CYLINDERS
Airport Terminal Building, Lambert Field,
St. Louis, Missouri
Architects – Hellmuth, Yamasaki, & Leinweber

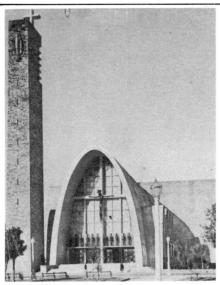

INTERSECTION OF
PARABOLIC CYLINDERS
Iglesia De La Purisima, Monterey, Mexico
(Church of the Most Pure)
Architect - Enrique De La Mora

Each horizontal cutting plane cuts a pair of circles. Note that points below cutting plane #1 are hidden in plan because they are located below the great circle of the sphere.

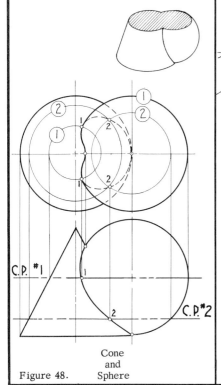

C.P. #1

C.P. #2

Cone and Sphere

Figure 48.

Radial cutting planes cut straight lines on the cone because they pass through the apex.

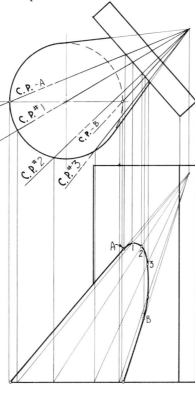

C.P. - A
C.P. #1
C.P. - B
C.P. #2
C.P. #3

A
B

Oblique Cone and Prism

Figure 49.

INTERSECTION OF
HYPERBOLIC PARABOLOIDS
Coyocan Market, Mexico
Designed by Felix Candela

INTERSECTION OF
HYPERBOLIC PARABOLOIDS
A Mausoleum at Karachi, Pakistan
From the Architectural Review
Architects – Raglan Squire and Partners

A R C H E S

See Architectural Graphic Standards For Geometric Construction Of Arches.

Corbelled
Model by
Moffitt & Crose

Figure 50.

Roman or Semi-Circular
Model by
Moffitt & Crose

Figure 51.

Segmental
Marston Hall
Iowa State University
Architects
Proudfoot & Bird

Figure 52.

Jack
Hospital
Iowa State University
Architects - Proudfoot,
Bird, & Rawson

Figure 53.

Gothic
St. Johns Episcopal
Church, Ames, Iowa
Architect - A.H. Kimball

Figure 54.

Ogee
Campanile
Iowa State University
Architect - Hallett

Figure 55.

Elliptical
Sigma Alpha Epsilon
Fraternity House, Ames, Ia.
Architects -
Kimball, Bailie, & Cowgil

Figure 56.

Tudor
Collegiate Presbyterian
Church, Ames, Iowa
Architects - Proudfoot,
Bird, & Rawson

Figure 57.

Parabolic
Holy Cross Lutheran Church
Wichita, Kansas
Architects - Ramey & Himes

Figure 58.

V A U L T S & D O M E S

Barrel Vault

Figure 59.

Models by Moffitt & Crose

Groin Vault

Figure 60.

Cloister Vault

Figure 61.

Models by Moffitt & Crose

Spherical Dome

Figure 62.

Dome on
Squinches

Figure 63.

Dome on Drum
& Pendentives

Figure 64.

Parabolic Dome
Model by Richard Campbell

Figure 65.

Bulbous Dome
Taj Mahal, Agra, India

Figure 66.

Bucks County Courthouse & Office Building
Doylestown, Pennsylvania
Architects: Carroll, Grisdale & Van Alen
Associate Architect: Fred F. Martin

CONVERGENCE IN ARCHITECTURE

Here are two buildings "IN PERSPEC-
TIVE" as seen by a camera.

This is what your eye would see if you
were in the same position as the camera.

The farther away an object is, the
smaller it appears.

Timken Mercy Hospital
Canton, Ohio
Schmidt, Garden & Erickson, Architects.

John Hancock Insurance Company, Kansas City, Missouri
Architect: Skidmore, Owings and Merrill, New York, New York

Further evidence of convergence is evident in this photograph where all three dimensions, length, width, and height become less with increased distance from the camera.

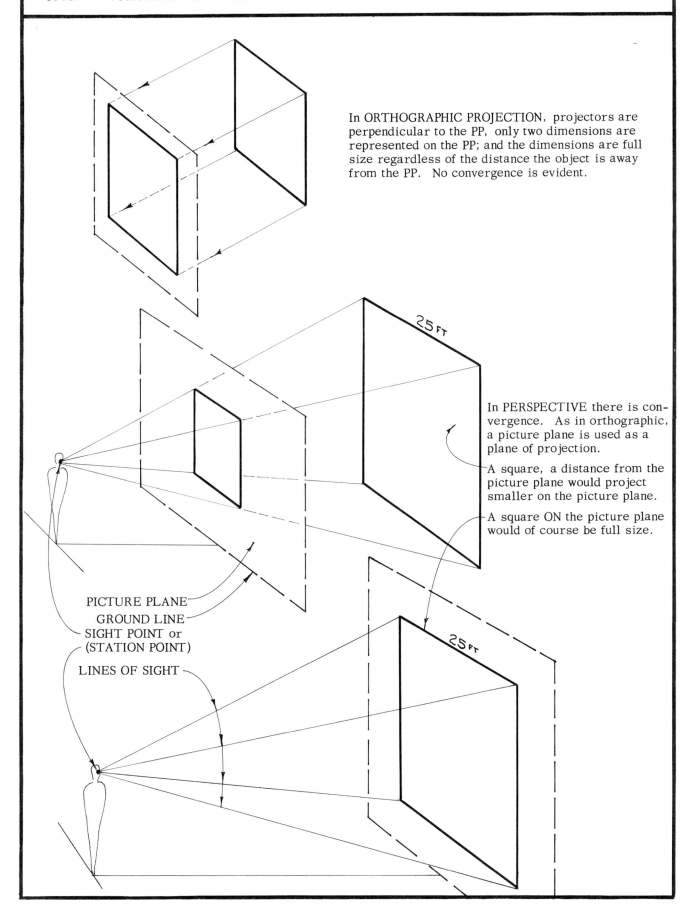

In ORTHOGRAPHIC PROJECTION, projectors are
perpendicular to the PP, only two dimensions are
represented on the PP; and the dimensions are full
size regardless of the distance the object is away
from the PP. No convergence is evident.

In PERSPECTIVE there is convergence. As in orthographic,
a picture plane is used as a
plane of projection.

A square, a distance from the
picture plane would project
smaller on the picture plane.

A square ON the picture plane
would of course be full size.

PICTURE PLANE
GROUND LINE
SIGHT POINT or
(STATION POINT)

LINES OF SIGHT

25 FT

25 FT

HORIZON LINE

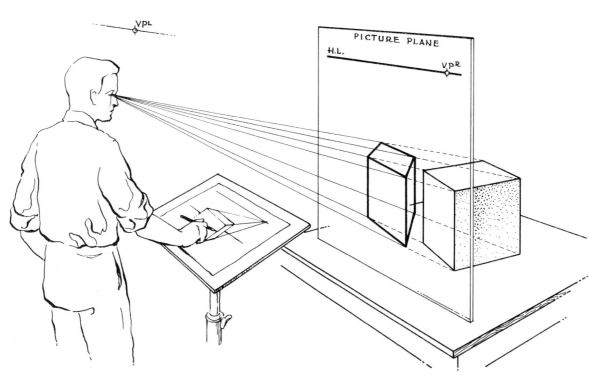

PICTURE PLANE

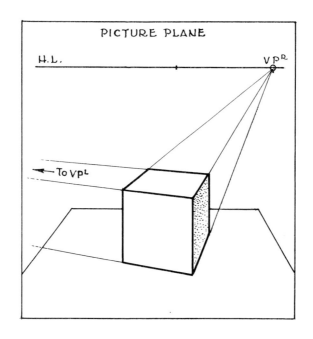

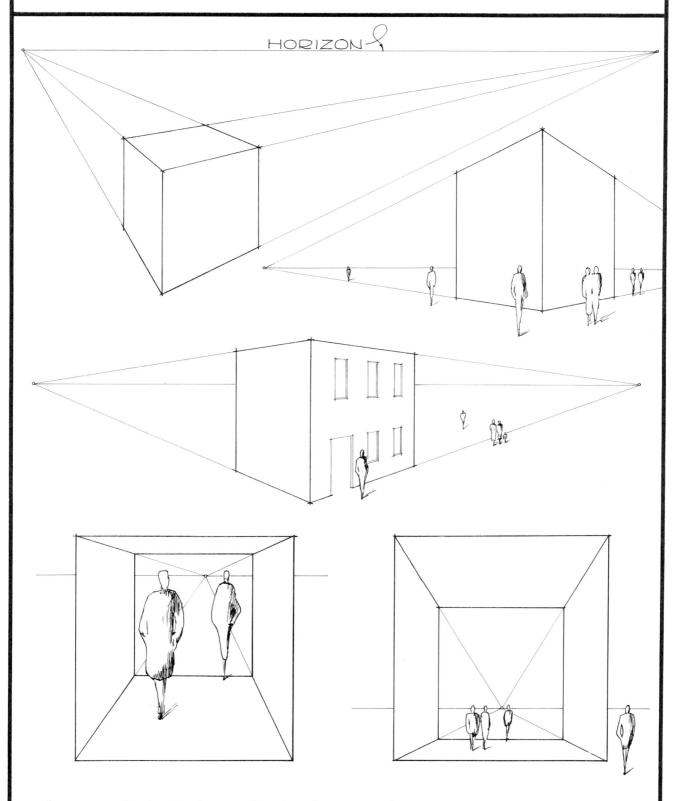

In a perspective drawing the true size of an object is not always apparent. The observer becomes aware of size when the object is shown in relation to the horizon, scale figures or familiar objects which are definitely related in size to the human figure, such as automobiles, doors, windows or stairs.

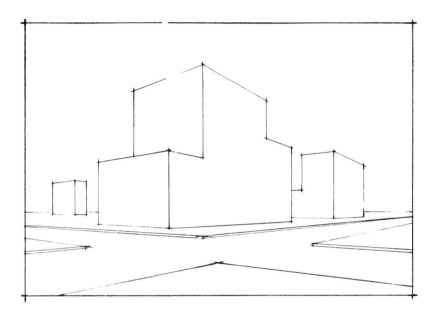

In line drawings without shading, depth or distance may be expressed by linear perspective.

According to The Columbia Encyclopedia "Perspective, in art, may be described as any method employed to represent three-dimensional space on a flat surface or in relief sculpture.

The two principal methods are linear perspective, which establishes the relative dimensions of objects as seen in space, and aerial perspective, which makes use of variations in color, light and dark, and contour to express depth."

In perspective drawings depth or distance may be accentuated by the use of aerial perspective which shows nearer objects in strong contrast of light and shade and color, and distant objects in subdued contrast and reduced color intensity.

In addition to linear and aerial perspective, depth may be accented by allowing near buildings or entourage (trees, bushes, etc.) to overlap more distant buildings or entourage.

The purpose of pages 4, 5, 6, 7, and 8 is to show the basic principles of how to draw a TWO-POINT PERSPECTIVE. The method presented here is the COMMON or OFFICE method. The two-point perspective was chosen to be introduced first because it involves the general principles characteristic of all other types of perspective and is probably the type used the most often.

This layout on page 7 is plan view only. It is in plan that the architect makes most of the decisions that will determine the effect he desires in the perspective picture.

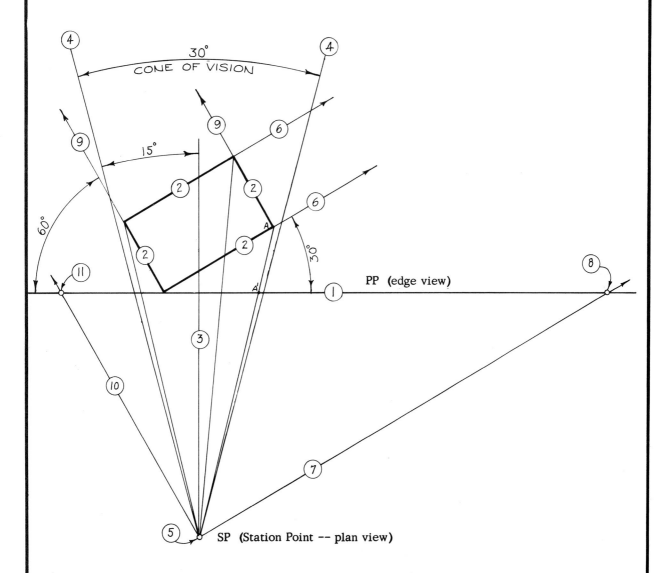

Step 1 Positions the picture plane (PP) vertically and here in plan it appears as an edge.

Step 2 Positions the building and indicates which wall will be emphasized to show the most desirable angle at which to "take the picture." This drawing of the plan of the building is positioned 30° and 60° with the PP. Other angles may be chosen for changes in emphasis. It is placed directly against the PP for ease of making vertical measurements which will be explained on page 10.

Step 3   A line is drawn perpendicular to the PP and through the Point of Interest of the building. On this line the STATION POINT, SP (position of the observer) will be located to show the building with minimum distortion.

Step 4   The 30° CONE OF VISION (15° on each side of line 3) must include the building. The observer must be able to see the entire building in width and height through a cone whose apex angle is 30°. This will locate the STATION POINT far enough away from the building to avoid distortion in the perspective picture. Page 7 shows the cone of vision includes the width of the building. Page 10 shows the cone of vision applied to the height of the building. There are occasions when distortion is desired to emphasize or exaggerate certain features.

Step 5   The STATION POINT will now serve as a point from which to draw the lines of sight from the observer (SP) to the points on the building. Point A on the building will appear to the observer to be at A' on the PP. Likewise all the other points that will appear on the perspective picture will appear on the PP where these lines of sight pierce the PP.

Steps 6, 7, 8, 9, 10, and 11 are probably the most difficult to comprehend, and are important to an understanding of the theory of perspective drawing.

Step 6   Imagine the horizontal lines 6 as extensions of all horizontal lines on the building that are in that direction. These lines are all parallel to each other and can be referred to as a "family" of lines. Imagine them extended for miles perhaps, until they reach the horizon. They remain parallel to each other all the way, but because the horizon is so far away it appears to the observer that they converge and meet at a point. The horizon is where all horizontal lines appear to meet.

Step 7   Now imagine the observer observing these horizontal lines and viewing this "point" on the horizon. His line of sight (line 7) is also horizontal and parallel to the other lines of the "family" and this "point" on the horizon appears to him to be on the picture plane at point 8. This "point" on the PP is called the RIGHT VANISHING POINT and will be the vanishing point for all the lines of this "family" on the perspective picture.

Steps 9, 10, and 11 similarly locate the LEFT VANISHING POINT which will be the vanishing point on the perspective picture, for all the lines of the other "family" of horizontal lines.

The plan layout is now complete and the ELEVATION considerations will be made as shown on page 10.

Decisions that have been made on page 7:

     1. Position of the PP.

     2. Position of the building plan with respect to the PP.

     3. Choice of the STATION POINT.

The Decision remaining is the position of the HORIZON which is the elevation of the observer's eye and is discussed on page 10.

Before proceding to page 10 for the completion of the office method of perspective, observe that height measurements of buildings must always be made <u>ON</u> the picture plane.

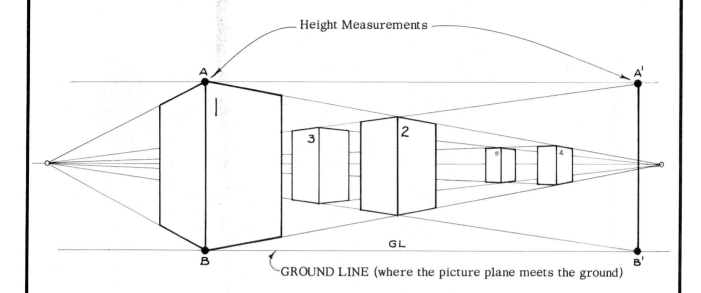

The drawing above shows five buildings all the same size. Their height measurements must all be made <u>ON</u> the PP, then transferred to each building by means of perspective lines.

Since building 1 touches the PP its true height can be measured on the edge that touches the PP, that is, AB.

The height of buildings 2 and 4 can be transferred to their locations by means of one perspective line. But the height of buildings 3 and 5 must be transferred to their locations by perspective lines in two directions, from the initial measurement on building 1.

If the height of buildings 2 and 3 were extended directly to the PP at A'B', the true height could be measured.

Before the perspective picture is drawn, one more decision needs to be made. The distance of observer's eye is above the ground will determine whether the "picture" will be "taken" to show as an AERIAL view when the eye is high enough to see the top of the building; or about 5 ft. high to be as it appears normally as the observer stands on level ground; or whether it will be a "worm's eye" view when the eye is assumed to be <u>on</u> the ground; or a view when the building may be on a hill higher than the position of the observer when the HORIZON would be below the ground line GL.

In the drawing below the HORIZON was chosen 5'-6" above the GL. A check with the side elevation view of the CONE OF VISION shows the entire building is now within the 30° cone of vision, in elevation as well as in plan.

Step 1. The edge of the building that is against the PP will appear in TL in the perspective drawing. This vertical edge will begin at the ground line (GL) since this is where the vertical PP intersects the ground on which the building rests.

Step 2. The true height of the building is projected from the ELEVATION, to 3.

Steps 4 and 5. These lines give the directions of the horizontal lines of the front wall. See Step 7, pages 7 and 8.

Step 6. The length of the front wall is determined, and line 7 can be drawn.

Lines 8, 9, 10, and 11 complete the perspective picture.

Drawing Scale: 1/16" = 1'-0"

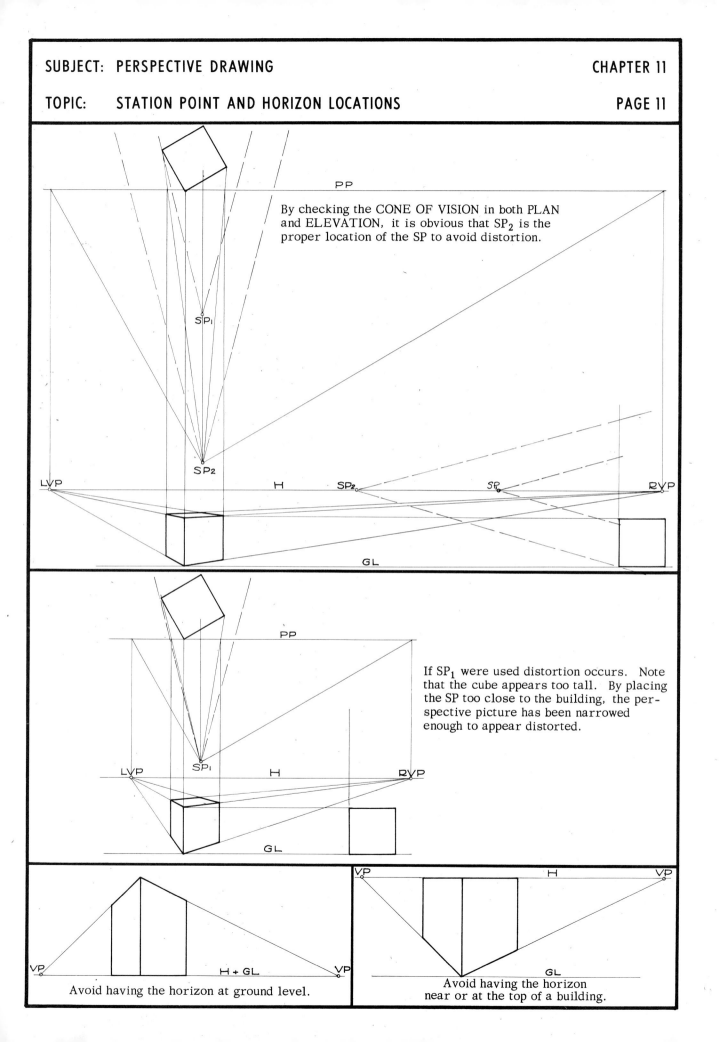

By checking the CONE OF VISION in both PLAN
and ELEVATION, it is obvious that SP_2 is the
proper location of the SP to avoid distortion.

If SP_1 were used distortion occurs. Note
that the cube appears too tall. By placing
the SP too close to the building, the perspective picture has been narrowed
enough to appear distorted.

Avoid having the horizon at ground level.

Avoid having the horizon
near or at the top of a building.

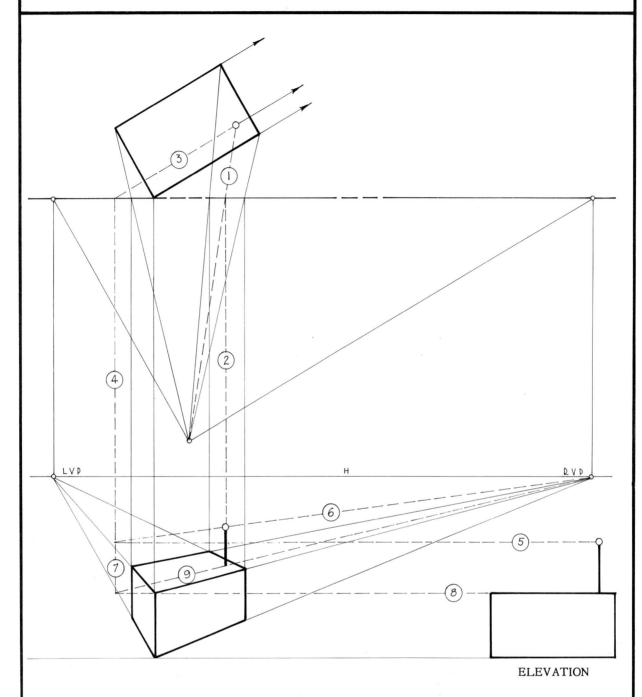

ELEVATION

This page demonstrates how to consider any point in space and locate it on the perspective picture.

The drawing above only emphasizes the general procedure known as the OFFICE METHOD shown on these pages 3, 4, 5, 6, and 7. An understanding of this procedure will make it possible to locate any point which could be one of a number of points on a curved line which does not have a vanishing point, or a point or points on a line for which no vanishing point has yet been determined.

Line 3 constitutes the "secret" or the "key" to being able to locate any point. This line 3 shows an imaginary and auxiliary line drawn in, to solve the problem. It is drawn through the top of the flag pole and drawn parallel to one of the "family" of lines for which a vanishing point has already been established. This line is extended until it pierces the PP.

Lines 4 and 5 locate this piercing point in elevation, where its true height can be measured or projected from the elevation view of the building shown in the lower right of the layout.

Line 6 is the perspective of the imaginary auxiliary line on which the top of the flag pole will be located.

Lines 7, 8, and 9 locate the bottom of the flag pole.

This could have been accomplished as well if the imaginary auxiliary line were drawn parallel to the other family of lines using the LEFT VANISHING POINT.

SUGGESTED PROCEDURE FOR BECOMING MORE FAMILIAR WITH MAKING PERSPECTIVE DRAWINGS:

To fully understand the effects of the variations of the positions of the PICTURE PLANE, STATION POINT, and HORIZON it is advisable to use the same figure or building. Then the different effects can best be compared.

Suggested variations and the expected effects:

1. Moving the PP farther out in front of the building would make the resulting perspective picture smaller.

2. Moving the PP farther back from the front edge of the building will make the resulting perspective picture larger.

3. Moving the station point closer than allowed by the cone of vision will cause distortion, such as making the dimensions not proportional to the actual dimensions.

4. Moving the station point farther away from the building than required by the cone of vision will have little effect on the resulting picture, except that the surrounding landscape, especially foreground, will not be as distorted.

5. The effect of moving the horizon into different positions has been discussed on page 5. If the horizon is placed too high to have the building included in the cone of vision, the distortion will be greater if the building is tall, compared to its length and width.

TWO-POINT INTERIOR PERSPECTIVE

Two-point perspective is used for interiors as well as exteriors and the principles are the same.

Below are shown three methods of locating the apex of a right pyramid in perspective.

1. <u>COORDINATE</u> (or box) method. Construct a box around the pyramid. Draw a center line through the top of the box. Draw the perspective of this center line, then project the apex to this perspective line.

2. Draw diagonals for the top of the box to locate the apex.

3. <u>PERSPECTIVE LINE</u> method.
    Draw a line through the apex, in plan, in the direction of a line for which there is a VP. Extend this line to the PP. Its actual height can then be measured on the PP. Then draw the perspective of this line and project the apex to the line.

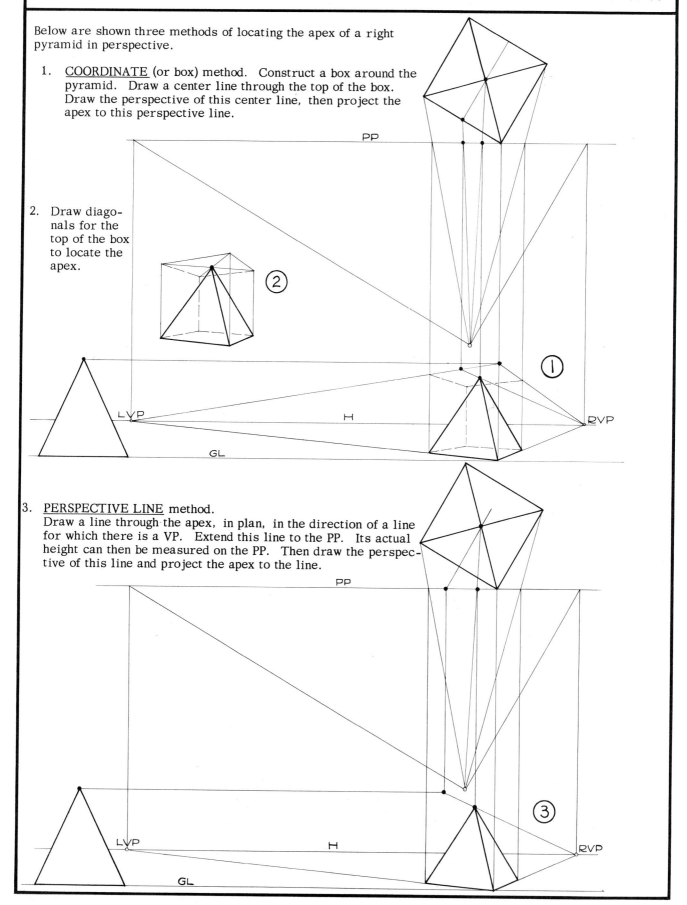

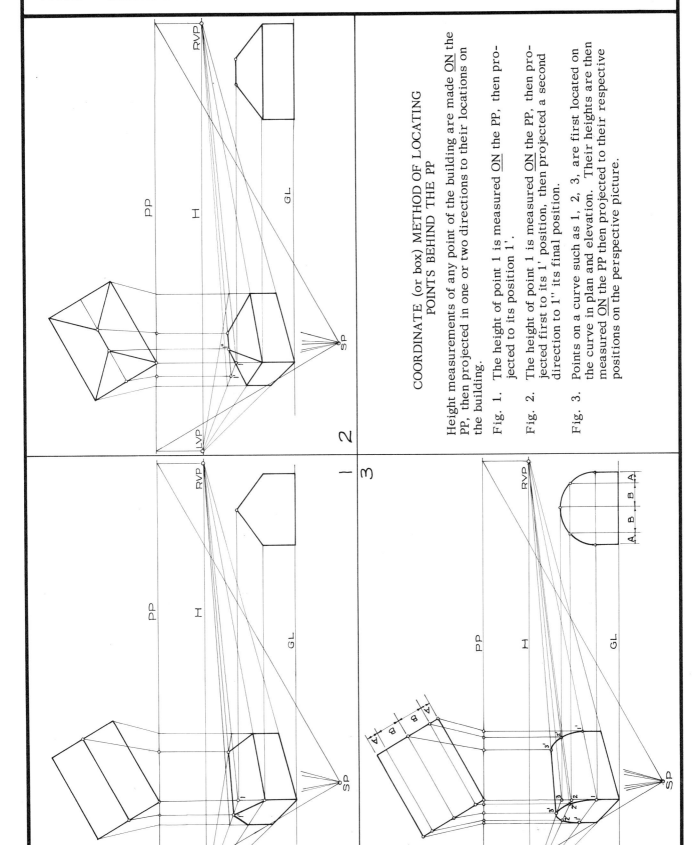

COORDINATE (or box) METHOD OF LOCATING
POINTS BEHIND THE PP

Height measurements of any point of the building are made ON the
PP, then projected in one or two directions to their locations on
the building.

Fig. 1. The height of point 1 is measured ON the PP, then projected to its position 1'.

Fig. 2. The height of point 1 is measured ON the PP, then projected first to its 1' position, then projected a second
direction to 1'' its final position.

Fig. 3. Points on a curve such as 1, 2, 3, are first located on
the curve in plan and elevation. Their heights are then
measured ON the PP then projected to their respective
positions on the perspective picture.

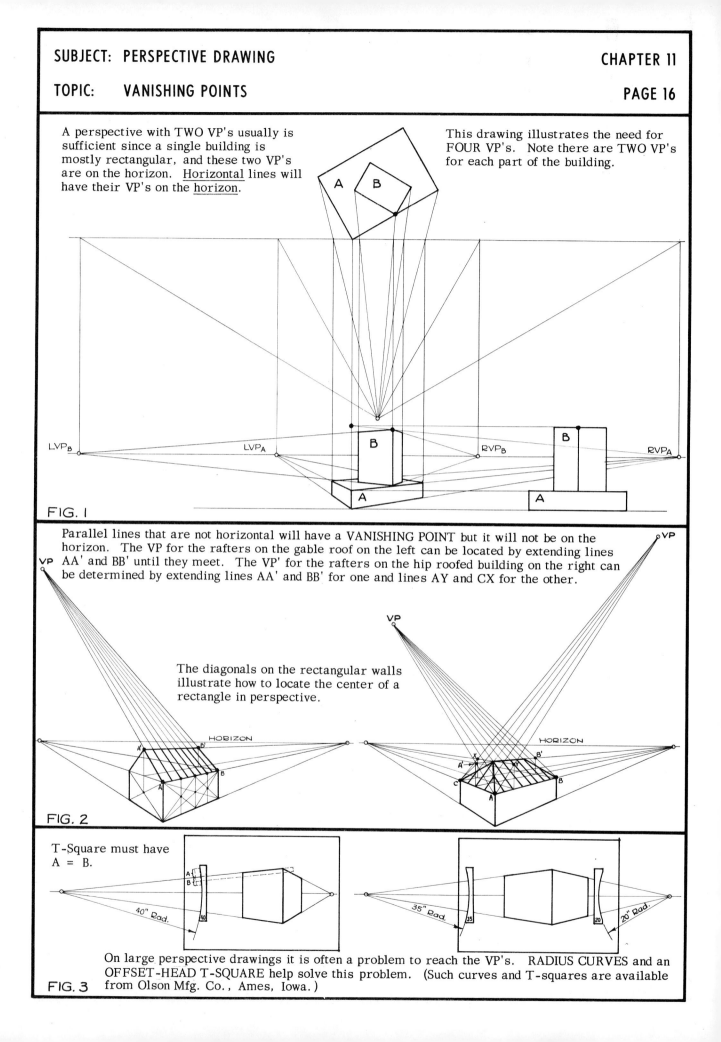

A perspective with TWO VP's usually is sufficient since a single building is mostly rectangular, and these two VP's are on the horizon. Horizontal lines will have their VP's on the horizon.

This drawing illustrates the need for FOUR VP's. Note there are TWO VP's for each part of the building.

FIG. 1

Parallel lines that are not horizontal will have a VANISHING POINT but it will not be on the horizon. The VP for the rafters on the gable roof on the left can be located by extending lines AA' and BB' until they meet. The VP' for the rafters on the hip roofed building on the right can be determined by extending lines AA' and BB' for one and lines AY and CX for the other.

The diagonals on the rectangular walls illustrate how to locate the center of a rectangle in perspective.

FIG. 2

T-Square must have A = B.

On large perspective drawings it is often a problem to reach the VP's. RADIUS CURVES and an OFFSET-HEAD T-SQUARE help solve this problem. (Such curves and T-squares are available from Olson Mfg. Co., Ames, Iowa.)

FIG. 3

VANISHING-POINT METHOD

See page 9, Chapter 12 for determining the VP for a sloping line, LR-VP. In the problem on this page the true slope of the hip rafters and the roof slope need to be determined before the VP's for the sloping lines can be located.

The disadvantage of this method is that often the VP's are inconveniently distant. If it were desirable to enlarge the perspective drawing of this building, Radius Curves would probably be needed, not only for the RVP but for at least three of the four VP's for the sloping lines.

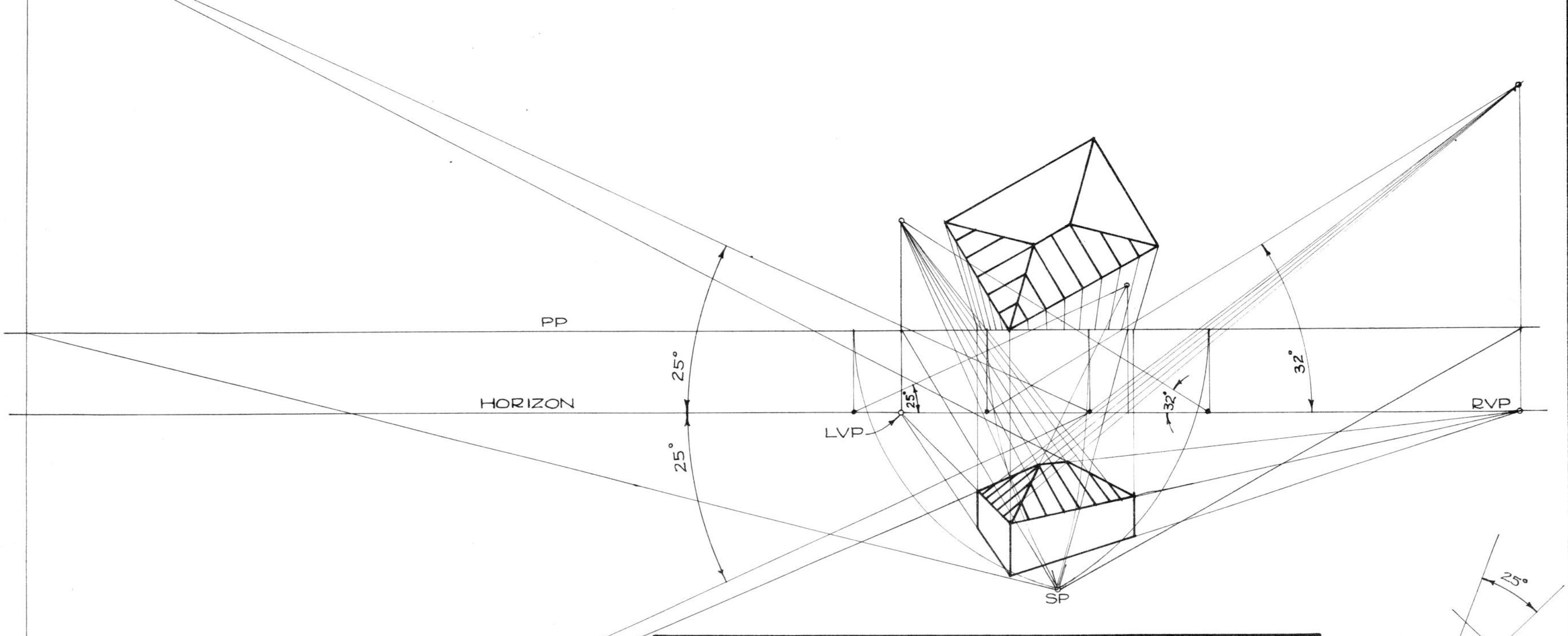

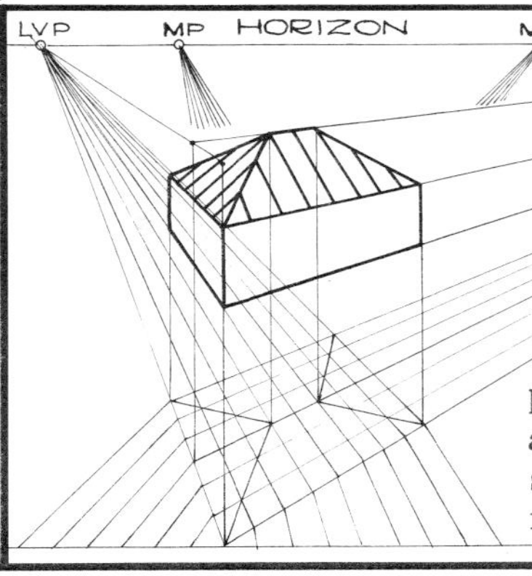

COORDINATE METHOD

Both ends of each sloping line are projected up from the perspective plan. This method requires less drawing space.

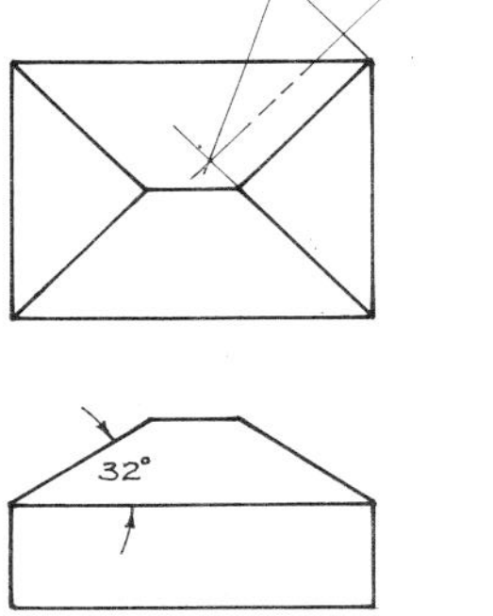

RVP

LVP

SP

PP

HORIZON

25°

25°

25°

32°

32°

32°

25°

ADVANTAGES OF THE PERSPECTIVE PLAN METHOD

1. In contrast to the OFFICE METHOD, it takes less room on the drawing board in the north-south direction.

2. The orthographic plan need not be redrawn in detail on the perspective layout, but its dimensions may be read from a set of plans that may have already been drawn for other purposes, and may have been drawn at a different scale than the perspective is to be drawn.

The PERSPECTIVE PLAN method of procedure is discussed on page 19.

SCALE: $\frac{1}{32}'' = 1'-0''$

SCALE: $\frac{3}{32}'' = 1'-0''$

MEASURING LINE AND G.L. FOR PERSPECTIVE PLAN

A small layout may be drawn at any convenient scale and only in block form without details such as doors, windows, etc., on any paper for the purpose of locating the distances between the VP's and MP's (measuring points) on the PP. The same considerations and decisions can be made on this simple drawing as discussed on pages 7, 8, and 10 of this chapter.

The distances between the VP's and MP's can then be scaled on the small drawing and transferred to the large actual perspective drawing layout at its scale.

The orthographic plan need not appear on the larger drawing layout and the measurements of all the plan details can be laid off on the measuring line, which is actually the GROUND LINE where the PP meets the ground.

The MEASURING POINTS are actually the VANISHING POINTS for the lines that transfer the plan measurements to the PP ground line. They are located on the small-scale drawing. Note the line SP-RMP is drawn parallel to MN and any other line parallel to MN that transfers dimensions from PP ground line to the floor plan. Similarly the line SP-LMP is drawn parallel to the line XY, and transfers the dimensions from walls in the other direction of the floor plan, to the PP ground line.

The PERSPECTIVE PLAN should be drawn as far as possible below the intended position of the PERSPECTIVE PICTURE for two reasons:

1. All the construction lines can then be made so as not to interfere with making a clean drawing of the "Picture."

2. Since usually the position of the horizon to the ground line of the actual perspective picture would make the floor plan appear so short in the depth direction, it would be difficult to measure and transfer the measurements accurately. An attempt to do this in most cases would be very convincing to the draftsman.

Figure 1: Note dimensions are all measured on the MEASURING LINE, then transferred to the BASE LINES, and then by perspective lines to the required places on the perspective plan.

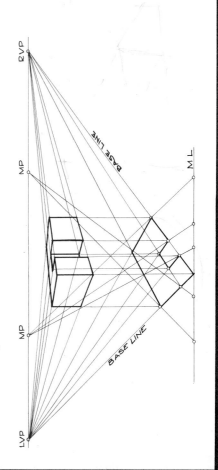

Figure 2: By studying page 18 it can be proven by plane geometry that SP-RVP = LMP-RVP and that SP-LVP = RMP-LVP because of similar triangles. Therefore a shortcut and usually more accurate method of locating the MP's is to draw arcs as shown below.

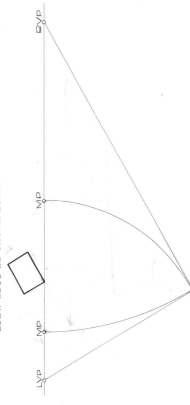

This two-point perspective drawing is of the St. Jude Hospital Expansion, Fullerton, California. Welton Becket & Associates, Architects.

This page illustrates how to measure plan distances not originating on the Picture Plane.

The dimensions 24'-0" and 14'-0" are laid off as was shown on page 8.

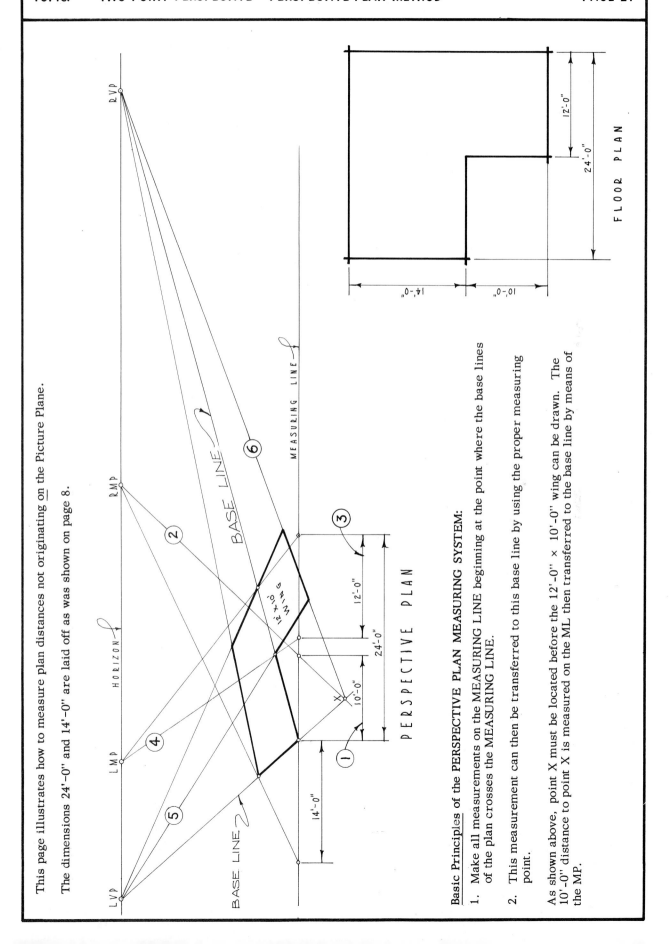

FLOOR PLAN

Basic Principles of the PERSPECTIVE PLAN MEASURING SYSTEM:

1. Make all measurements on the MEASURING LINE beginning at the point where the base lines of the plan crosses the MEASURING LINE.

2. This measurement can then be transferred to this base line by using the proper measuring point.

As shown above, point X must be located before the 12'-0" × 10'-0" wing can be drawn. The 10'-0" distance to point X is measured on the ML then transferred to the base line by means of the MP.

The two-point interior perspective is a drawing by George Alfred Parenti.
Photo of drawing courtesy -- Masonite Corporation.

This type of rendering is accomplished by first drawing the perspective with instruments, then tracing it in ink, freehand.

It is often more effective and more convenient to use ONE-POINT PERSPECTIVE instead of two-point. Two parallel walls on an interior can both be shown in one perspective picture, as in the drawing below. The fronts of buildings on both sides of a street can be shown in one perspective picture. See page 15. The draftsman needs less drawing board width to construct one-point perspective.

1. First draw the plan and elevation. Theoretically there is only one "family" of lines that is not parallel to the picture plane. This means there will be only one vanishing point for the perspective drawing.

2. In choosing the STATION POINT, distortion can be avoided if the cone of vision angle is approximately 60°.

3. The VANISHING POINT is of course on the HORIZON but can be varied from left to right for the desired emphasis in the picture.

4. Depth measurements of the floor plan are determined as they are in two-point perspective.

5. Height measurements must be made on the PP and transferred to the other walls with the use of the VP.

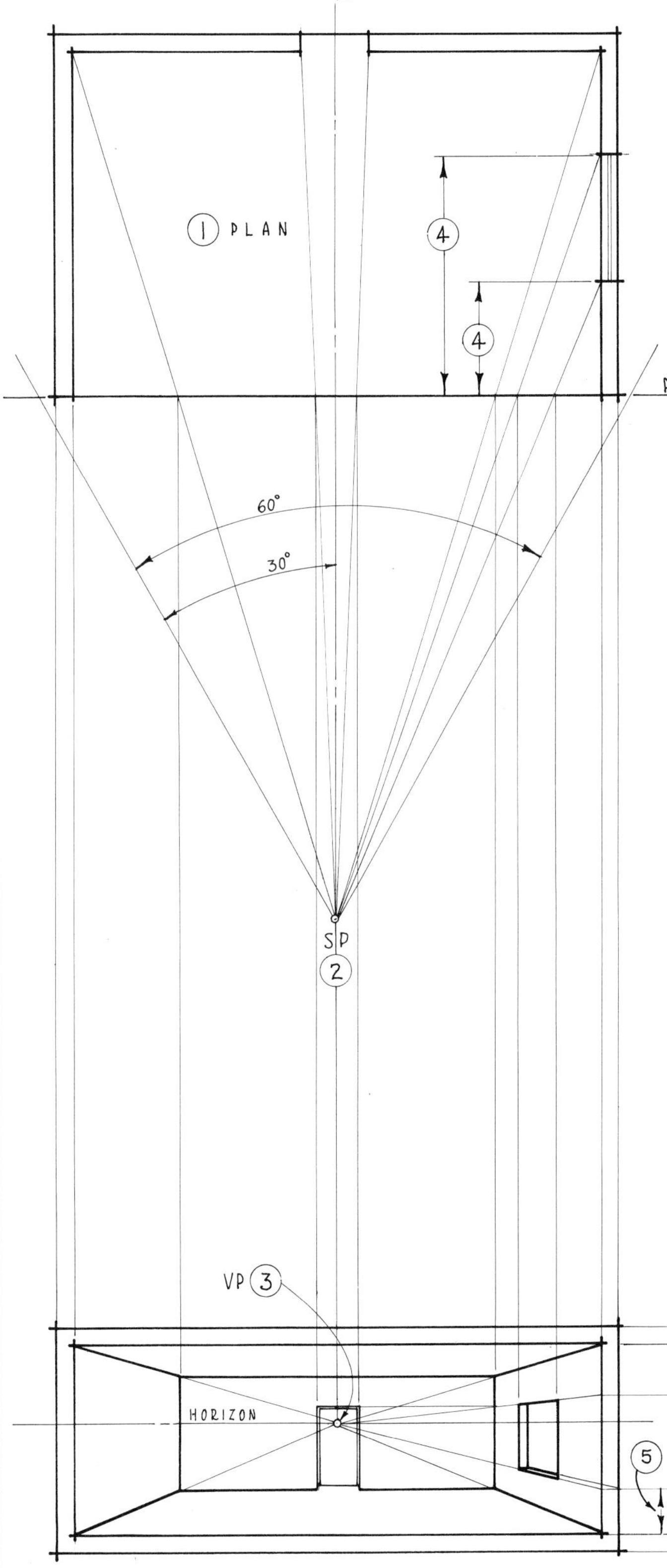

① PLAN

④

④

PP

60°

30°

S P ②

VP ③

HORIZON

⑤ ⑤ ⑤

PERSPECTIVE PICTURE

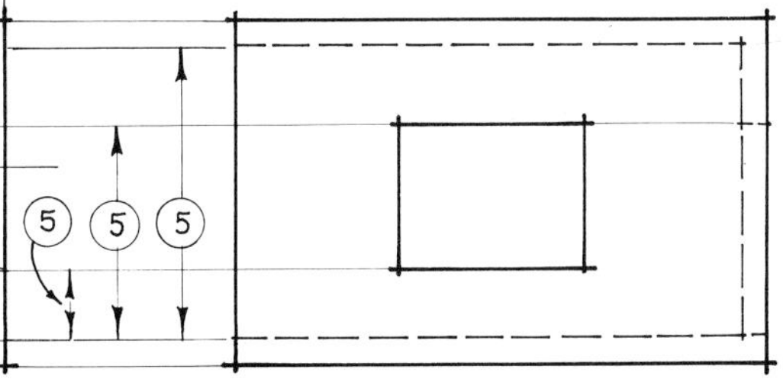

ELEVATION ①

Entrance Lobby, Hallmark Cards, Kansas City, Missouri.
Welton Becket & Associates, Architects.
Photo by Wayne Wright.

This page illustrates EXTERIOR one-point perspective, showing the fronts of two parallel rows of buildings.

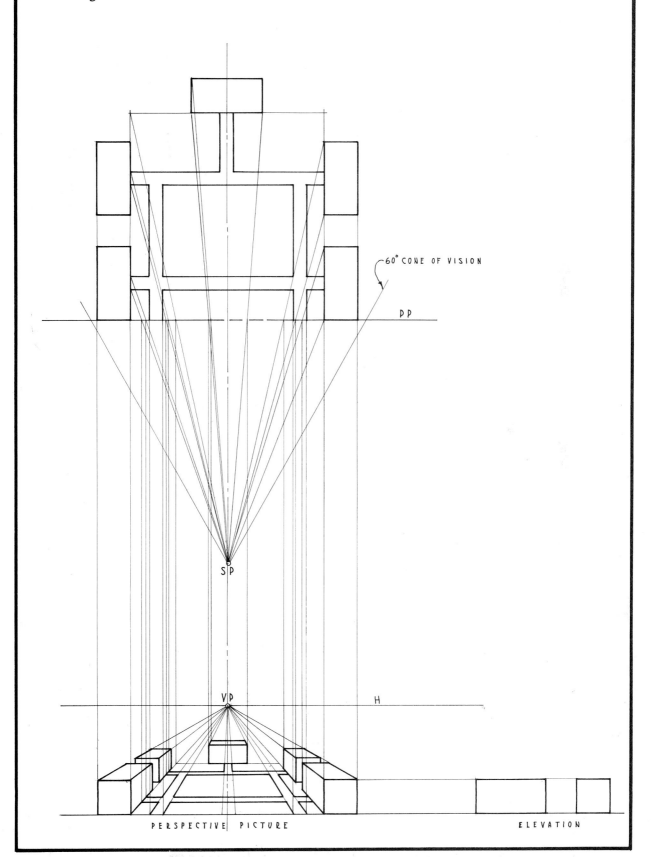

60° CONE OF VISION

PP

SP

VP   H

PERSPECTIVE PICTURE   ELEVATION

One-point perspective drawing by George Alfred Parenti.
Photo of drawing, courtesy – Masonite Corporation.

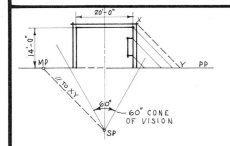

The general procedure for this method is similar to the
PERSPECTIVE PLAN METHOD used in two-point perspective
explained on pages 18 and 19.

Note on the above drawing that the MP (measuring point) is the
vanishing point for line XY and lines parallel to XY that transfer
the depth dimensions from the GL of the PP, to the building wall.

In the drawing below, the ELEVATION could have been drawn on the MEASURING LINE as well as on
the GL; and the ELEVATION could have been drawn so that point A would have been at B. The results
would be the same, but to avoid confusion of lines on the drawing it was placed farther to the right.

The depth dimensions are therefore transferred to the BASE LINE and then to the perspective plan,
from where they are projected to the perspective picture.

Heights are again measured only on the PP and transferred to the other parts of the perspective picture by perspective lines to the VP.

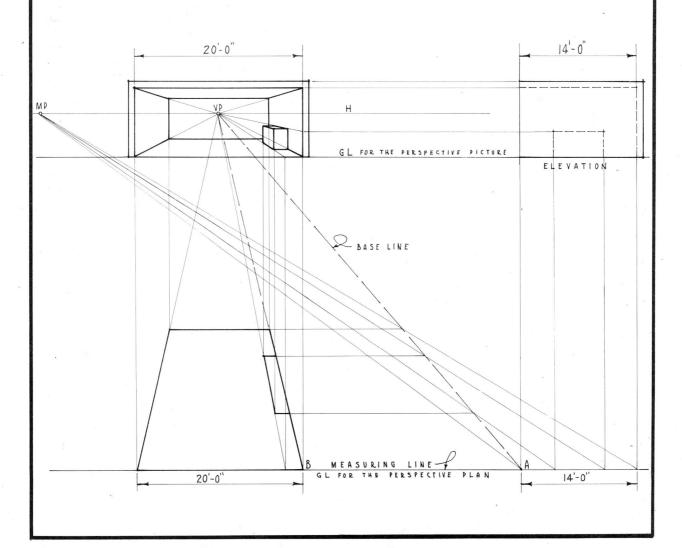

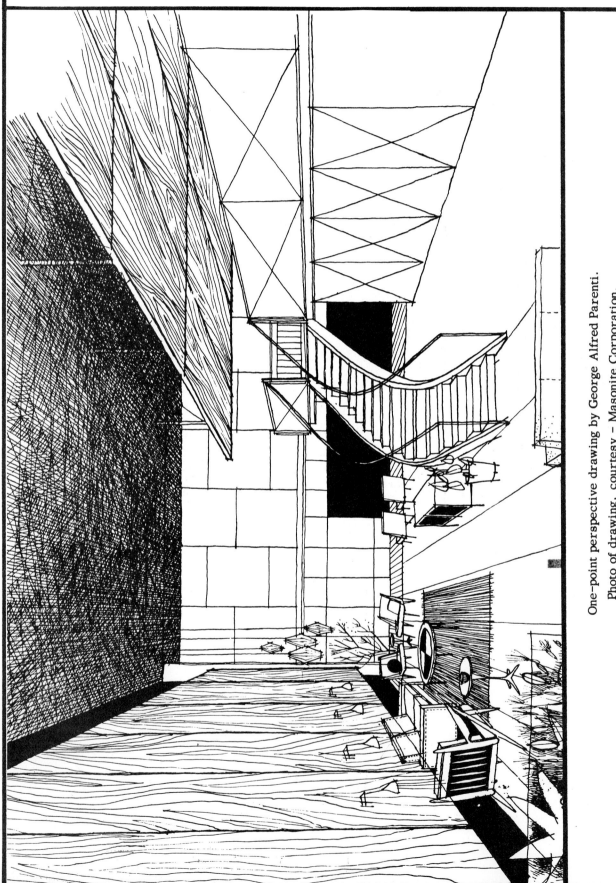

One-point perspective drawing by George Alfred Parenti.
Photo of drawing, courtesy – Masonite Corporation.

1. Camera (or axis of the Cone of Vision) was pointed downward causing vertical lines to <u>converge downward</u>, in this photograph of the Chase Manhatten National Bank. Skidmore, Owings and Merrill, Architects.

2. Camera (or axis of C of V) was pointed upward causing vertical lines to <u>converge upward</u>, in this photograph of the Alcoa Building in Pittsburg. Architects are Harrison and Abramoviz.

3. Camera (or axis of C of V) is horizontal causing <u>no convergence</u> in vertical lines in the photograph of St. Paul's Evangelical Lutheran Church in Glen Burnie, Maryland. Charles Edward Stade & Associates, Architects.

Before attempting to understand THREE-POINT PERSPECTIVE an understanding of TWO-POINT PER-SPECTIVE is necessary. See the discussion at the beginning of this chapter.

For the following discussion refer to the drawing on the next page.

LOCATION OF THE STATION POINT FOR CONVERGENCE UPWARD

If a building is much taller than it is wide, a "Skyscraper" effect can be obtained if the STATION POINT is near the ground and if the SP is close enough to the building so that the entire building cannot be viewed through the CONE OF VISION without pointing the C of V upward.

Care must be taken again with the C of V to avoid distortion. The plan must locate the SP at least far enough away from the PP to show no distortion in width.

However, if the side elevation shows that the entire height of the building will be seen with the AXIS OF THE C of V perpendicular to the vertical PP, then there will be no convergence upward and the resulting perspective will be a 2-POINT, and a 3-POINT is not possible.

On the other hand, if the side elevation shows that the entire height of the building will not be seen with the AXIS OF THE C of V perpendicular to the vertical PP, but that the entire height can be seen by tilting the C of V upward then there will be convergence upward, and no distortion should occur.

But, if in the side elevation the entire height of the building cannot be seen even with the tilted C of V, then the SP needs to be moved far enough away from the building so its entire height can be seen with the C of V in its tilted position, to avoid distortion.

LOCATION OF THE VERTICAL VANISHING POINT (VVP)

Now that the SP and the AXIS OF THE C of V have been determined, the PP must be redrawn perpendicular to the newly established AXIS OF THE C of V.

The VVP is located in the same manner as LVP and RVP in that from the SP (side elevation) a line parallel to the vertical lines of the building will locate the VVP on the newly positioned PP.

CHANGES IN LVP AND RVP

When the AXIS OF THE C of V is not horizontal, a slight change does actually occur in the location of the LVP and RVP, as well as a slight change in the position of the horizon.

PERSPECTIVE PICTURE

Because it is inclined, the PP must be revolved into a vertical position before projections are made to the perspective picture in the front elevation, in order that the PERSPECTIVE PICTURE will be in its true shape.

CONVERGENCE DOWNWARD

The above explains the theory involved when the SP is near the ground and the resulting convergence is UPWARD. Convergence DOWNWARD occurs when the SP is above or near the top of the building and similar theory is involved.

CONCLUSION

Since it has been proven the change of LVP and RVP from 2-point to 3-point perspective is so slight, it is practical to use the LVP and RVP for 2-point perspective and not attempt to locate the actual new positions of LVP and RVP for the 3-point perspective.

Therefore, only the new vanishing point (VVP) need be located to successfully make a 3-point perspective drawing.

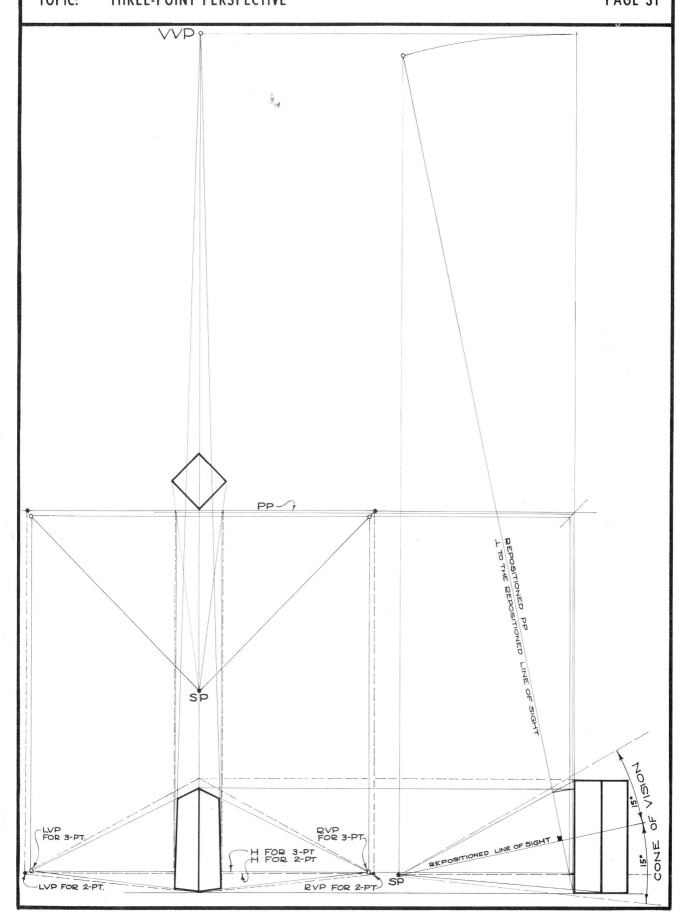

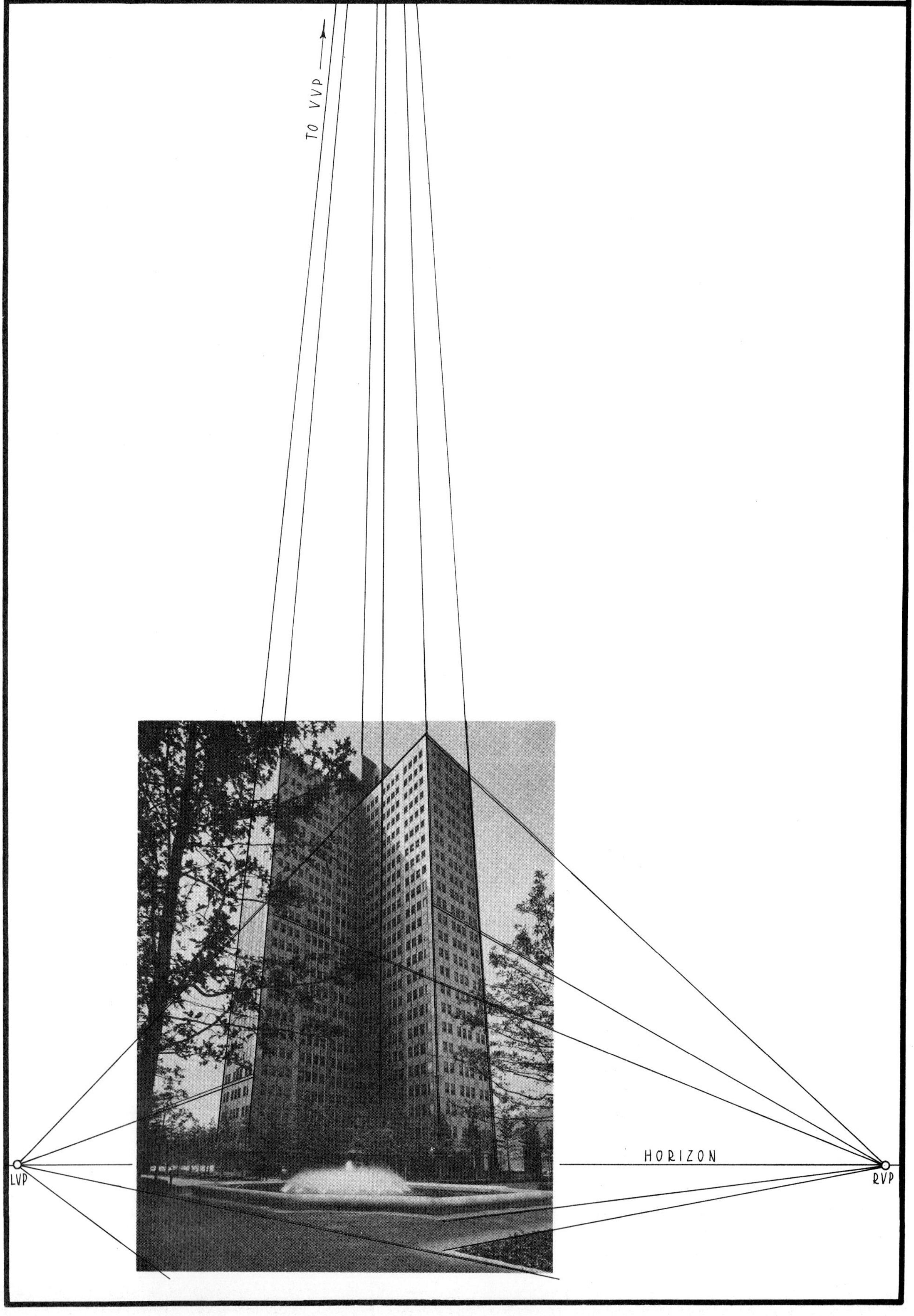

TO VVP

HORIZON

LVP

RVP

In perspective drawing the lines alone suggest shape and form in three dimensions, but the addition of shades and shadows correctly placed make the "picture" more realistic. It is then easier for the observer to judge the aesthetic effect created by the design.

It is the purpose of this chapter to present the theory of SHADES AND SHADOWS.

In the following drawings, on pages 1 through 8, the light rays are assumed to be parallel to the picture plane, and are assumed to be at some convenient angle, such as 45°, 30°, or 60°.

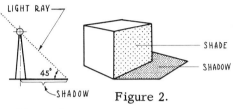

Figure 1.

Figure 2.

THE TWO FUNDAMENTAL PRINCIPLES:

1. A VERTICAL LINE CASTS ITS SHADOW ON THE GROUND OR ON ANY HORIZONTAL SURFACE, IN THE DIRECTION (bearing) OF THE RAYS OF LIGHT.

2. THE SHADOW ON A PLANE, CAST BY A LINE PARALLEL TO THAT PLANE, IS PARALLEL TO THE LINE.

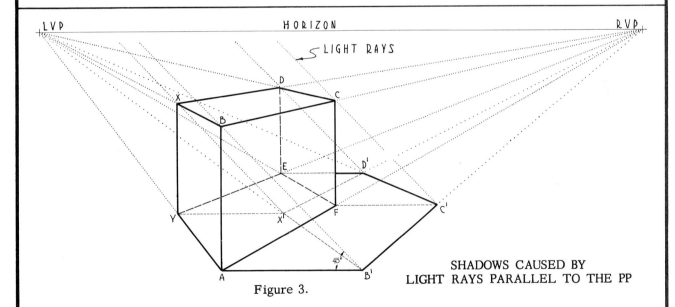

Figure 3.

SHADOWS CAUSED BY
LIGHT RAYS PARALLEL TO THE PP

VERTICAL LINES AB, CF, DE, and XY cast their shadows parallel to the PP since the light rays are parallel to the PP. The light rays are assumed to be parallel to each other, since the sun is larger and such a great distance from the earth. The angle of the rays depend upon the time of day and season of the year, but is usually arbitrarily chosen by the designer, to best show the effect created by the design.

HORIZONTAL LINE BC will cast a shadow that is parallel to BC because BC is parallel to the ground. On a perspective drawing the shadow line B'C' will be drawn to the same vanishing point as the line BC. The length of the shadow line B'C' will be determined by the light projection through point C to C'.

HORIZONTAL LINES CD, DX, and XB will cast their shadows in a manner similar to BC.

In Figure 3, the VERTICAL LINES cast their shadows according to PRINCIPLE 1, and the HORIZONTAL LINES cast their shadows according to PRINCIPLE 2.

Hidden shadow lines are not shown on a pictorial drawing, but are sometimes determined to aid in completing the direction of shadow lines that will show.

A little experience will enable the student to readily choose the lines that will determine the visible shadow.

Figure 4 below shows Figure 3 redrawn, omitting the unnecessary construction, showing only the visible shadows.

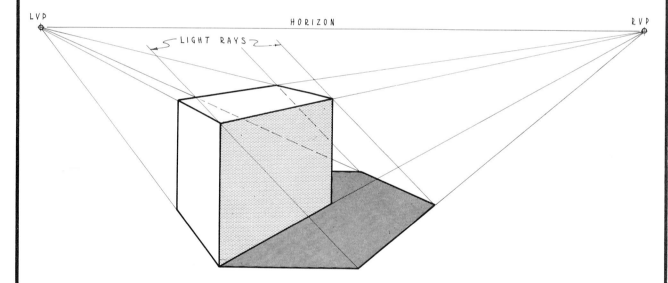

Figure 4. Showing Only Visible Shadows

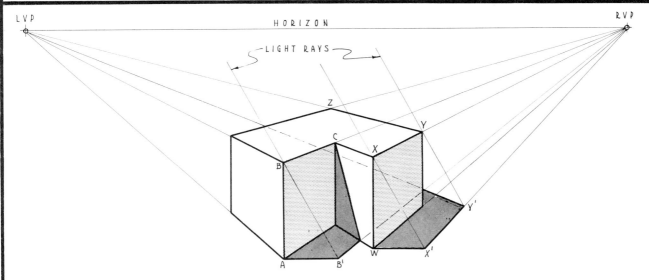

Figure 5.   Shadow of a Horizontal Line Falling Partially on
Level Ground and Partially on a Vertical Wall.

FUNDAMENTAL PRINCIPLE 1 applies to shadow line AB' and WX'.

FUNDAMENTAL PRINCIPLE 2 applies to part of the shadow line B'C until it meets the wall.   The
remaining shadow of line BC must end at C.

FUNDAMENTAL PRINCIPLE 2 also applies to X'Y' and Y'Z'.

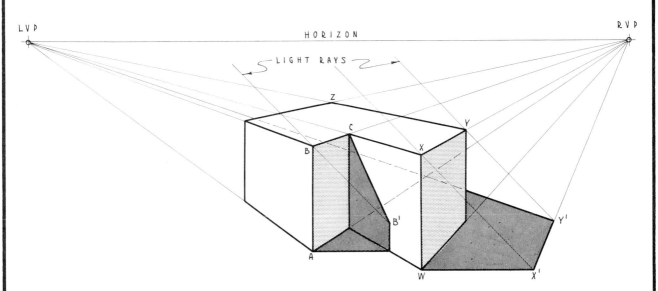

Figure 6.   Shadow of a Vertical Line Falling Partially on
Level Ground and Partially on a Vertical Wall.

FUNDAMENTAL PRINCIPLE 1 applies to the shadow of line AB until it meets the wall.

FUNDAMENTAL PRINCIPLE 2 applies to remainder of the shadow of AB since the line AB is parallel
to the wall.

The entire shadow of line BC will begin at B' and end at C.

The shadow WX'Y'Z' is determined as in Figure 5.

Stonestown Medical Building, San Francisco. Welton Becket & Associates, Architects. Illustrates SHADOWS ON WALLS.

NOTES

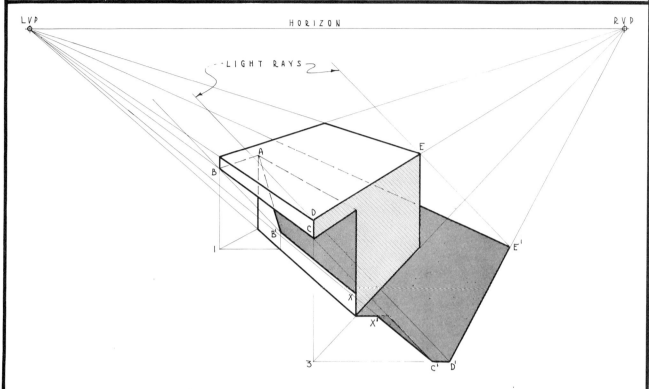

Figure 7. Shadow of a Building with an Overhang

The solution of this problem involves only the FUNDAMENTAL PRINCIPLES 1 and 2.

First construct points 1 and 3 to resolve the problem into a basic shape of the building shown in Figure 4 on page 2, so the FUNDAMENTAL PRINCIPLES can be applied.

Point B' is located in the same manner as point B' in Figure 6, page 3.

The shadow of BC falls partially on the wall and partially on the ground. The portion on the wall is drawn according to FUNDAMENTAL PRINCIPLE 2. This will locate point X on the wall. X' is located according to FUNDAMENTAL PRINCIPLE 1. X'C' is simply the remainder of the shadow of line BC according to FUNDAMENTAL PRINCIPLE 2.

C'D' is located according to PRINCIPLE 1, using D3 as the construction line.

The rest of the shadow follows FUNDAMENTAL PRINCIPLE 2.

The overhang casts a shadow on the wall of Goldwater's Park Central Shopping Center, Phoenix, Arizona. Welton Becket and Associates, architects. A Marlow Photo.

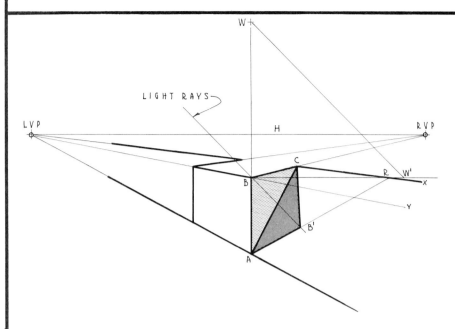

Figure 8.   Shadows on Sloping Ground

The solution of this problem involves only the FUNDAMENTAL PRINCIPLE 1.

Construct an extension of line AB infinitely upward towards W.   Construct the level ground BCXY.

The shadow of this vertical line, BW, will fall in the direction of BRW' on level ground.   R is the point on the upper edge of the sloping ground.   Therefore, AR would be the shadow of that part of AW that falls on sloping ground.

Point B is on the line AW, therefore its shadow will fall on AR at B'.

The shadow of this building on the sloping surface is then AB'C.

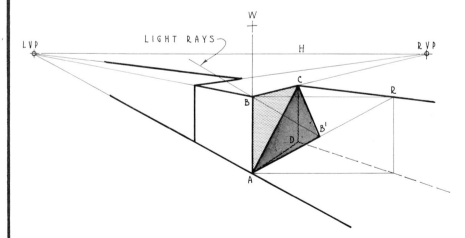

Figure 9.   Shadow on Sloping Ground (Alternate Solution)

Construct AW as in Figure 8, then construct an imaginary vertical wall in line with the imaginary vertical line CD.   According to FUNDAMENTAL PRINCIPLE 1, the shadow of AW will be parallel to the PP until it meets this vertical wall, then its shadow will be vertical according to PRINCIPLE 2, until it reaches R.   The remainder of the construction needed to determine the shadow on sloping ground is the same as in Figure 8.

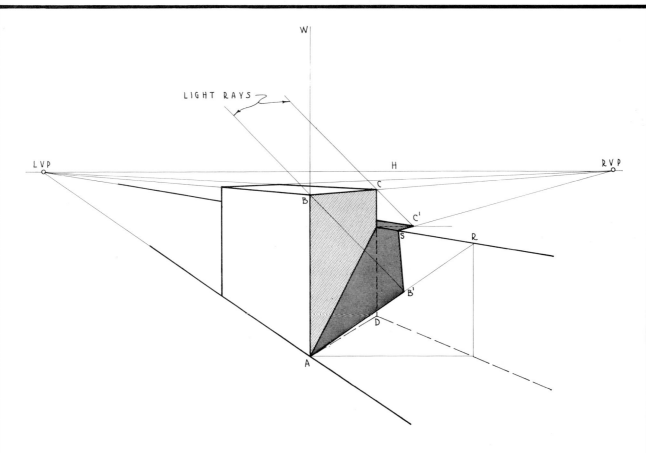

Figure 10. Shadow on Sloping Ground

B' is located as shown in Figure 9. C' is located according to FUNDAMENTAL PRINCIPLE 1.

Once B' and C' are located, C'S can be drawn according to FUNDAMENTAL PRINCIPLE 2, and B'S is simply a straight line drawn between two established points.

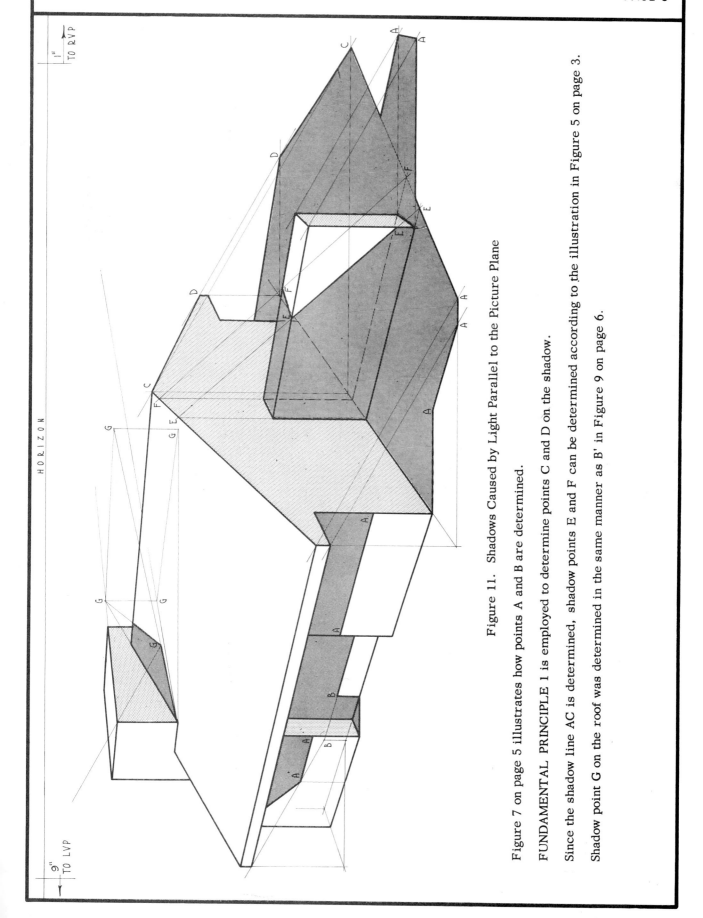

Figure 11. Shadows Caused by Light Parallel to the Picture Plane

Figure 7 on page 5 illustrates how points A and B are determined.

FUNDAMENTAL PRINCIPLE 1 is employed to determine points C and D on the shadow.

Since the shadow line AC is determined, shadow points E and F can be determined according to the illustration in Figure 5 on page 3.

Shadow point G on the roof was determined in the same manner as B' in Figure 9 on page 6.

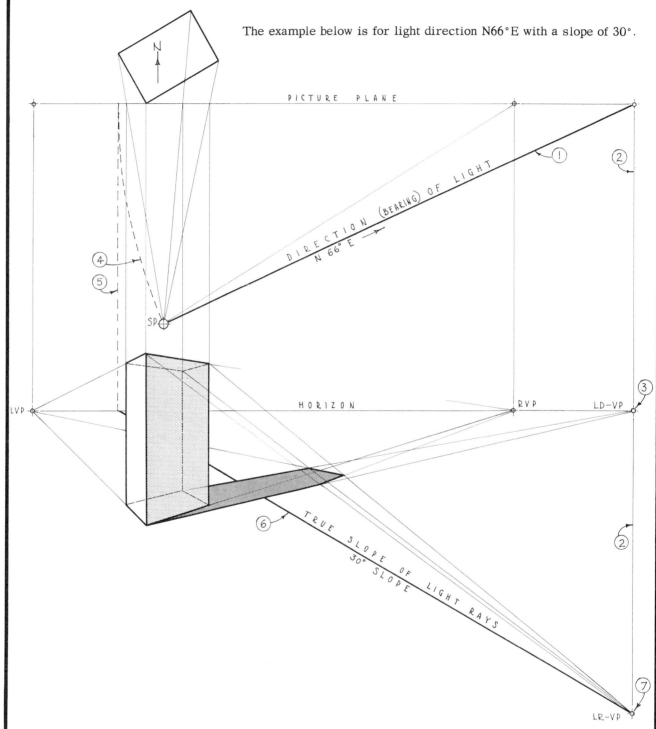

The example below is for light direction N66°E with a slope of 30°.

Figure 12. Light Oblique to the Picture Plane

In drawing shadows cast by light rays that are not parallel to the PP (oblique to the PP), the principles involved are the same as for light rays that are parallel to the PP. It is assumed the student knows how to find vanishing points as discussed in Chapter 11.

When the light rays are not parallel (oblique) to the PP, they do converge in perspective and meet at a common point LR-VP (Light Ray Vanishing Point). LR-VP is located by first locating LD-VP (Light Direction Vanishing Point).

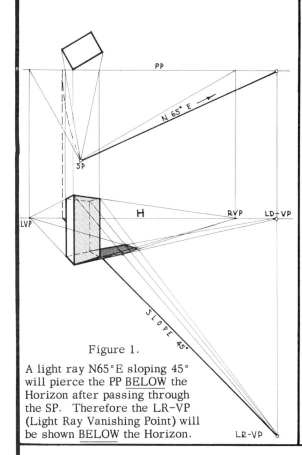

Figure 1.

A light ray N65°E sloping 45° will pierce the PP <u>BELOW</u> the Horizon after passing through the SP. Therefore the LR-VP (Light Ray Vanishing Point) will be shown <u>BELOW</u> the Horizon.

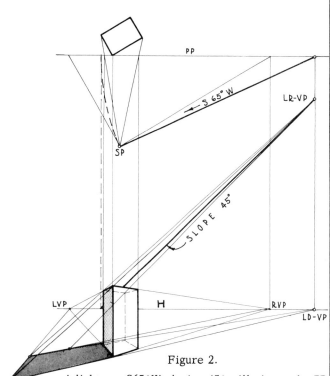

Figure 2.

A light ray S65°W sloping 45° will pierce the PP <u>ABOVE</u> the Horizon before it reaches the SP. Therefore the LR-VP will be shown <u>ABOVE</u> the Horizon.

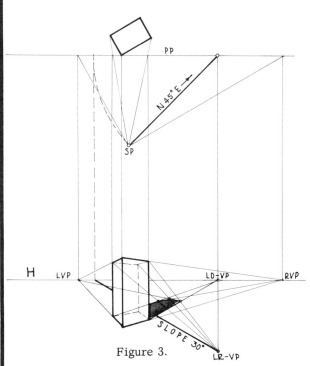

Figure 3.

A light ray N45°E sloping 30° will pierce the PP <u>BELOW</u> the Horizon after passing through the SP. Therefore the LR-VP will be shown <u>BELOW</u> the Horizon.

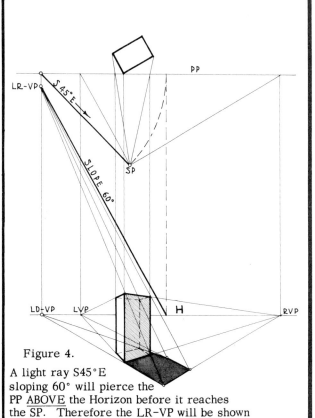

Figure 4.

A light ray S45°E sloping 60° will pierce the PP <u>ABOVE</u> the Horizon before it reaches the SP. Therefore the LR-VP will be shown <u>ABOVE</u> the Horizon.

SUN CONTROL DATA varies for different areas on the earth and are shown here for the area including Ames, Iowa. These data are computed for architectural use from the AMERICAN NAUTICAL ALMANAC 1964, and the TABLES OF COMPUTED ALTITUDE AND AZIMUTH (U. S. Navy Hydrographic Office). Computed data do not differ significantly from year to year for identical dates, and the varience should not affect architectural solar design.

LAT 42° N LONG 93°40' W

	JANUARY 20			FEBRUARY 19			MARCH 21			APRIL 20		
	Time	Alt	Az	Time	Alt	Az	Time	Alt	Az	Time	Alt	Az
Sunrise	7:39	000	117	7:07	000	105	6:19	000	90	5:28	000	73
	8:26	07	125	8:29	13	119	7:22	11	100	6:14	08	81
	9:26	15	137	9:29	22	131	8:22	22	111	8:14	30	102
	10:26	22	150	10:29	30	146	9:22	32	123	9:14	41	115
	11:26	26 1/2	164	11:29	35	162	10:22	40	139	10:14	50	131
	12:26	28	180	12:29	36 1/2	180	11:22	46	158	11:14	57	153
	1:26	26	196	1:29	35	198	12:22	48 1/2	180	12:14	59 1/2	180
	2:26	22	210	2:29	30	214	1:22	46	202	1:14	57	207
	3:26	15	223	3:29	22	229	2:22	40	221	3:14	41	245
	4:26	07	235	4:29	13	241	3:22	32	237	5:14	19	269
Sunset	5:13	000	245	5:51	000	255	6:27	000	270	7:00	000	287

	MAY 22			JUNE 22			JULY 23			AUGUST 24		
Sunrise	4:48	000	60	4:39	000	57	5:00	000	61	5:31	000	73
	5:11	04	66	5:17	05	63	6:21	13	75	6:17	07	82
	7:11	24	84	7:17	26	81	8:21	35	94	8:17	30	102
	9:11	47	105	9:17	48	102	10:21	56	122	10:17	49	131
	11:11	65	145	10:17	59	117	11:21	64	145	11:17	56	153
	12:11	68 1/2	180	11:17	68	141	12:21	68	180	12:17	59	180
	1:11	65	215	12:17	71 1/2	180	1:21	64	215	1:17	56	207
	3:11	47	255	1:17	68	219	3:21	46	254	3:17	40	245
	4:11	36	266	3:17	48	258	4:21	35	266	4:17	30	258
	5:11	24	276	4:17	37	269	5:21	24	276	5:17	18	268
	6:11	13	286	6:17	15	288	6:21	13	285	6:17	07	278
Sunset	7:36	000	299	7:54	000	302	7:42	000	298	7:04	000	296

	SEPTEMBER 23			OCTOBER 23			NOVEMBER 23			DECEMBER 22		
Sunrise	6:02	000	88	6:36	000	105	7:16	000	117	7:40	000	122
	7:07	11	100	7:59	13	119	8:01	07	125	8:14	04	127
	9:07	31	124	8:59	22	131	9:01	15	137	9:14	12	138
	10:07	39	139	9:59	30	146	10:01	21	150	10:14	19	151
	11:07	45	158	10:59	35	162	11:01	26	164	11:14	23	165
	12:07	47 1/2	180	11:59	36 1/2	180	12:01	27 1/2	180	12:14	24 1/2	180
	1:07	45	202	12:59	35	198	1:01	26	196	1:14	23	195
	2:07	39	221	1:59	30	214	2:01	21	210	2:14	19	209
	3:07	31	226	2:59	22	229	3:01	15	223	3:14	12	222
	4:07	22	249	3:59	13	241	4:01	07	235	4:14	04	233
	5:07	10	260	4:59	03	253						
Sunset	6:12	000	272	5:23	000	255	4:47	000	243	4:46	000	238

SUN CONTROL DATA used is for January 20, 10:26 A.M. which has 22° ALTITUDE and 150° AZIMUTH.

Since the AZIMUTH is the same direction as the PP then all light will be parallel to the PP with no convergence and the angle of ALTITUDE will show no convergence for the light rays.

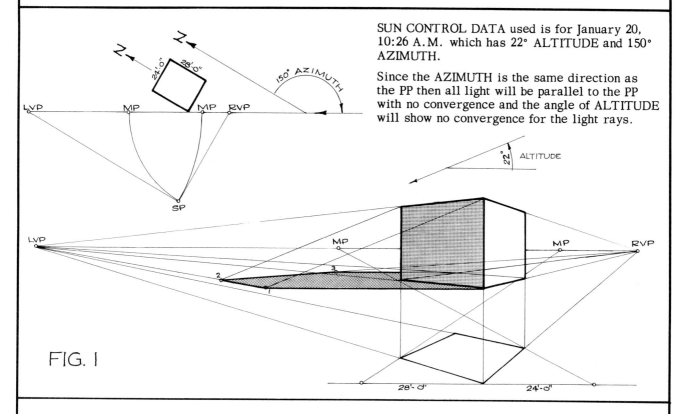

FIG. 1

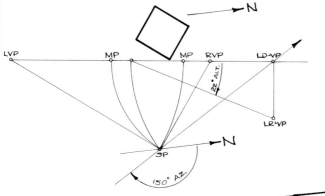

The same SUN CONTROL DATA is used here as was used in the problem above. Since NORTH in this case was different the light is not parallel to the PP and convergence takes place in both the AZIMUTH and ALTITUDE to LD-VP and LR-VP, respectively.

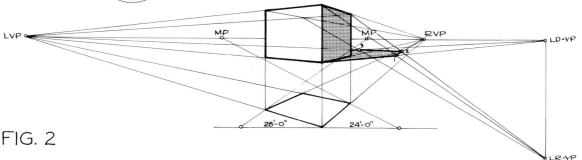

FIG. 2

In both FIG. 1 and FIG. 2 the same principles are used as are used on pages 9 and 10, except that AZIMUTH is used instead of BEARING and ALTITUDE is used in place of SLOPE.

In review of page 1, the above problems illustrate:
    PRINCIPLE 1 for the shadow lines from 1 and 3 to the building, and
    PRINCIPLE 2 for the shadow lines 1-2 and 2-3.

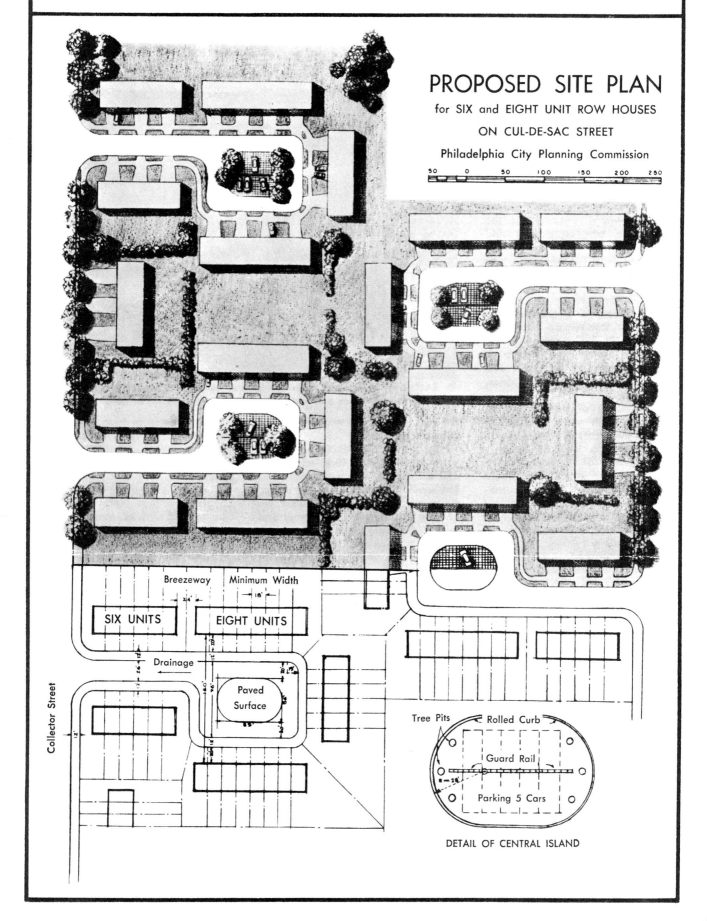

PROPOSED SITE PLAN
for SIX and EIGHT UNIT ROW HOUSES
ON CUL-DE-SAC STREET
Philadelphia City Planning Commission

50 0 50 100 150 200 250

Breezeway   Minimum Width

SIX UNITS   EIGHT UNITS

Drainage

Collector Street

Paved
Surface

Tree Pits   Rolled Curb

Guard Rail

Parking 5 Cars

DETAIL OF CENTRAL ISLAND

Review THE TWO FUNDAMENTAL PRINCIPLES on page one of this chapter.

It is conventional practice to show shades and shadows on PLANS and ELEVATIONS using a standard bearing and slope of light.

This standard BEARING is N 45° E and the standard SLOPE is 35°15'52", both of which describe the DIAGONAL OF A CUBE.

FIG. 1 shows pictorially the DIAGONAL direction of light and the resulting SHADOW.

FIG. 2 shows the same in orthographic projection. Note the 45° projection lines in both plan and elevation.

FIG. 3 shows the shadow only on the ground.

FIG. 4 shows the shadow partially on the ground and partially on the wall.

FIG. 5 shows the shadow of a cube when it falls entirely on the wall.

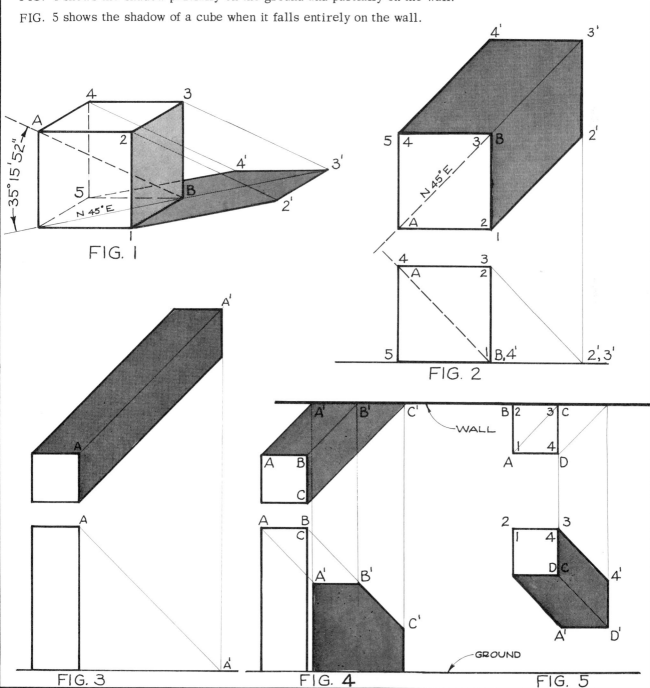

FIG. 1

FIG. 2

FIG. 3

FIG. 4

FIG. 5

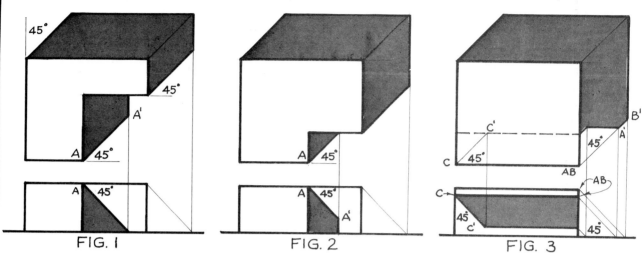

FIG. 1   FIG. 2   FIG. 3

Figures 1, 2, 3, 4, and 5 illustrate shadows in ORTHOGRAPHIC from building shapes similar to those in PERSPECTIVE shown on pages 3, 5, 6, and 7 of this chapter. Note point A' in Figure 4 is located with the aid of the side view, and point A' in Figure 5 was located with the aid of a CP (Cutting Plane) and without the aid of the side view. Either method is adequate.

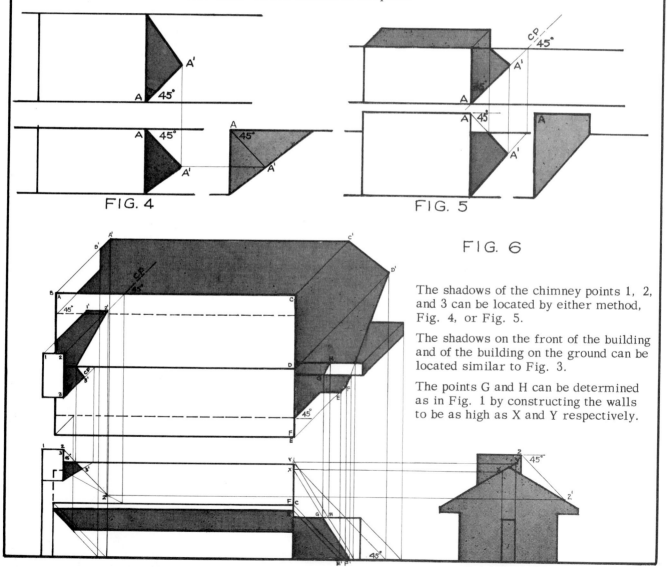

FIG. 4   FIG. 5

FIG. 6

The shadows of the chimney points 1, 2, and 3 can be located by either method, Fig. 4, or Fig. 5.

The shadows on the front of the building and of the building on the ground can be located similar to Fig. 3.

The points G and H can be determined as in Fig. 1 by constructing the walls to be as high as X and Y respectively.

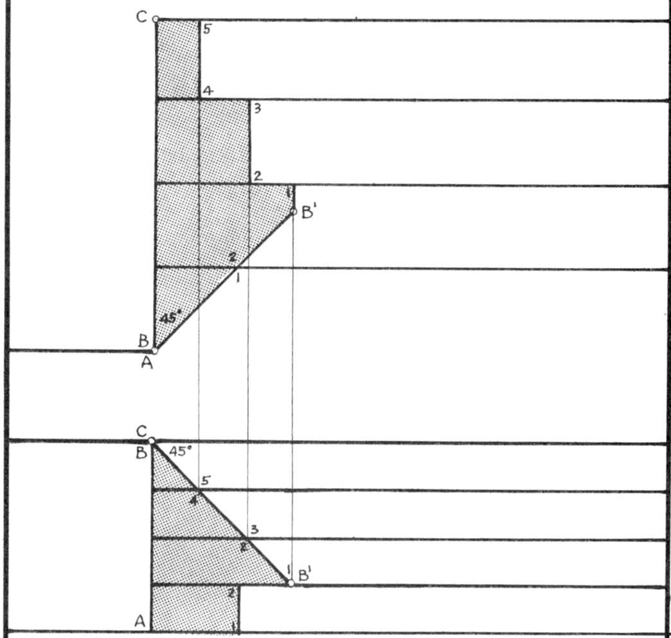

Figure 1: Shadows on steps.

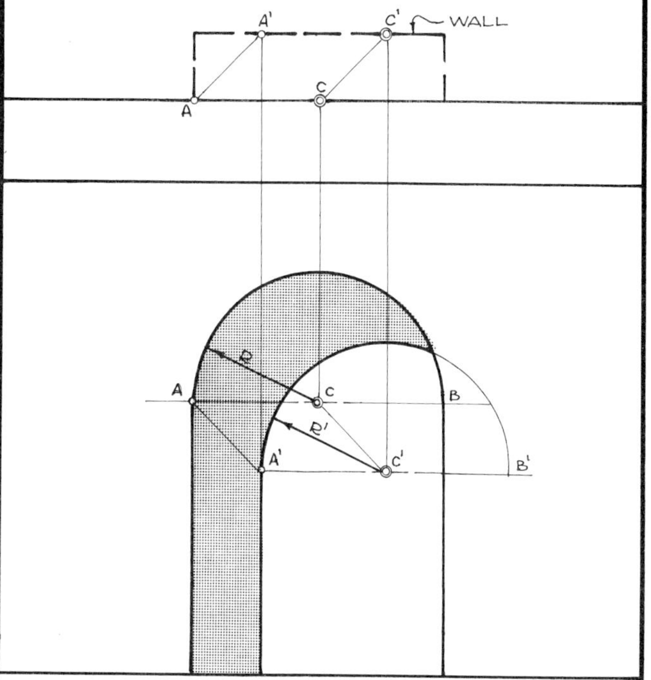

Figure 2: Shadow of a circular line on a wall parallel to the line.

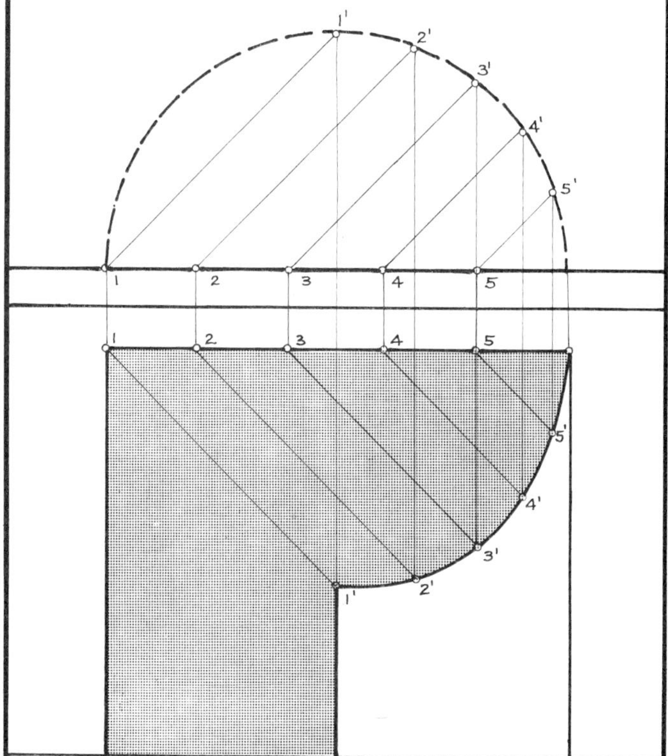

Figure 3: Shadow of a straight line on a circular wall.

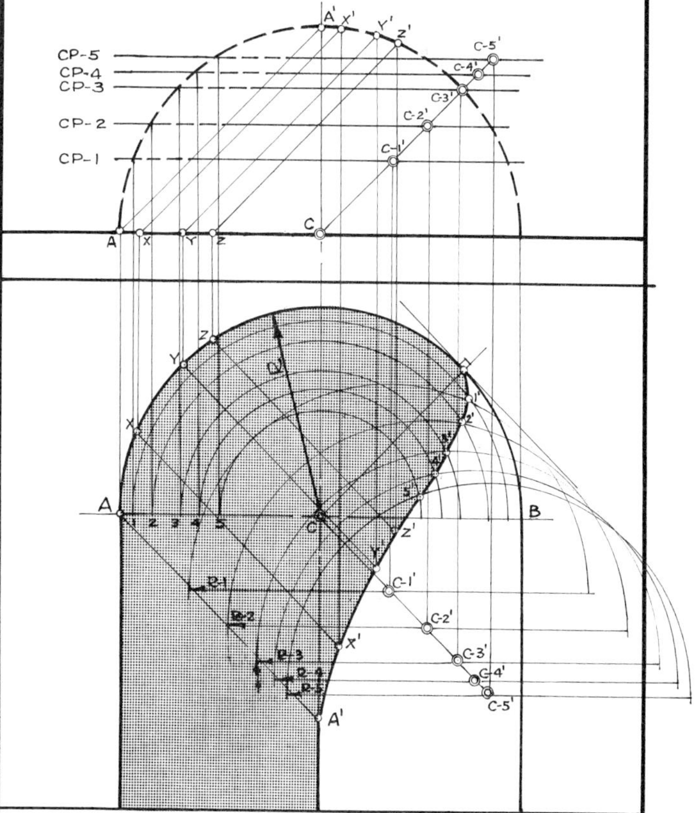

Figure 4: SHADOW IN A SPHERICAL NICHE
For shadow A'X'Y'Z' see Fig. 3. For shadow 1'2'3'4'5' see Fig. 2.
The CP's are used as walls similar to the wall in Fig. 2.

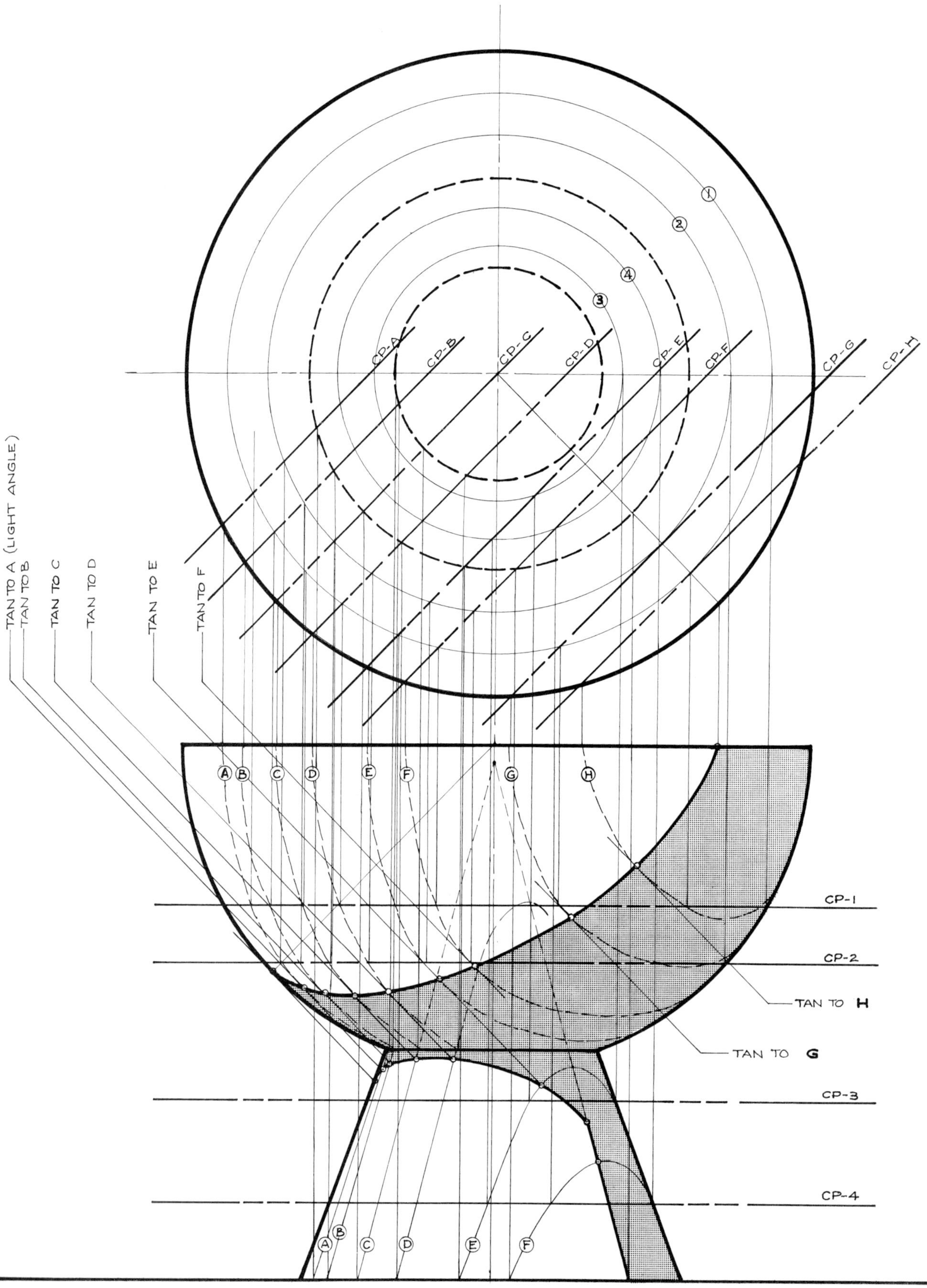

CP-A
CP-B
CP-C
CP-D
CP-E
CP-F
CP-G
CP-H

TAN TO A (LIGHT ANGLE)
TAN TO B
TAN TO C
TAN TO D
TAN TO E
TAN TO F

CP-1
CP-2
TAN TO **H**
TAN TO **G**
CP-3
CP-4

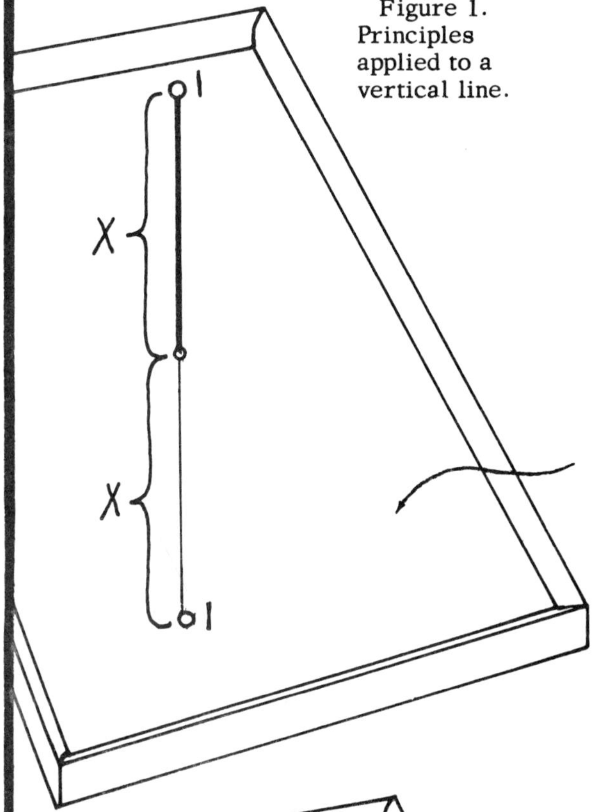

Figure 1.
Principles
applied to a
vertical line.

PRINCIPLES

1. In perspective, the reflected image of a point will fall directly below the point.

2. The depth of the reflection of a point will be equal to the distance that point is above the reflecting surface.

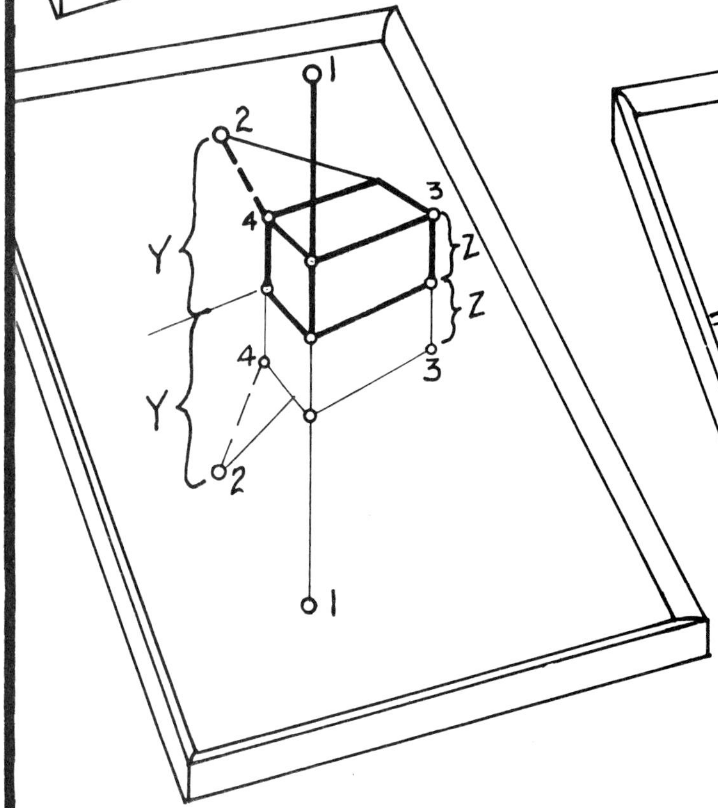

Mirror or water as a reflecting surface.

Figure 2.

Y and Z show principles applied to oblique and vertical lines.

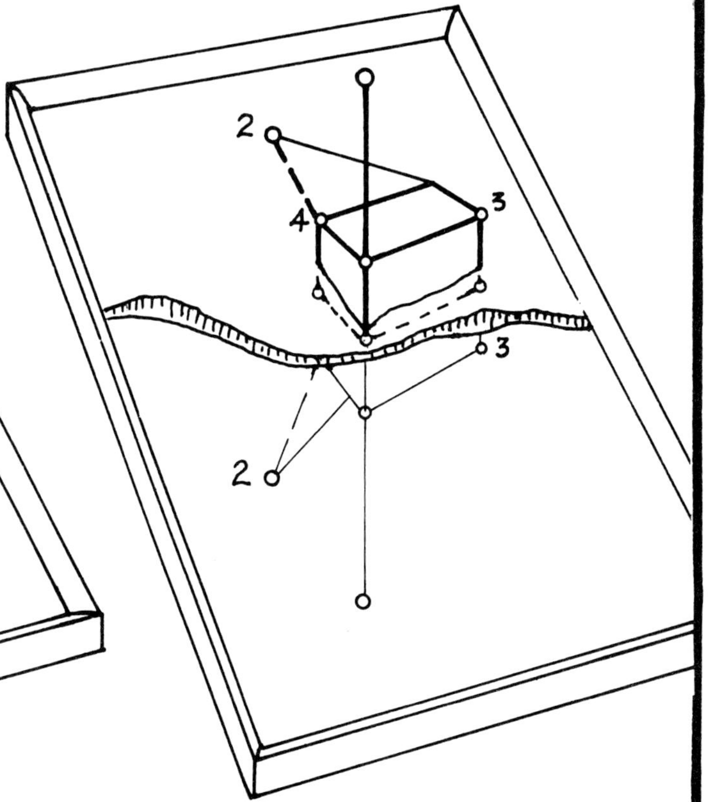

Figure 3.

Point 4 will not show since the "shore line" hides it.

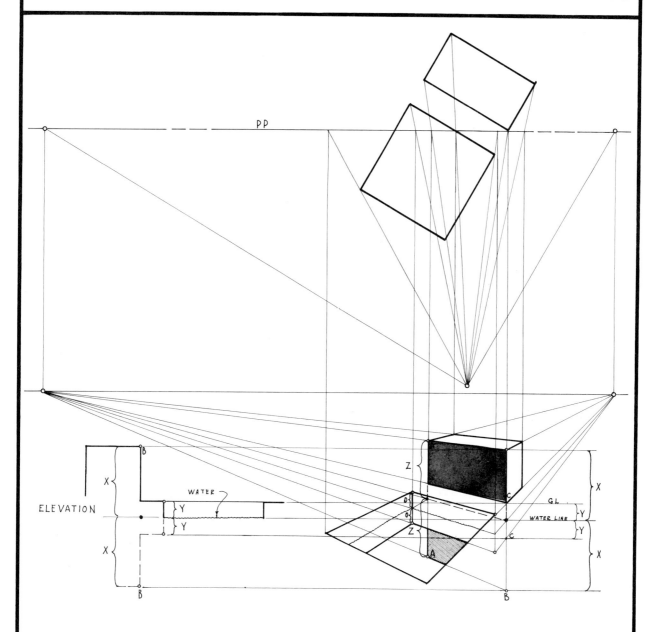

PRINCIPLES OF REFLECTIONS:

1. In perspective, the reflected image of a point will fall directly below the point.

2. The depth of the reflection of a point will be equal to the distance that point is above the reflecting surface.

The X distance is the actual height of A above the elevation of the water level. The reflection will be the X distance below the water level. This can be measured on the measuring line according to the principles of perspective measurements.

Likewise Point C can be determined by the Y measurement.

However, the reflection of point A can also be measured directly below A on the building to A in reflection by using the distance Z.

The time-exposed photo shows an interesting reflection of the Chevrolet Engineering Administration Building in Warren, Michigan.

The Caernarvon Castle, Wales, with its thirteen towers and castellated battlements, built by Edward the First of England, is clearly reflected in the sea.

The lake reflects the sky, mountains and the city of HALLSTATT, AUSTRIA.

Photo courtesy Hubert Raab of Klagenfurt, Austria.

An architect makes presentation drawings in an attempt to show his client how the building will look after it is built.

Perspective drawings are "rendered" to look like a photograph or to give the impressions created by seeing the building.

Unrendered drawings show all surfaces equal in value with no contrast and with no shades or shadows.

Successful RENDERING of a drawing will give the perspective more depth by varying the dark and light treatment of surfaces IN LIGHT, IN SHADE, and IN SHADOW. By contrasting these surfaces with respect to each other, and by varying the degree of light to dark of each surface, the three dimensions of space are emphasized.

By proper control of these contrasts, the building can be emphasized, making it the most important part of the composition.

When the building occupies the center of interest but is not dominated by entourage, that is, its surroundings, trees, bushes, etc., the drawing can be properly called an ARCHITECTURAL PRESENTATION.

The optical illusions demonstrated on this page illustrate the effects of contrast. The dots do not appear alike and each of the swatches appear to be graded. The understanding of this behavior will aid the architect in preparing presentation drawings.

The following pages attempt to call attention to these features of presentation in photographs and drawings.

Photographs and renderings shown in previous chapters may also be examined and compared in this respect.

1.

2.

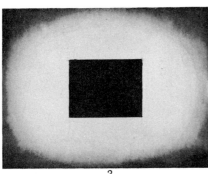

3.

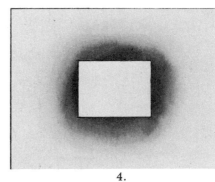

4.

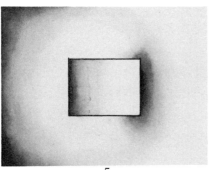

5.

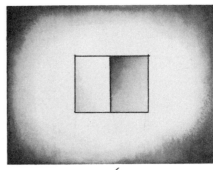

6.

Emphasis is greater in 3 and 4 than in 1 and 2 due to the treatment of the area directly next to the square. The emphasis is the greatest where the contrast is the greatest. Varied emphasis by contrast is evident in 5 and 6.

Before rendering a presentation drawing, it is advisable to determine the effectiveness of the composition, that is, placement of building, figures and entourage, and the contrast of values throughout the rendering by making small scale, preliminary studies similar to those shown on this page.

Step 1: Begin "rendering" a drawing at the most important points of contrast. This will serve as a guide in determining the degree of contrast necessary for proper emphasis.

Step 2: Complete the study, maintaining interest and perspective depth by means of contrast.

In rendering presentation drawings, various media, paper, and techniques are used. Delineators often have favorites of their own but vary them depending upon the size of the drawings, the time they are allowed to work on them, whether black and white, color, or monochrome is to be used, etc.

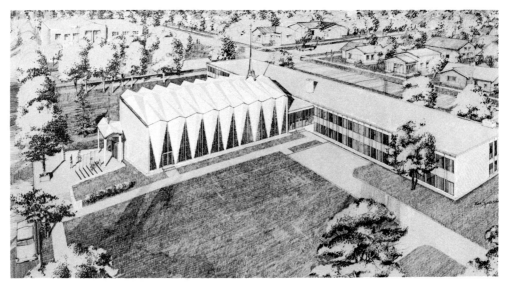

The above rendering is of Trinity Lutheran Church of Minnehaha Falls, Minneapolis, Minnesota. Architects: Sövik, Mathre and Madson.

Executed on grey illustration board.
A Wolff pencil, grade BB was used.
The white highlights were emphasized with a charcoal white pencil, grade No. 558.

The above rendering is of the Evangelical Lutheran Church of Mt. Horeb, Wisconsin. Architects: Sövik, Mathre and Madson.

Executed on Whatman's cold press illustration board.
Sky was rendered with pastels.
Watercolor was used for the remainder of the rendering.

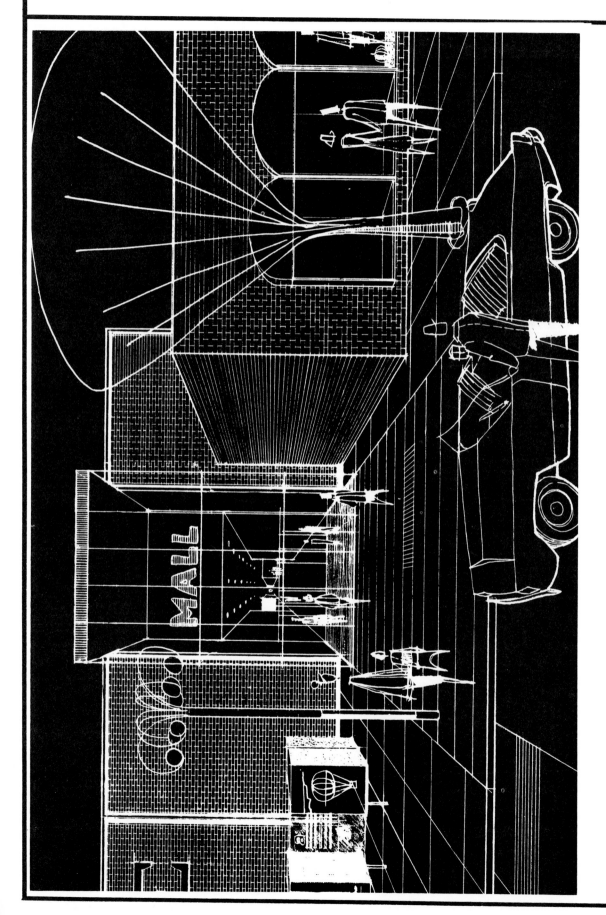

An unrendered one-point perspective drawing by Welton Becket & Associates, architects.
See previous chapters for other unrendered perspectives executed with black lines on white paper.

A RENDERING of the Los Angeles Custom House and Federal Office Building, Welton Becket and Associates, Architects.

The Santa Monica, California, Civic Auditorium, Architects: Welton Becket and Associates. Extreme contrast is achieved by the photographer giving dramatic emphasis to the building.

The administration building of Phoenix-Rheinrohr AG in Düsseldorf, Germany is an example of the behavior of shade on a tall building.

Due to the reflections from the surroundings and other buildings, the lower part of tall walls in shade will be lighter than the upper part.

The wall in shade is darker at the top. The wall in shadow is partially in sunlight; the top edge of the shadow is the darkest. Note the far windows appear lighter.

Mount Sinai Hospital & Clinic, Los Angeles.
Architects: Walton Becket and Associates.

The near edge of the window wall appears the lightest. The windows appear darker where they do not reflect the sky. The shadow on the low wall at the left is an example of the optical illusion described on page 1.
The Parker Pen Company, Janesville, Wisconsin. Architects: John J. Flad & Associates.

This photograph of the circular Memorial Sports Arena in Los Angeles, by architects Welton Becket and Associates, provides an example of how to render curved surfaces.

On both sides of the highlight, the sloping wall becomes increasingly dark, both towards the left where the wall is in light and towards the right where the wall is in shade.

The foreground shadows of trees give the perspective more depth by providing a contrast from dark in the foreground to light near the building.

The glass of the windows and doors appear black. This is usually true except (1) when the glass catches reflections of nearby objects or the sky, (2) has drapery behind it, or (3) when the interior is light enough to be seen through the glass.

The near windows appear darker. Shaded buildings across the street appear black in the window reflections. The photograph borders were masked to help frame the picture. Texaco, Los Angeles, California. Architects: Welton Becket & Associates. Photo by Julius Schulman.

St. Martha's Mission, West Covina, California; Architect: Carleton Winslow.
In spite of the entourage simplicity, perspective depth is indicated.

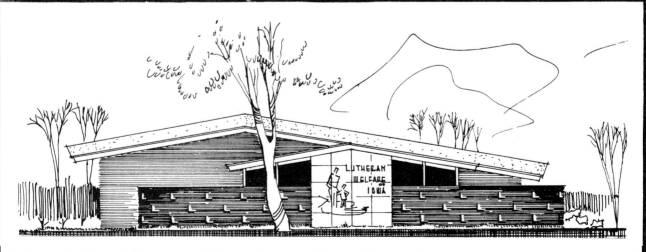

Lutheran Welfare Building, Des Moines, Iowa; Architects: Thorson & Brom.
Simply rendered elevations with mere suggestions of entourage are typical studies often used as auxiliary presentation drawings.

OVER THE RIVER...THE HILLS OF IOWA

Courtesy of Caradco Co.,
Dubuque, Iowa

This drawing by C. P. Ferring shows leafless tree structures as foreground, providing added depth to the perspective.

The architect William P. Wenzler's watercolor rendered presentation drawing of his design for St. Edmund's Episcopal Church, Elm Grove, Wisconsin is compared below with a photograph of the church after it was built.

NOTES

The appearance of sketches and drawings is often greatly improved by proper mounting and matting. One recommended method of mounting and matting a drawing is shown on this page. The procedure is similar for all compositions, whether horizontal, vertical, or square.

If a drawing is placed under a mat having the same width all around the drawing, an optical illusion may result, making the bottom margin look smaller. As a guide to those who may be inexperienced in matting, it is suggested that the minimum width of 3" and 4", as illustrated, be used.

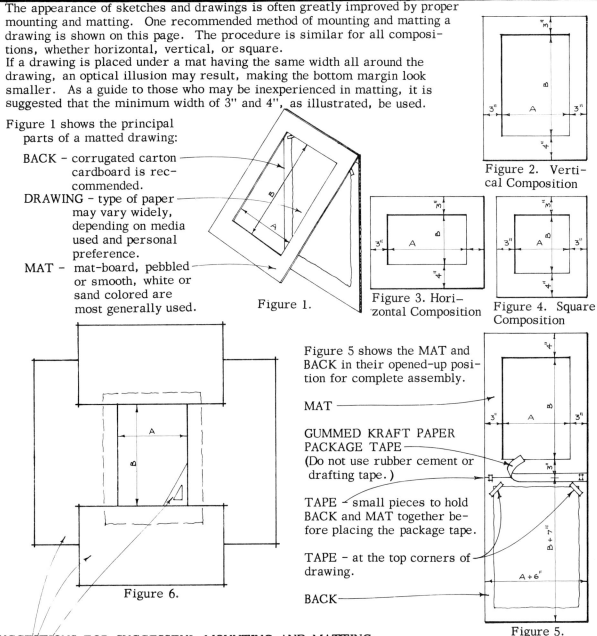

Figure 1 shows the principal parts of a matted drawing:

   BACK - corrugated carton cardboard is recommended.

   DRAWING - type of paper may vary widely, depending on media used and personal preference.

   MAT - mat-board, pebbled or smooth, white or sand colored are most generally used.

Figure 1.

Figure 2. Vertical Composition

Figure 3. Horizontal Composition

Figure 4. Square Composition

Figure 5 shows the MAT and BACK in their opened-up position for complete assembly.

MAT

GUMMED KRAFT PAPER PACKAGE TAPE (Do not use rubber cement or drafting tape.)

TAPE - small pieces to hold BACK and MAT together before placing the package tape.

TAPE - at the top corners of drawing.

BACK

Figure 6.

Figure 5.

SUGGESTIONS FOR SUCCESSFUL MOUNTING AND MATTING:

Step 1. Use four pieces of cardboard or stiff paper, moving them back and forth until you decide on the portion of the drawing or sketch you wish to appear through the mat opening, that is, the dimensions A and B.

Step 2. Place a triangle in the corners to square the opening. Mark the corners. Measure the opening.

Step 3. Cut the BACK and MAT each A + 6" × B + 7".

Step 4. Measure in from edge of mat 3" on top and sides, and 4" at the bottom.

Step 5. Cut the A × B opening in the MAT using an EXACTO knife or other sharp blade. Cut on the front side. Use a straight-edge such as a T-square, and cut slightly past each corner to insure clean 90° corners.

Step 6. Place two small pieces of tape to hold the BACK and MAT together while placing the HINGE tape. The package tape serves as the hinge tape.

Step 7. Close the mat over the back; insert the sketch or drawing to its desired position, then open the mat and tape the drawing at the top corners.

     The matted drawing is now ready to be displayed, or to be placed under glass in a wood frame for more permanent display and protection.

Since buildings should always be beautiful, they should be so in all seasons. Therefore presentation drawings often show trees without foliage.
Architects: Brooks and Borg.

The background trees and plantings next to the building walls are drawn with a flattened soft pencil. The foreground trees show foliage drawn with a wedge-pointed soft pencil.
Architects: Brooks and Borg.

The drawings on this page are examples of students' work, showing various techniques of indicating entourage.

Above are suggested pencil techniques that may be used in drawing entourage on presentation drawings.

Above are suggested pencil techniques that may be used in drawing entourage on presentation drawings.

STYLIZE — KEEP FIGURES SIMPLE

6'-0"

SCALE 1/8" = 1'-0"

GROUP FIGURES

6'-0"

SCALE 1/4" = 1'-0"

ACTION

Show Figures in Action Where Appropriate - Figures Should Not Detract

GATE 5

Too Much Action — Suggests a Poorly Planned Air Terminal Building

FLY

Show Character - Avoid Grotesque Distortion

Brush Draw Figures — For Ink Wash Renderings & Water Colors.

Above are suggested pencil techniques that may be used in drawing entourage on presentation drawings.

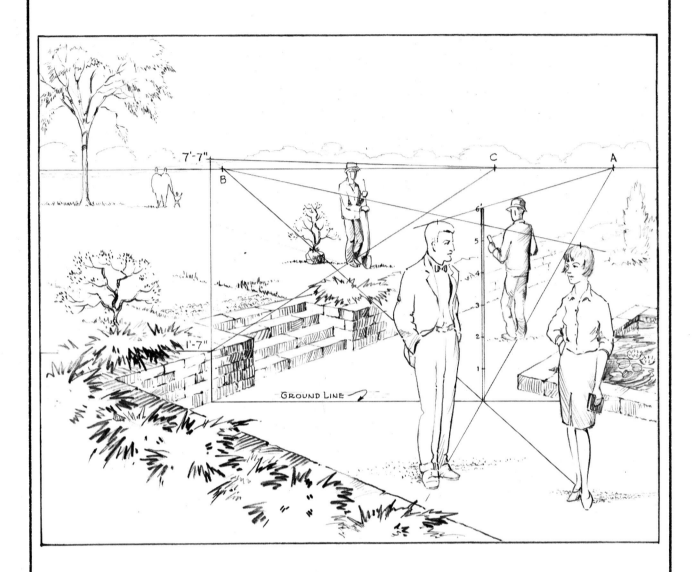

In the above perspective drawing the men are 6'-0" and the girl is 5'-6". The gardener is standing on the same ground level as the observer, therefore his eye level coincides with the horizon. The other people are standing on ground 1'-7" below the ground level of the observer, therefore their eye levels are below the horizon.

PROCEDURE FOR PLACING FIGURES IN A PERSPECTIVE DRAWING:

1. On any true height line establish the figure height.

2. From any convenient point on the horizon draw a line through the base of the figure height, then draw a line from the point on the horizon through the top of the figure height.

3. These two lines or their extension in front of the picture plane establish proper heights for figures placed anywhere along them.

4. Figures may be either sketched in between these lines or a figure previously drawn may be moved along the lines until its proper position is found.

In preparing preliminary designs for buildings, an architect often compiles data in the form of charts and graphs. It is often necessary that he be able to present this information in preliminary reports to clients, building committees, or civic bodies for their study before approving the building plans.

Typical subjects of these charts and graphs are as follows:

1. WEATHER: The severity of weather influences the type of structure chosen. These elements of weather include temperature, rainfall, floods, snowfall, wind and tornadoes.

2. SOIL CONDITIONS: This important consideration influences the foundation requirements of the structure to be erected. A study of borings made on the site, other geological data, and a study of a graph on BEARING CAPACITIES OF SOILS as shown on page 6, would furnish data necessary to design the required footings and foundations.

3. TOPOGRAPHY: Topographical maps such as shown on page 21 of Chapter 8 need to be consulted as preliminary information in conjunction with the soil study.

4. EARTHQUAKES: Although this consideration is more important in some areas than others, it is a factor to be considered. The east and west coast of the United States offer more risk than other parts of the country. For that reason building codes in these areas have requirements for the structural design of buildings on the basis of the anticipated risk.

5. NATURAL RESOURCES: The natural resources of building materials and their proximity to the building site need to be considered in the interest of economy, since the cost of the material is often affected by the distance it needs to be transported.

6. POPULATION TRENDS: Population growth often affects the consideration of the future needs of the building under study. These trends are obtainable from the State Bureau of Census and from local statistics pertinent to the phases of the project.

A few typical charts and graphs are shown on the following pages:

1. Table -- page 2.

2. Rectangular Coordinate Graphs -- page 2 and 6.

3. Maps -- pages 3, 4, and 5.

4. Area Diagrams -- page 4.

5. Bar Charts -- page 5.

6. Pie Charts -- page 5.

A TABLE

Figure 1. Monthly and Annual Iowa Normals

MONTH	TEMPERATURE (°F)	PRECIPITATION inches	SNOWFALL inches	SUNSHINE %possible	HOURLY WIND SPEED mi/hr	PREVAILING DIRECTION
January	20	1.0	7.1	51	8.9	NW
February	23	1.1	6.7	55	9.2	NW
March	36	1.7	5.7	58	9.7	NW
April	49	2.6	1.5	58	9.9	S
May	60	4.0	0.1	62	9.0	S
June	70	4.5	0.0	69	8.1	S
July	75	3.6	0.0	76	7.3	S
August	73	3.8	0.0	70	7.1	S
September	64	4.0	0.0	63	7.8	S
October	53	2.3	0.5	59	8.3	SW
November	37	1.7	2.5	50	8.9	NW
December	24	1.1	5.7	45	8.7	NW
ANNUAL	49	31.4	29.8	60	8.6	NW

A RECTANGULAR COORDINATE GRAPH

(Courtesy Iowa State University Press)

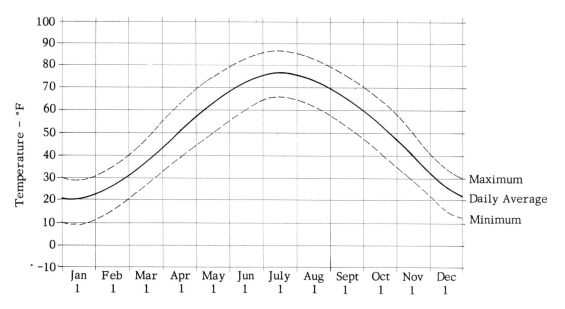

Annual March of Temperature, Central Iowa*

Figure 2.

*The average curve is for the 20 years 1925-44.
The maximum and minimum curves are from
approximately a 55-year period of record ending
with 1950.

MAXIMUM FROST PENETRATION in inches

Use for Foundations

(United States Weather Bureau)

TORNADO FREQUENCY BY STATES
(United States Weather Bureau)
(1916 – 1951)
A MAP

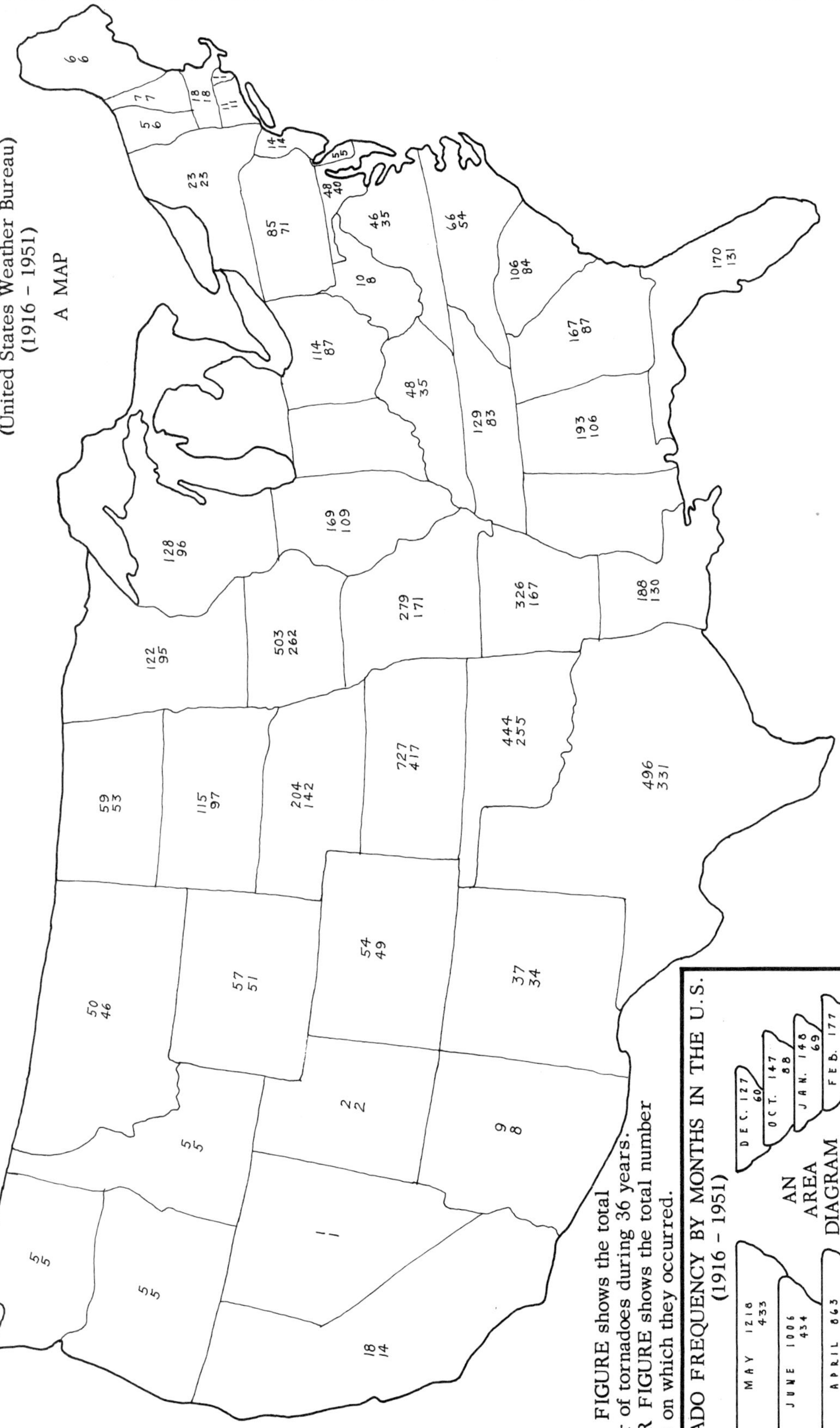
6 6
7 7
18 18
11 11
5 6
14 14
5 5
23 23
48 40
85 71
46 35
66 54
170 131
106 84
10 8
167 87
114 87
48 35
129 83
193 106
169 109
128 96
188 130
326 167
279 171
503 262
122 95
444 255
496 331
727 417
204 142
115 97
59 53
54 49
37 34
57 51
50 46
2 2
9 8
5 5
1 1
5 5
5 5
18 14

UPPER FIGURE shows total number.
LOWER FIGURE shows total days.

UPPER FIGURE shows the total number of tornadoes during 36 years. LOWER FIGURE shows the total number of days on which they occurred.

TORNADO FREQUENCY BY MONTHS IN THE U.S.
(1916 – 1951)

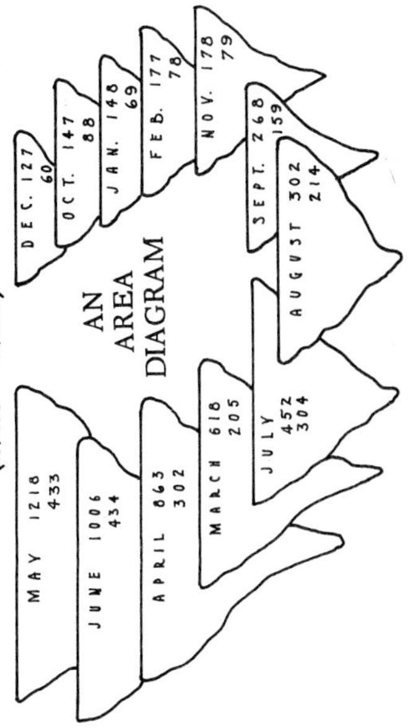
AN AREA DIAGRAM
MAY 1218 433
JUNE 1006 434
APRIL 863 302
MARCH 618 205
JULY 452 304
AUGUST 302 214
SEPT. 268 159
NOV. 178 79
FEB. 177 78
JAN. 148 69
OCT. 147 88
DEC. 127 60

EARTHQUAKE FREQUENCY
  IN THE UNITED STATES
(From information obtained from "Earthquake
  Damage and Earthquake Insurance" by
John R. Freeman.)

A MAP

1 CALIFORNIA and WESTERN NEVADA
Frequent shocks of high intensity.

2
+
3 WASHINGTON, OREGON and ATLANTIC COAST
Frequent shocks, sometimes destructive.

4 ROCKY MOUNTAIN REGION
Few severe shocks recorded, perhaps because
of sparse settlement and brief, incomplete
record.

5 GREAT LAKES and MISSISSIPPI VALLEY
Low frequency of severe shocks.

6 GREAT PLAINS REGION
No severe shocks recorded.

A PIE CHART

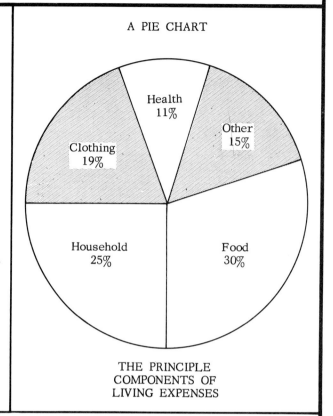

Health
11%

Other
15%

Clothing
19%

Household
25%

Food
30%

THE PRINCIPLE
COMPONENTS OF
LIVING EXPENSES

A BAR CHART

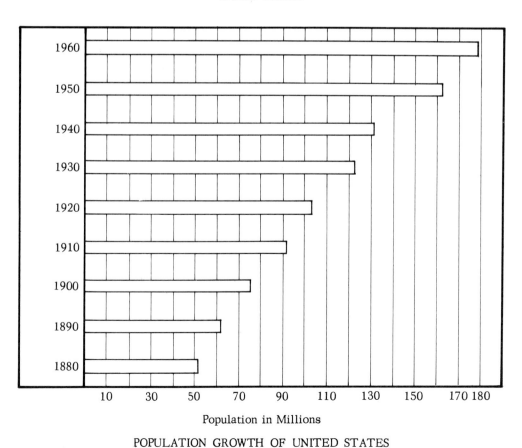

Population in Millions

POPULATION GROWTH OF UNITED STATES

A RECTANGULAR COORDINATE GRAPH

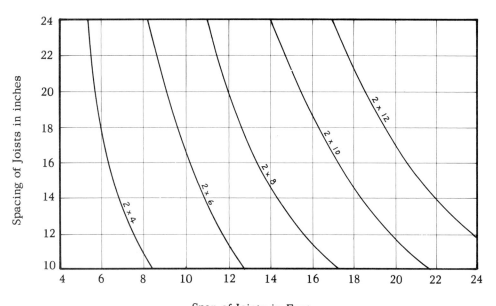

Span of Joists in Feet

SIZES, SPACING, AND SPANS OF JOISTS

A RECTANGULAR COORDINATE GRAPH

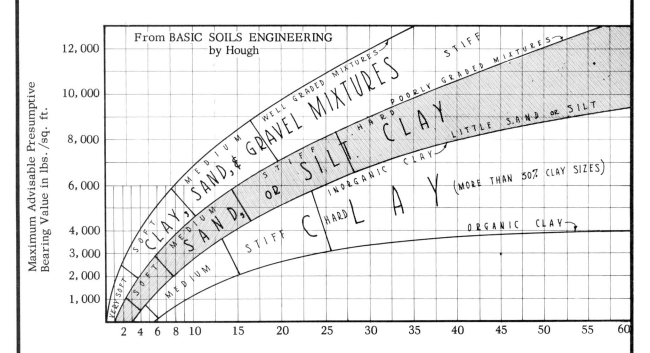

STANDARD PENETRATION RESISTANCE* in blows/ft.

*Number of blows of 140-lb. pin-guided drive weight falling 30-in./blow required to drive a split-barrel spoon with a 2-in. outside diameter 12-in.
(Higher values may be used for precompressed (or compacted) clays of low sensitivity than for normally loaded or extra-sensitive clays.)